Notes on Mathematics in Primary Schools

Notes on Mathematics in Primary Schools

By members of the

Association of Teachers of Mathematics

Association of Teachers of Mathematics

Published by the Association of Teachers of Mathematics
Kings Chambers, Queen Street, Derby, DE1 3DA.

© Association of Teachers of Mathematics 1979
ISBN 0 900095 06 7
Library of Congress Catalogue Card Number: 67-10775

First published by the Cambridge University Press 1967

Reissued by the Association of Teachers of Mathematics 1979
Reissued by the Association of Teachers of Mathematics 1984

First printed in Great Britain by
Percy Lund, Humphries & Co. Ltd., Bradford and London
Reprinted in Great Britain by
F. H. Brown Ltd., Nelson 1979
M. J. Phelan Printers, Ripley 1984

Contents

CONTENTS

Prefatory note

Most of the material for this book was written and compiled at two five-day residential sessions in January and April, 1965. Although it is the result of intense co-operative activity, the book is not intended as in any sense an 'agreed' report or a permanent record.

The following members of the Association of Teachers of Mathematics shared in the writing of it:

(Mrs) R. M. Bevan
H. Bracewell
(Miss) B. I. Briggs
W. M. Brookes
(Mrs) S. N. Cheetham
W. R. Cowderoy
W. B. Foster
C. Frisby
(Mrs) R. M. Fyfe
J. Hames
I. Harris
R. P. G. May
S. A. Morley

(Miss) K. Northcroft
J. W. Oliver
(Mrs) R. J. Peachey
D. J. Pitman
(Mrs) A. I. G. Renton
B. Simcox
W. B. Sloan
N. V. Smith
D. A. Sturgess
D. G. Tahta
(Mrs) V. L. Underwood
(Miss) N. M. Usher
D. H. Wheeler (executive editor)

Preface to the 1984 Edition

This book, first published 17 years ago is still popular and widely recommended on pre-service and in-service courses. Many of the issues raised in the introduction have become universally accepted as important and we believe that the book still provides a valuable stimulus to research and development. No attempt has been made to update the book by altering units of measurement as this would undermine the authenticity of the anecdotes that are used to illustrate arguments.

Introduction

The mathematical experiences of a child before the age of eleven, and the responses he has been encouraged to make to them, largely determine his potential mathematical development. It is no longer possible to believe that the learning of mathematics properly begins in the secondary school, and that the only essential preparation for this stage is a certain minimum of computational skill in arithmetic. The learning of mathematics, in the widest sense, begins before the child goes to school and continues throughout the primary school and beyond, except when impoverished experience and unimaginative teaching stop the development. We have written this book at a time when an increasing number of teachers accept this viewpoint and when changes are taking place in the mathematics taught in primary schools. We strongly support all those changes which are designed to enrich the mathematical experiences of young children, and which emphasize the central importance of their activity and their ways of thinking.

In an earlier book [40] we discussed the case for a reform of mathematics teaching in secondary schools, and expressed ourselves in favour of the teaching of modern mathematics. Many of the arguments we used there, and some of the illustrations we gave, have an obvious relevance to mathematics in primary schools, but we are aware that we may easily be misunderstood if we baldly say that we think modern mathematics should be taught to primary school children. Modern mathematics, as we understand it, has special characteristics which tell us something important about the nature and role of the subject. It is the implications of these that we follow, rather than the label that has been attached to certain relatively new mathematical topics.

Mathematics is the creation of human minds. A new piece of

mathematics can be fashioned to do a job in the same way that, say, a new building can be designed. This is the first lesson to be learnt from modern mathematics. The invention of new algebras and new geometries, together with the investigations into the foundations of mathematics at the turn of the century, have shown that mathematics cannot be an absolute, given *a priori*, or a science built entirely on observations of the real world. Mathematics is made by men and has all the fallibility and uncertainty that this implies. It does not exist outside the human mind, and it takes its qualities from the minds of men who created it.

Because mathematics is made by men and exists only in their minds, it must be made or re-made in the mind of each person who learns it. In this sense mathematics can only be learnt by being created. We do not believe that a clear distinction can be drawn between the activities of the mathematician inventing new mathematics and the child learning mathematics which is new to him. The child has different resources and different experiences, but both are involved in creative acts. We want to stress that the mathematics a child knows is, in a real sense, his possession, because by a personal act he has created it.

A second characteristic of modern mathematics is closely related to the first. Mathematics is now applied to a very wide range of situations and is not confined, as it once was, to the mechanics of the physical world. Completely new fields of mathematical applications have sprung up, some only a few years old. Operational research and cybernetics, to choose just two examples, are applications of mathematics to problems which formerly would not have been thought susceptible to mathematical analysis. Much of this work may seem a long way from the classroom and particularly from the primary school classroom. But its significance for the teacher lies in its demonstration of the vast number of things that are worth thinking about in a mathematical way. Mathematics is not just about number and space; it can be said to happen whenever the mind classifies and creates structures. This increases tremendously the range of experiences which turn out to be mathematically relevant, and it makes it easier for the teacher to create occasions for his pupils to use mathematics, and find situations which release mathematical thinking. One practical consequence of this is that, in the classroom, mathematics becomes more varied and therefore more enjoyable. Another is that the child can explore situations which are within his experience, which yield quite profound mathematics, and yet which do not require the technical equipment of memorized relationships and algorithms that traditional number work so often does.

If mathematics is not seen as restricted to a few conventionally accepted areas of experience, or constrained to follow a simple linear development, the teacher can encourage his pupils to range far and wide in their mathematical activity. They can explore situations which are incredibly rich in their mathematical yield. There are situations, some of which we mention, which are direct enough to be grasped by all children, and yet which provide such a wealth of possibilities that they are difficult to exhaust. Faced with the responses of children to such situations, confident judgments about the mathematics appropriate for a particular age, or the precedence of some piece of mathematics over another, have to be abandoned. It becomes obvious that the learning of mathematics is a complex activity and that children can work happily within this complexity.

We believe, then, that teaching which tries to simplify learning by emphasizing the mastery of small isolated steps does not help children, but puts barriers in their way. They need the general techniques and strategies of mathematics rather than the ability to answer easy questions accurately. They have been grossly deprived if accuracy in a tiny field is all that their learning brings them. It can be said, of course, that general techniques and strategies are very abstract and that children should not be expected to acquire them. But the child's first steps in learning to talk, for example, show that he is capable of forming classifications at a high level of abstraction, and it seems to us that the teaching he often receives ties him much too closely to the particular. Mathematics may then become difficult for him, not because it demands abstract thought but because it does not allow him to be abstract enough. We do not mean by this that mathematics should be (or can be) detached from the concrete and from experience. We believe that in the early stages of his learning a child oscillates between an absorption in some particular feature of his immediate situation, and a free-ranging survey of the similarities and differences that appear to him when he remembers other situations from his experience. His activity may look unfocused and unpredictable, and the jargon may say that he has not formed such-and-such concepts; but introspection of our thinking when we are learning something new appears to us to show that the child's thinking is not essentially different in this respect from our own.

The creation of mathematics by the child does not take place in a vacuum. From the beginning he belongs to a social environment which influences him in a multitude of ways. This environment offers him certain experiences and a language to use in talking about them. His thinking is mainly controlled by his need to understand his environment and to make himself understood in it. He watches what people do and imitates them; he talks to them about his activities and he listens to the words they use. By these means he gradually constructs a view of the world which satisfies himself and is acceptable to the social group to which he belongs. In any society he learns to use a particular language, he plays particular games and he masters certain skills. He also acquires certain ways of behaving and thinking which are approved and encouraged by the people around him. Some of these lead him to mathematics. He learns to build stable structures, to arrange and classify objects, to order and count them. He learns to discriminate properties and to distinguish relationships. In all these activities his choice of significant actions is largely governed by the social acceptance and rejection of his attempts.

We believe that the learning of mathematics has to be seen in this way as individual creative (or re-creative) acts taking place in a social context. It is clear to us that there is not just one mathematics, for the mathematics that is socially acceptable is different for different cultures, and in any society it changes from time to time, as it is changing in ours now. Each society has its mathematical currency, and this mathematics is accessible to the children born into it. On the other hand, although there is some consensus of opinion about mathematics at any one time this does not completely determine how each individual sees it, or prevent a few from going beyond what is generally known. This interaction between the structures created by the individual, and the structures made accessible through other people, operates at all levels: in the child, the teacher and the research mathematician.

It can be argued that the teaching of mathematics has concentrated exclusively on the attempt to transmit known mathematics, and that it has done this in an incredibly narrow way. Our view of mathematics makes us see the job of the teacher differently. We are concerned with the creative side of the child's learning and with minimizing the teacher's interference with this. Every time a teacher insists on his way of doing a piece of mathematics, rejecting any responses which do not seem to fit, he nibbles away at his pupils' ability to act mathematically. We believe in the value of the child's mathematics; that he should have freedom to make it and use it and talk about it. The child may sometimes make mathematics that to an adult is not valid. Provided the teacher avoids *ex cathedra* judgments, and has sympathy with what the child is trying to do, it is then proper for the child's mathematics to be put to the social test. In this way the sensitive teacher can balance his pupils' need to think their own thoughts with their need to share and communicate with other people. The preservation of some degree of equilibrium between the demands of mathematics to be socially acceptable and the freedom to invent mathematics which may have meaning only for the inventor is the chief pedagogical task. In this sense the teaching of mathematics is not unlike the teaching of art or English.

We believe, then, that modern mathematics, with its wide range of application and its awareness of itself as a fabrication of human beings, has changed the way in which mathematics should be taught. In this book we try to talk about these consequences. We have not written a text-book for children, but a book for primary school teachers based on our observations of children learning mathematics. Many of the things we have said are not easily conveyed in words and we have had to be content with some passages which are suggestive rather than explicit. For these to be meaningful the reader will have to meet us halfway. We are conscious that without a willingness to become personally involved in at least some of the things we have written, the reader will find this book ineffective and empty. This is as true of the mathematics we discuss as of our reporting and our commentary. We do not think that a teacher can teach mathematics effectively without experience of some mathematical activity, and we have tried to write some passages that put mathematical questions to the reader. We hope he will follow up those that intrigue him; on his own with paper and pencil, through discussion with colleagues, or in the classroom with his pupils.

It is clear that we associate with the words 'modern mathematics' an attitude to mathematics rather than a list of particular mathematical topics. There is little point in making a simple value distinction between 'modern' and 'traditional' mathematical topics, and using the former to oust the latter. Apart from a reduction in the amount of time spent on doing imitative routine work, there is no need to jettison any of the mathematics that is traditionally taught in the primary school. But although the mathematics will stay, the methods of teaching it must change.

We reject an exclusive concentration on the acquisition of computational skills. We also reject the separation of computation from other mathematical activity and the attempt to deal with it as if it were learnt differently. This distinction has no reality for us (or for children, as far as we can see). One characteristic mathematical activity is the generation of algorithms and routine procedures. The choices that are made in the creation, selection and operation of these procedures are important mathematical decisions and an integral part of mathematical strategy. It is not that children now need to know less about numbers and how to compute with numbers. On the contrary they should know much more about number relationships and the operations that can be performed with numbers. Through games with numbers, play with patterns of numbers and free compositions with numbers, children can learn, without drill, to deal empirically with situations involving numbers, and develop a flexible set of procedures for handling such routine as is necessary.

Primary school mathematics, though, is not only about numbers. We approve the teaching of some plane and solid geometry, the use of co-ordinates, graphs, simple numerical algebra, and some topics usually called 'modern': sets, simple examples of algebraic structures, elementary topology, and so on. But what do these words mean? 'Plane geometry' may just mean the tedious and useless ruler and compass constructions brought down unchanged from the first year of the secondary school; 'sets' may stand for the manipulation of Venn diagrams to solve pseudo-problems; 'graphs' may mean a formalized routine for illustrating relationships. If these are the meanings the words carry in practice, we want nothing of them. We do not identify any of these areas with the formal treatments that we find in the majority of text-books. As we said in our earlier book, mathematics begins with situations. We try here to talk in terms of these situations rather than the mathematical topics to which they may lead. At all levels this is the right place from which to start; it is especially so in the primary school where codification and formalization are the least important activities.

Our experience with young children has shown us that we do not know the upper limit to the mathematics they can learn, and that we are always underestimating their powers. We have therefore deliberately abstained from writing a syllabus and saying what we think primary school children *should* learn. We do not want, in any case, to suggest that there is any finality in our thinking about primary school mathematics. Our ideas have changed and developed in the course of writing the book and we know they will have changed and developed still further by the time it is in print. We take the risk that some of the things we have written will be read as considered, authoritative statements. We have indeed considered what we have written, jettisoned much of it and modified more; but the only authority our words have is the correspondence a few of them may bear to the reality of children learning mathematics.

As yet we have hardly mentioned the teacher in the classroom and the demands that our views of children and mathematics make. We have implied some features of his role: that he should have personal experience of some mathematical activity; that he should be sensitive to the conflicts that can arise in communicating mathematics; that he should give his children freedom to make their own mathematics. We cannot hide the fact that if a teacher adopts these aims his job is made immensely difficult. It is easy to say that children must be allowed to make their own mathematics. How is the teacher to act if their responses are so varied and unfamiliar that he is at a loss? He may have difficulty in understanding a child's response, or in recognizing whether it has any mathematical value, or in knowing where to go next. Perhaps we can only say that this is not a problem which is peculiar to the primary school teacher, although he may feel it most acutely. The secondary school pupil will outpace his teachers and the research student go beyond the knowledge of his professor. At all levels, where freedom is permitted, teachers may be nonplussed. The problem of inadequacy, in this sense, has to be lived with as part of the price to be paid for doing the job better. The ability to support a degree of insecurity may be a higher teaching qualification than the ability to keep a step ahead.

The aim of this book is not to provide a programme for primary school mathematics but to stimulate experiment. We have therefore excluded many things that other writers have said. The time in which we wrote the book, and our personal resources, have set other limits to the material. What remains seems to us to fall roughly into three categories. We have reported some classroom events as faithfully as we can; we have commented on some learning processes as we have understood them; and we have inserted some other material, in incomplete and suggestive form, in the hope that it will urge readers to make mathematical investigations of their own. We have chosen to avoid putting too tight a structure on the book, and the sequence of material does not follow logic or chronology or order of difficulty. It is a book to be dipped into rather than read straight through.

This book is offered as a contribution to the on-going research and development that every teacher should experience throughout his professional life.

2

Number patterns

A square array such as the one shown below offers many opportunities for the discovery of number patterns. In particular, consideration of the patterns of multiples can open an interesting field of enquiry. Many teachers will be able to draw from their own experience in the class-room and so extend or supplement what is discussed here. No attempt is made either to exhaust the situation, or to claim that the sequence of ideas presented has intrinsic merit. It is the underlying freedom of choice, permitting this or that sequence to emerge, which merits our attention.

1	2	3	4	5	6	7	8	9	10
11	12	13	14	15	16	17	18	19	20
21	22	23	24	25	26	27	28	29	30
31	32	33	34	35	36	37	38	39	40
41	42	43	44	45	46	47	48	49	50
51	52	53	54	55	56	57	58	59	60
61	62	63	64	65	66	67	68	69	70
71	72	73	74	75	76	77	78	79	80
81	82	83	84	85	86	87	88	89	90
91	92	93	94	95	96	97	98	99	100

Fig.1

Although we show here a particular square array of numbers (sometimes called the Pythagorean square), and investigate certain patterns within it, we need not keep strictly to this framework, for we may use our freedom to vary the number of elements in the columns and in the rows. If we allow the simple extension of varying the number of elements in each row, we generate, as we shall see, a wealth of possibilities which are mathematically relevant. We can often miss opportunities of extending mathematical activity by sticking rigidly to a particular situation (the Pythagorean square, in this case) because we are not conscious of the fact that *we* have the power to make changes in the situation, to study the consequences of our actions, and that this is an integral part of mathematical thinking, even at an elementary level. To extend the columns of the array may produce little of interest. But the mere fact that we have recognized that this specific alteration does not affect the structure of the situation is in itself important.

Let us look more closely at the Pythagorean square: a natural starting-point since we normally work in base ten. Some properties are readily apparent and we can expect a variety of comments from children if we ask a question as 'open' as, 'What can you say about this?' Alternatively we can direct the enquiry by asking a series of questions:

How many numbers are there in each row?

Where are the numbers which have a 4 in the unit position?

Where are the numbers having a 4 in the tens position?

Where is the number which has a 4 in both positions?

What can be said about the numbers in the 7th row? in the 5th column?

Which number is in the 3rd row and the 2nd column?

If we extend the array beyond 100, in which column will you find 104, 638, 7625, 38276391762? How do you know?

Can you name any large number which will be in the 6th column? What do you take into account when you make your choice?

Can you think of any number which cannot be fitted into the array?

Look for the set of even numbers and put a ring round each one. What do you notice? Can you describe the 'pattern' of the even numbers? Do the odd numbers form a similar pattern?

What about the multiples of 3? Do they make a pattern? If so, can you describe it?

Let us pause for a moment and consider these two approaches to the situation. On the one hand, the teacher asks, 'What can you say about this?', and waits to hear the replies of the children. On the other, the teacher asks questions which direct the children's perceptions and subsequent thoughts along predetermined channels. This is, of course, far too simple a distinction to make, for in practice the two merge in varying degrees. Nevertheless, it is useful for discussion purposes, particularly as the tendency for one or the other type of approach to

*dominate tells us something about attitudes towards the learning situa-
tion. By asking more open questions, we are allowing the children (at
least,* some *of them – it is important to recognize this limitation) to talk
about what the situation reveals to them personally.*

In this sample of questions an effort has been made to extend the
awareness from the particular to the more general. Having focused
attention on the relation between the rows and column positions, and
the units and tens digits, we have taken a further step toward abstraction by considering the column positions of numbers greater than
100, and gone on to talk about numbers so big that it is inconceivable
that any child should actually continue the array far enough to
include them.

Multiples

The preliminary set of questions ended with a glance at the patterns
formed by the sets of even and odd numbers and the multiples of 3.
What can we say about the positions of the multiples of other
numbers? Do they form patterns?

*It will be convenient at this stage to introduce a notation for the sets of
multiples; children will be able to invent other possibilities. Here we
shall denote the set of multiples of 2 by M(2), the set of multiples of 6
by M(6), etc.*

The multiples of 2 are to be found in alternate columns, and we can
refer to this as a 'column pattern.' Are there other sets of multiples
which generate column patterns? M(5)? M(10)? In each case, all the
numbers in the columns are part of the total pattern. What about
M(4)? This forms a column pattern in a way, although there is a
difference in that every number in each column of the pattern is not
within the set. We may even say that M(3) is a column pattern in this
sense, but the eye more readily sees this as a 'diagonal' arrangement.
In M(4) some columns are not a part of the pattern, whereas in M(3)
elements are to be found in every column.

We can remove some of these ambiguities if we wish by restricting
our use of words. A definition may satisfy our intuitive insight into a
situation for a while, but as a result of further investigation and discussion with others, it seems inadequate in that it is too broad; it
allows too much. We shall describe as 'column' patterns those in
which every number in the columns belongs to the pattern. With this
use of the word M(2), M(5) and M(10) are column patterns; M(4)
is not.

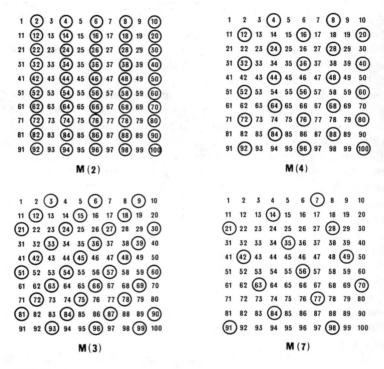

Fig.2

Exercises

1. Why is it that M(2), M(5) and M(10) produce column patterns in this array?

2. Why does the 'diagonal' pattern for M(3) arise? Can it be described as a shift of 1 down and 1 to the left? (Or 1 down and 2 to the right?) Describe M(4) in this way. And M(5).

    Can the variations in the horizontal shifts for these patterns be explained? Is it linked with the number of elements in each row?

3. Describe the patterns generated by M(6), M(7), M(8), M(9), M(11), etc.

4. Compare M(9) with M(11). Are they similar? Different? Compare M(7) and M(13).

5. Which of the patterns in question 3 spread over every column in the array? Can a reason for this be given? What about M(14) and M(21)?

Some patterns are completely contained in others: M(4) in M(2), M(8) in M(2) and M(4), M(6) in M(3) and M(2), etc. The numbers contained, for example, in both M(6) and M(4) are the common multiples of 4 and 6 (12, 24, 36, ...), and these form a pattern of their own.

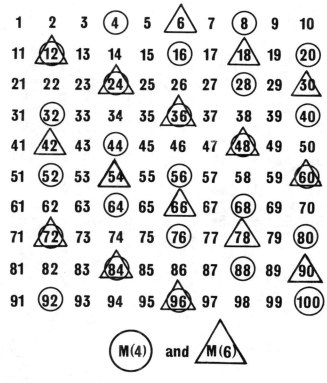

Fig.3

A convenient device for exploring the patterns of common multiples of sets of numbers is the superposition of sheets of acetate (see the article 'Searching for Patterns' by M. Beberman in [14] for more detail on this). The pattern of M(3), say, can be shown by colouring on one sheet and the pattern for M(5) by a different colour on another. If these are put on top of each other, the intersection of the two sets of numbers can be seen where the two colourings coincide. In this case it will show the set of common multiples of 3 and 5, i.e. M(15).

This method can of course be extended to the common multiples of three or more numbers. In the example we have suggested, the two numbers are co-prime (they have no common factor other than 1). By superposing M(6) on M(3), say, we see that all the numbers in M(6) are also in M(3), so in this case the intersection is M(6).

In a 'diagonal' pattern, other diagonals can be observed. Look at the pattern of M(4) below.

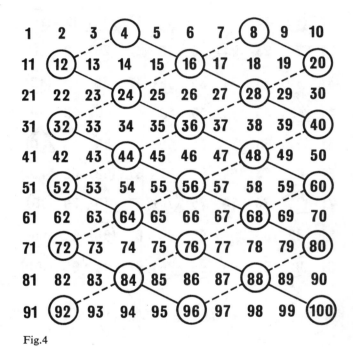

Fig.4

We may notice, for example, that along the unbroken diagonals the numbers increase by 12 each time; the sum of the digits increases by 3 each time. How far is this true? When does this relationship break down, and why? These are not properties of this pattern only. If we begin with any number in the array, move 1 square down and 2 squares to the right, and go on repeating this movement, we obtain sequences with comparable properties. Explore what happens when we make other horizontal and vertical displacements.

What do we find if we look at the broken lines?

Prime numbers

Still considering the Pythagorean square, suppose we cross out 1, and then all the multiples of 2 except 2 itself, all the multiples of 3 except 3 itself, and do the same for 5 and 7, we are left with all the prime numbers less than 100. We do not need to go beyond the multiples of 7. Why not? How far would we need to go if we extended the square and wanted to select all the prime numbers less than 256?

Look at the positions of the prime numbers in the square relative to the positions of M(6):

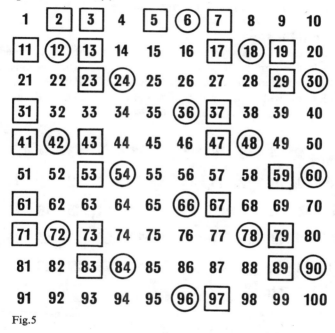

Fig.5

The prime numbers, with the exception of 2 and 3, either precede or follow a multiple of 6. Is this generally true?

Excluding 2, all prime numbers are odd; every odd number lies between two even numbers. In every set of three consecutive whole numbers, one and only one of them, is divisible by 3. (Why?) If we now consider any three consecutive whole numbers in which the middle one is prime, we know that this prime number is flanked by two even numbers, one of which must be divisible by 3. (The prime number cannot, by definition, be divided by 3 unless it is itself 3.) So this number is divisible by 2 and by 3, and therefore by 6. Hence any prime number (except 2 and 3) precedes or follows a multiple of 6.

The crossing-out method of selecting prime numbers is usually called Eratosthenes' Sieve. By crossing out 1 at the start we have assumed that 1 is not a prime number. As so often in dealing with number properties, we find that 1 is an odd man out. Does 1 satisfy the definition of a prime number or not? In fact we have a choice here since the definition is not clear at this point. Having made our choice, certain other consequences must follow if we are to be consistent. Mathematicians in general choose to regard 1 as neither prime nor composite.

Changing the rows

We recognized at the beginning of this chapter that we had freedom to change the number of elements in each row. Let us use this freedom and see what effect it has (see 'Searching for Patterns' [14]). As examples, we will consider two arrays, the first with seven and the second with six elements in each row.

1	2	3	4	5	6	7		1	2	3	4	5	6
8	9	10	11	12	13	14		7	8	9	10	11	12
15	16	17	18	19	20	21		13	14	15	16	17	18
22	23	24	25	26	27	28		19	20	21	22	23	24
29	30	31	32	33	34	35		25	26	27	28	29	30

etc.   etc.

(A)   (B)

Fig.6

In the Pythagorean square, we found certain basic types of visual pattern:

    (i) column   e.g. M(2), M(5), M(10),

    (ii) diagonal, with numbers in all columns

                     e.g. M(3), M(9), M(11),

    (iii) diagonal, with numbers appearing only in certain columns

                     e.g. M(4), M(6), M(8), M(12).

In (i) the generating numbers (2, 5, 10) were factors of 10, the number of elements in each row. In (ii) they were co-prime to 10. In (iii) they each had a factor which was also a factor of 10.

Can we find corresponding properties for the patterns of multiples in the arrays (A) and (B)?

1. Which sets of multiples now give column patterns?
2. Which give a pattern running through all columns?
3. Which patterns are limited to certain columns?
4. The multiples of 2 appear in 'chessboard' fashion in array (A). Is this true if there are 8, 9, 13 elements in a row? When is it true in general?
5. In array (B) the multiples of 3 appear in columns. What variation can we make in the number of elements in each row so that the multiples of 3 remain in columns? Is there more than one answer?
6. What will the number of elements in each row have to be for the multiples of 8 to appear in only two columns?
7. Can we make multiples of 7 behave like the multiples of 3 in the Pythagorean square? Is there more than one answer?
8. Make up more questions.

An addition game

Consider again one of the variants of the Pythagorean table – the one with seven elements in each row. This time we will label the columns for reference.

Choose any two columns. *C and F*. Choose a number in C and another in F. Yes, any number you like in these columns. Add them together. Which column contains your answer? *B*. And yours? and yours? Are all of them in B?

Let's try again. Choose two different columns. *E and A*. Where is the answer this time? *In F*. For all choices of numbers in E and A? *Yes*. Imagine the number array to be extended, still keeping seven numbers in each row. Now take two numbers in the extension, one in A and the other in B. Add them. Where is the answer? *In C*. Is it true that the answer is in C for all possible choices of numbers from columns A and B? *Yes*. Why? (See p.83 for some further discussion which may help in the search for a proof.)

How shall we write what we have discovered? $C+F=B$ and $E+A=F$. Is it true that $D+F=C$? that $A+B=C$? *Yes*.

What is the unknown in the statement $E+?=C$? *It can only be E. That is, $E+E=C$. But can we do this? You said 'Choose any two columns', and here we have a case where both of the added numbers*

A	B	C	D	E	F	G
1	2	3	4	5	6	7
8	9	10	11	12	13	14
15	16	17	18	19	20	21
22	23	24	25	26	27	28
29	30	31	32	33	34	35
36	37	38	39	40	41	42
			etc.			

Fig. 7

come from the same column. Well, shall we allow ourselves to do this? If we want to be able to add together *any* two numbers our rules must cover the possibility of adding two numbers from the same column. Let us agree, then, that we can take the two numbers from any columns, and that we permit the special case of taking the same column twice.

What are the answers to $A+A$, $B+B$? Does $D+D=A$? *One of them seems very peculiar: $G+G=G$.*

Let us look carefully at column G. Choose another column. *B.* Add any number in G to any number in B. Where is the answer? *Still in B.* Try again: add any number in G to any number in E. *The answer is in E.* So we have $B+G=B$ and $E+G=E$. Is $C+G=C$? *Yes.* We also know that $G+G=G$. What happens, then, if we add a number in G to any other number? *The answer stays in the same column as the second number.*

Will the same kind of adding game work with the Pythagorean square? Which column behaves like G in this case? Why does it work like this? *In the Pythagorean square, it looks as if the property depends only on the units digits of the numbers chosen.* What is the generalization for other arrays? The units digit is the remainder on dividing the number by 10. What is the analogue when there are seven elements in each row? Is it a property of the remainders on division by 7? (see p.83, note 3).

Suppose now that we keep the rules of the game the same, but replace the operation of addition by multiplication. Explore the development of this game.

Exercises

1. There are many other kinds of number array. Investigate the following and try to find some properties, however trivial they may seem to be.

(a)

0	1	2	3	4	5	6	7	8	9	10
1	2	3	4	5	6	7	8	9	10	11
2	3	4	5	6	7	8	9	10	11	12
3	4	5	6	7	8	9	10	11	12	13
4	5	6	7	8	9	10	11	12	13	14
5	6	7	8	9	10	11	12	13	14	15
6	7	8	9	10	11	12	13	14	15	16
7	8	9	10	11	12	13	14	15	16	17
8	9	10	11	12	13	14	15	16	17	18
9	10	11	12	13	14	15	16	17	18	19
10	11	12	13	14	15	16	17	18	19	20

(b)

0	1	2	3	4	5	6	7	8	9
1	2	3	4	5	6	7	8	9	0
2	3	4	5	6	7	8	9	0	1
3	4	5	6	7	8	9	0	1	2
4	5	6	7	8	9	0	1	2	3
5	6	7	8	9	0	1	2	3	4
6	7	8	9	0	1	2	3	4	5
7	8	9	0	1	2	3	4	5	6
8	9	0	1	2	3	4	5	6	7
9	0	1	2	3	4	5	6	7	8

2. Decide how to continue the following parts of arrays, and try to find some properties.

(a)

1	1	1	1	1	1	1	1	1	1	.	.
1	2	3	4	5	6	7	8	9	10	.	.
1	3	6	10	15	21	28	36	45	55	.	.
1	4	10	20	35	56	84	120	165	220	.	.
.	.	.	.	.	.	.	.	.	.	.	.
.	.	.	.	.	.	.	.	.	.	.	.

(b)

$$1$$
$$1 \quad 1$$
$$1 \quad 2 \quad 1$$
$$1 \quad 3 \quad 3 \quad 1$$
$$1 \quad 4 \quad 6 \quad 4 \quad 1$$
$$1 \quad 5 \quad 10 \quad 10 \quad 5 \quad 1$$

. . . . .

. . . . .

(c)

1	1	1	1	1	1	1	.	.	.
2	4	8	6	2	4	8	.	.	.
3	9	7	1	3	9	7	.	.	.
4	6	4	6	4	6	4	.	.	.
5	5	5	5	5	5	5	.	.	.
6	6	6	6	6	6	6	.	.	.
7	9	3	1	7	9	3	.	.	.
8	4	2	6	8	4	2	.	.	.
9	1	9	1	9	1	9	.	.	.

Can you hazard any guesses about the origin of array (c)?
The examples on p.287 may offer a clue.

3. (A number pattern of a different kind.)

$1 \times 1 = 1$

$11 \times 11 = 121$

What are the values of the products 111×111 and $1,111 \times 1,111$? What are our expectations about the value of $1,111,111 \times 1,111,111$? What causes the pattern of digits in the products? What happens after the result 12,345,678,987,654,321 is reached? What will be the next result?

These answers all have an odd number of digits, and the largest digit is in a certain position. Is it possible to obtain the answer 1,221 or 123,321 or 12,344,321 as the results of similar multiplications?

What numbers *can* be multiplied together to give 123,321?

What is the product $111,111 \times 11,111$?

How far are the results of the explorations you have made dependent on the numbers being expressed in the scale of ten (i.e. in base ten)?

Paper folding

It is interesting to attempt to evolve some patterned activity *in which the mind is not concerned directly with numbers in the first instance, but rather with some repetitive action out of which number patterns can arise. As illustrations of this idea, we shall consider a few examples. Paper folding provides us with a simple and convenient starting point.*

Take a rectangular sheet of paper and fold it once to make a four-page booklet. Number the pages 1 to 4. Open the sheet and notice that the sum of the numbers on either side of the sheet is 5.

Now take two sheets of paper, fold each as before and insert one inside the other to make an eight-page booklet. (If 15 sheets are used how many pages will the booklet have? How is the number of pages related to the number of sheets?) Number the pages, detach the sheets and open them out. What do you find? Each pair of numbers sums to 9.

Imagine a booklet made from six sheets. What will be the number on the last page? Is it true that each pair of numbers on one side of a sheet sums to 25 this time? Can you find 1 and 24, 2 and 23, 3 and 22 etc.?

What is the relationship between the sums of the pairs of the numbers and the number of pages in the booklet? In the booklet made from six sheets, which numbers face each other in the centre?

12 and 13? What numbers will face each other in a booklet made from 19 sheets?

The action involved in the construction of the booklet can go on indefinitely; more and more sheets can be used. Moreover, it is a repetitive action; we can perform the operation as many times as we wish and observe the emerging number pattern. At any moment we can decide to continue the action virtually – in our heads, as it were – and begin to make generalizations (see p.57 for a further discussion of 'action proofs'). The continuing pattern within this activity suggests to us that if p is the number of pages in the booklet and n is the number of sheets, then $p = 4n$. What is the sum of the page numbers on either side of any sheet? $p + 1$ or $4n + 1$?

Notice that the attention we give to the page numbers on each side of a sheet is encouraging a particular way of looking at the sequence of numbers. For example, the eight sheet booklet has page numbers running from 1 to 32, and our attention is fixed on certain pairs:

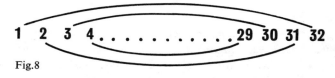

Fig.8

Can this observation be used to find the sum of all the page numbers in the booklet, i.e. $1 + 2 + 3 + \ldots + 31 + 32$? Explain why, for a booklet with p pages, this sum will be

$$\tfrac{1}{2}p \times (p+1) \text{ or } \frac{p(p+1)}{2}$$

What are the corresponding results if we use n (the number of sheets) instead of p?

Without performing the actual addition, find the sum of the series $1 + 2 + 3 + \ldots + 71 + 72$ and $1 + 2 + 3 + \ldots + 99 + 100$. What about the sums $1 + 2 + 3 + \ldots + 65 + 66$ and $1 + 2 + 3 \ldots + 38 + 39$? Can the last two series be generated by the booklet activity? Are the formulae valid in these cases?

Now consider an eight-page booklet obtained by French-folding the original sheet (say 10×8) first into 5×8 and then, at right angles to the first fold, into 5×4. (Fig.9)

Have the folded edge at the top. Number the pages from 1 to 8 in the bottom right-hand corners (without cutting the fold). When the sheet is opened out, what do you expect to observe about the page

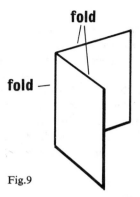

fold

fold —

Fig.9

numbers? (Check!) Is it true that the 'horizontal' pairs sum to 9?
This reminds us of the first example. What about the 'vertical' pairs?
They appear to sum to 5 or to 13. We notice 2 and 3, 4 and 1, 6 and 7,
5 and 8.

Now make (or imagine) a 16-page booklet by folding again and
making a page size $2\frac{1}{2} \times 4$. As before, put the folded edge at the top
and number the pages without cutting any folds. What do we anticipate this time?

Which pairs sum to 17? Which pairs sum to 9 or 25?

Imagine a 32-page booklet (the usual folio used in the production
of a book) and find the corresponding totals. Is a pattern beginning
to emerge?

Number of pages	Sum of 'horizontal' pairs	Sum of 'vertical' pairs	
8	9	5	13
16	17	9	25
32	33	17	49
64	?	?	?
.	.	.	.
.	.	.	.
p	?	?	?

Can you devise other questions that might be asked about this
booklet-making activity? Or devise some further folding actions that
can generate a number sequence?

Patterns of rods

Here and in other places in this book, the colour names used are those of the Cuisenaire material. The descriptions can easily be translated into the Colour-Factor system of colouring, or recast in terms of other forms of apparatus.

We do not suggest that children should be directed step-by-step through the following sequence (or any other that we describe in this book). It serves here merely as an illustration of 'patterned activity'. If children are asked, let us say, to 'make something with squares', it is possible that the particular patterns we discuss will arise along with others.

Make a square with four red rods.

Fig.10

Choose four rods of the same colour that will border the red square. Repeat the action. And again.

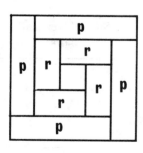

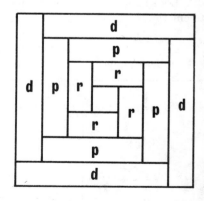

Fig.11

What is the area of the red square (including the unfilled part)? What is the area of the unfilled part? If the area of the white rod is taken to be 1, can we describe the situation by writing

$$1+(4\times2)=3^2?$$

What shall we write for pattern (ii)?

$1+(4\times2)=5^2$ or $3^2+(4\times4)=5^2$.

Pattern (iii) will give

$1+(4\times2)+(4\times4)+(4\times6)=7^2$ or $5^2+(4\times6)=7^2$.

Write down a few more statements of this sequence. Does the repetitive nature of the action justify a generalization?

Notice that in this pattern we have used only the even lengths. Now make a similar square pattern with the rods not already used.

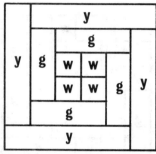

Fig.12

This can give $2^2+(4\times3)=4^2$

and $4^2+(4\times5)=6^2$.

What will follow if we add more rods?

Combining the results from both square patterns, we have

$1^2+(4\times2)=3^2$ (writing 1 as 1^2 to match the rest of the pattern)

$2^2+(4\times3)=4^2$

$3^2+(4\times4)=5^2$

$\cdot$ $\cdot$ $\cdot$ $\cdot$ $\cdot$ $\cdot$

$\cdot$ $\cdot$ $\cdot$ $\cdot$ $\cdot$ $\cdot$

$8^2+(4\times9)=10^2$.

Can this number pattern be continued virtually without reading it off from the pattern of rods? If we imagine a square in which the four outer rods are of length $(n+1)$ units can we write

$n^2+4(n+1)=(n+2)^2$?

Exercises

1. Make a rectangle using two green and two red rods, as drawn in the diagram. (Fig.13)

Continue this pattern with the rods, by bordering with two pink and two yellow rods, and so on. What number pattern (or patterns) do you observe?

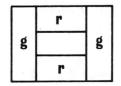

Fig.13

2. Make a square from four staircases of white, red and green rods as shown.

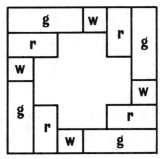

Fig.14

Continue this pattern by increasing the number of rods in the staircases one at a time. What patterns do you observe? Is

$$4(1+2+3)+2(2+4)=6^2$$

a possible interpretation?

3. Make a square with green rods laid side-by-side. Put a red square made similarly on top, in one corner. Do the same thing with other squares of consecutive rods. What patterns do you notice? What can you say if you put a green square on a yellow square, a pink square on a dark green square, and so on? Investigate further.

Dot patterns

In the first part of this chapter we used a square grid as an underlying structure, and the patterns observed were basically patterns of squares on the grid which contained the symbols for particular numbers. This led us to investigate the connection between the visual pattern of squares and the corresponding number properties. Now we can use the words 'number patterns' to mean something rather different. We are familiar, for instance, with the conventional ways in which we put spots on a domino; the perception of $\cdot\!\cdot\!\cdot$ suggests

to us the number five. It is in this sense – seen as a spatial arrangement of the units composing a number – that we can speak of a
number having (or suggesting) a pattern. Take, for instance, the
familiar sequences of triangular and square numbers:

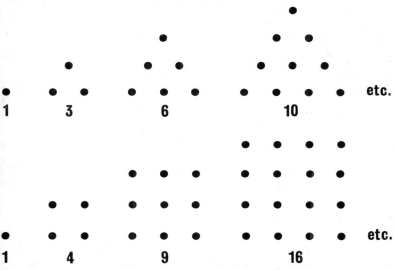

Fig.15

Here we can perceive a pattern for each individual number and any
single pattern contains all the preceding ones in the sequence. For
the triangular numbers,

$3=1+2$, $6=1+2+3$, $10=1+2+3+4$, etc.

Notice, too, that the sum of two adjacent triangular numbers gives a
square number.

Is this result true for any pair of adjacent triangular numbers? Does
the regularity in the growth of the pattern make the statement

Fig.16

plausible? Are we ready to accept the property without further ado?
For the square numbers,

$4 = 1+3$, $9 = 1+3+5$, $16 = 1+3+5+7$,

or $2^2 = 1+3$, $3^2 = 1+3+5$, $4^2 = 1+3+5+7$, etc.

How can we express, say, 64, 144? We see that the sum of the first two odd numbers is equal to the square of 2; the sum of the first three odd numbers is equal to the square of 3, etc.

Let us glance again at the square number pattern and notice, in particular, the *differences* between consecutive square numbers:

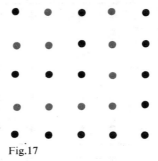

Fig.17

More generally, let us consider the squares $n \times n$ and $(n+1) \times (n+1)$: the number of dots in each square will be n^2 and $(n+1)^2$ respectively. If we start with n^2, the number of extra dots we need to make $(n+1)^2$ is $n+n+1$ or $2n+1$. The diagram below illustrates this when $n=5$.

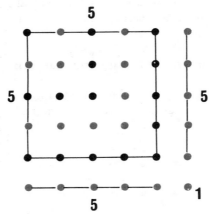

Fig.18

These observations suggest one way in which we can find the square root of a number. If we subtract successive odd numbers starting with 1, from the given number, the number of subtractions we can make gives the square root, or an approximation to it. For example, let us start with 81 and subtract 1, then 3, then 5, and so on, until we can subtract no more:

$$81 - \ 1 = 80$$
$$80 - \ 3 = 77$$
$$77 - \ 5 = 72$$
$$72 - \ 7 = 65$$
$$65 - \ 9 = 56$$
$$56 - 11 = 45$$
$$45 - 13 = 32$$
$$32 - 15 = 17$$
$$17 - 17 = 0.$$

We have subtracted nine successive odd numbers, and there is no remainder, and so the square root of 81 is 9.

Certainly for small numbers this is not a very practicable method. But it is a safe and sure way of finding square roots of large numbers if one has a calculating machine to handle the successive subtractions quickly.

It is interesting to notice that we can sometimes use a modification of this method by starting with a rough approximation. For example, let us find the square root of 594. Now we know that 400 has a square root of 20. (If we know another square nearer to 594 we will, of course, use that.) We must add 41 to get the next square to 400, then 43 to get the next, and so on. (Why?)

Now we find that $400 + (41 + 43 + 45 + 47) = 576$
$$400 + (41 + 43 + 45 + 47 + 49) = 625.$$

This tells us that the square root of 594 lies between 24 and 25. (Why?) To get nearer to the value of the square root we must develop other methods which are beyond the scope of this book.

Since we have mentioned square roots, it is perhaps worth suggesting that children can explore the square roots of two, three and four-figure numbers with the Dienes Multibase Arithmetic Blocks or similar material. The problem is one of taking pieces from the 10-box to represent the original number (without using the blocks), and arranging the pieces to form as large a square as possible. The square root, or an approximation to it, is given by the length of a side of the square. Plenty of practical work on these lines can soon lead children to a method of computing square roots which makes sense of the 'long method' now banished from our secondary school text-books.

Patterns on pegboard

The triangular and square patterns we have discussed owe their interest to their very special configurations, but we can, if we wish, choose to represent numbers by dot patterns in a variety of ways. We *might* choose to represent four by the pattern $\cdot\,\vdots\,$ or five by the pattern $\,.\,.\,\vdots\,$. (In the context of the preceding paragraphs, the latter is a particularly meaningful way of representing an odd number.) As we stress so often in this book, the recognition that an element of choice is involved is the real point that we are making.

We illustrate this by a brief account of a number of experiments with a group of children on the theme, 'How many patterns can be made by putting a given number of pegs into the holes of a piece of pegboard?' We observe before we give the account that

(i) the basic lattice structure of the holes on the board is a built-in restriction on the range of possible patterns, but that without this or some other restriction the possibilities would be too extensive to classify; and that

(ii) a good deal of the early discussion is an attempt, by the teacher and the children, to clarify the remaining ambiguities of the question and make the solution manageable.

'How many patterns can be made with two pegs?' The first attempt usually produces an enormous number of patterns, as the two pegs can be put anywhere on the board. After discussion of these various possibilities, one way of limiting these to something more convenient is to restrict the use of the word 'pattern' to those arrangements in which the two pegs are in holes next to one another (children usually suggest this). This, however, is still not precise enough, as the following are 'next to one another' in one particular direction.

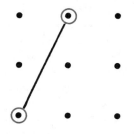

Fig.19

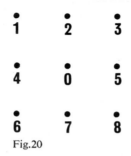

Fig.20

In order to be more precise, we can say that if we put the peg in any hole on the board (position O in Fig.20) another peg is 'next' to it if it is in any one of the positions 1 to 8.

'Can we now say how many different patterns can be made with two pegs?' Even after this lengthy discussion of what is meant by 'next to', children will spend a long time experimenting with the various possible positions for the two pegs. Most children seem to feel that the positions 2, 4, 5, 7 produce the 'same pattern', and justify this in some way such as 'It is the same when you turn the board round'. Sometimes children consider that positions 1,3,6,8 give the same patterns as 2, 4, 5, 7; at other times they think of them as 'different' because they are farther apart.

'How many different patterns can be made with three pegs?'

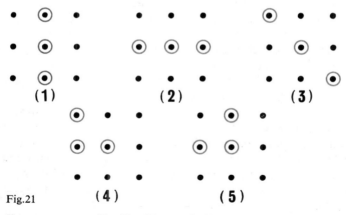

Fig.21 **(4)** **(5)**

The linear patterns (1), (2), (3) are similar to those produced with two pegs, and again we have the problem of whether they are the same as each other or whether they are essentially different. (4) and

(5) give us something new, although they are of course the same pattern turned round or turned over; this was not always discovered.

'How many different patterns can be made with four pegs?'

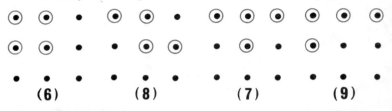

Fig.22

Can we include?

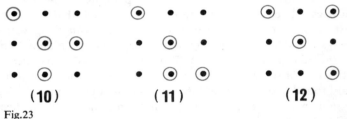

Fig.23

Is (12) the same as (7)?

There were also the usual linear patterns.

Many of the patterns were given names by the children: (6) square, (8) parallelogram, (7) triangle, (9) most often called L-shaped.

'How many patterns can be made with . . . ?'

The more pegs there are, of course, the more patterns one gets, and the children may well become interested in classifying the number according to the shape of the patterns.

The fact that some numbers can be expressed in the form $a \times b$ (neither a nor b equal to 1), some in the form $a \times a$, and that others do not fit into either of these patterns was usually arrived at fairly quickly and led to the idea of rectangular, square and prime numbers. Although triangular patterns were made, only some of them corresponded to the usual definition of triangular numbers. (Fig. 24)

Thus, only pattern (iii) is a representation of a triangular number in the usual sense of the words.

Is this kind of exploration worth initiating? What are your views about the ambiguities of the questions and the possibility of confusion

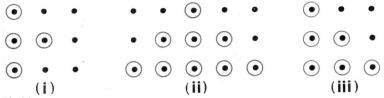

(i) (ii) (iii)

Fig.24

and disagreement among the children? Should the teacher always take care not to ask ambiguous questions?

Is it possible that the teacher does not always see in advance the ambiguities in his questions and statements until the reaction of his pupils surprise him by their variety?

Products

The number relationships which are examined in school and which emerge in, for example, the study of number arrays which we sketched earlier in this section, are overwhelmingly of an additive kind. Even the triangular or square numbers seem interesting because a pattern exists in what we have to add to one of them to get the next. When we talk of multiples of a number (as when we recite a 'table'), we are only calling attention to the results of successively adding a particular number. But sequences of numbers can be generated multiplicatively.

We launch what follows with some talk of rods, as this is a convenient starting-point for children who are familiar with their use. We refer readers to the Cuisenaire or Colour-Factor literature for a description of the ways in which the 'cross' and 'tower' conventions can be introduced. Briefly, 'towers' are formed by placing rods on top of each other so that each is at right angles to the one underneath. These symbolize successive multiplication by the appropriate numbers. A 'cross' is a tower made of only two rods.

(a) Compose a tower of red rods, step by step, starting with a single rod, crossing it with another red rod, crossing this with a third, and so on. With white rod as unit, the number name of the red rod is 2, so that the corresponding number names for successive stages in the construction of the tower are 2, 4, 8, 16, etc. (Fig.25)

We have used an action corresponding to the mental operation of multiplying, and we notice, as in our generation of square or triangular numbers, that each pattern includes all preceding patterns.

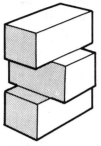

Fig.25

Similarly construct a tower of light-green rods, step by step, saying 3, 9, 27, 81, etc.

Although there are physical limitations to the height of a tower, we recognize that we can perform the virtual action of putting another rod indefinitely.

The products (which are all powers of 2 or 3 so far) can be found in the first two lines of the accompanying table. The table only contains products less than 1000, and is divided by the vertical lines into hundred lots.

Notice that a pink tower is equivalent to a red tower containing twice as many rods. A pink tower yields the numbers 4, 16, 64, etc., which are contained in the sequence already obtained from the red tower.

(b) Take some light-green and red rods and construct towers containing a mixture of the two colours. Does the order in which we put them in the tower affect the value of the product? We probably start with a tower containing one red rod and some greens, or one green and some reds; then perhaps a tower with two reds and some greens, or two greens and some reds. We can develop some systematic strategy for covering all the possibilities. The table shows these products in the 3rd, 4th, 5th and 6th rows. Can you detect the principle used to generate each row?

(c) Take some red, light-green and yellow rods and form mixed towers. Do we need to consider $2 \times (3 \times 5)$, $3 \times (2 \times 5)$, $5 \times (2 \times 3)$, etc., separately? We may notice, however, that our mental calculations can be made easier by taking the numbers in some orders rather than others. Which lines in the table show the corresponding products?

(d) We discover that we can restrict ourselves to the rods represent-

Factors	Products									
2	2 **4** 8 **16** 32 **64**	128	**256**			512				
3	3 **9** 27 **81**	243					**729**			
2,3	6 12,24,48 96	192		384			768			
	18, 54	162			486					
	36 72	108	216	**324**	432	**576**	648		864	972
	144		288							
5	5 **25**	125					**625**			
2,5	10,20,40,50,80	**100**	200	320	**400**	500	640		800	
		160	250							
3,5	15 45 75	135	**225**	375	405		675			
2,3,5	30 60 90	120	240	300	450	540	600	720	810	**900**
		150	270	360	480			750		960
		180								
7	7 **49**			343						
2,7	14,28 56 98	112	224	392	448		686	**784**	896	
		196								
3,7	21, 63	147		**441**	567					
		189								
2,3,7	42 84	126	252	336		504	672	756	882	
		168	294	378		588				
5,7	35	175	245							
2,5,7	70	140	280	350	490	560		700		980
3,5,7		105		315		525		735		945
2,3,5,7			210		420		630		840	

Fig.26. Table of powers.

ing prime numbers, as all the products we can make can be made with these alone. (The remark at the end of (a) may give us a clue to the reason.)

(e) When do the towers represent square numbers? Do any of the following towers represent squares?

$$r\times r\times r,\quad r\times g\times r\times g,\quad r\times g\times r\times y\times y\times g,\quad r\times r\times g\times y\times y,$$
$$r^4\times y^6\times g^2.$$

(In the last part, r^4 is an abbreviation for $r\times r\times r\times r$ and y^6 an abbreviation for $y\times y\times y\times y\times y\times y$.)

(f) The table stops with the factor 7. Can you extend it to include products involving the factor 11?

The preceding exercise has its own fascination. It is useful, though, as a technique – one among very many – by which one can generate numbers from others. It is a set of such techniques, rather than a limited store of 'number facts', that give children mastery in the field of numbers.

Relational patterns

When we are calculating the powers of 2, as in the last section, we may become absorbed in certain properties that we find. Our first contact with simple logarithms may arise from this situation (see p.283).

Let us begin again: start with 1 and double successively:

1, 2, 4, 8, 16, 32, 64, 128, 256, ...

If we suddenly find ourselves looking at the units digits of these numbers, we may be surprised to see the recurring pattern 2, 4, 8, 6.

We may represent this schematically, using arrows to lead from one unit digit to the next. Then it is clear that, if we begin with 1, we find ourselves in a cycle from which we cannot escape by continuing to double.

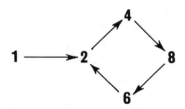

Fig.27

What happens if we begin with 3 and double successively?

3, 6, 12, 24, 48, 96, 192, 384, ...

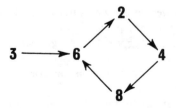

Fig.28

What about the sequences starting with 7 and 9?

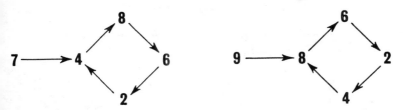

Fig.29

What happens if we start with 2, 4, 6, or 8? What happens if we start with 5? 5 leads to 0, and however many times we continue to double, the units digit will stay 0.

We can combine all our information into one diagram:

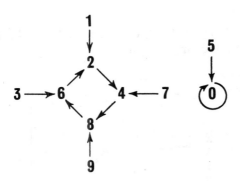

Fig.30

Can we now say what pattern of units digits we shall get, whatever the number we start with? Yes, for we have considered all the possible units digits that can occur in our original number.

Once we have recognized a particular doubling pattern, we might expect to find similar patterns emerging if we successively multiply by 3, by 4, and so on. Are they going to be very different? Will they be linked in any way? Let us see.

Trebling

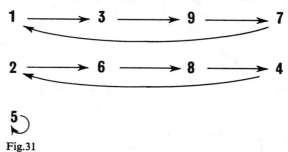

Fig.31

We can redraw this as:

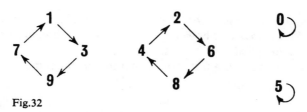

Fig.32

There is something familiar here. The cycle 2, 6, 8, 4 is the reverse of the cycle in the doubling pattern.

Multiplying by 4

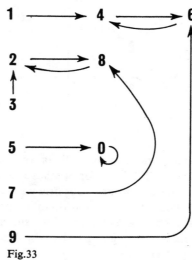

Fig.33

Reorganizing, this becomes:

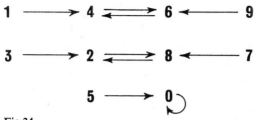

Fig.34

Can we make any observations about this? How could we have derived this from our doubling pattern?

Multiplying by 5

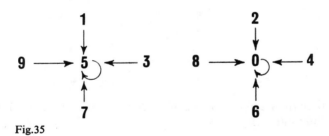

Fig.35

Multiplying by 6

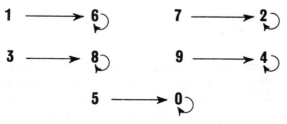

Fig.36

Multiplying by 7

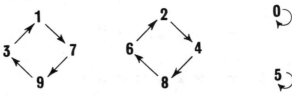

Fig.37

Compare this with the pattern for trebling.

Multiplying by 8

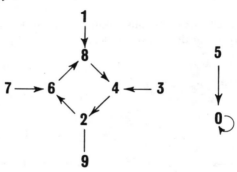

Fig.38

This pattern is similar in design to another. Which? And how do they differ internally?

Multiplying by 9

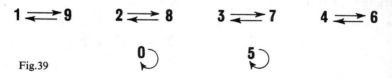

Fig.39

Vast numbers of observations can be made about these patterns. Look, for instance, at the occurrence of certain sub-patterns such as **a⇌b** and **a→b⤵** . Various interrelations appear to exist between the several patterns. Are there any obvious ways in which patterns can be combined? Consider doubling and trebling.

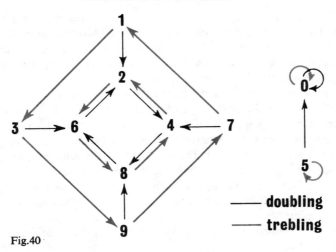

Fig.40

How could we obtain the pattern for multiplying by 6 from this? Can we combine any others?

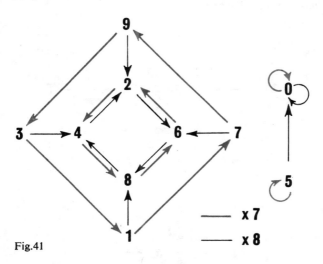

Fig.41

There is (of course!) an element of choice in the way we schematize the patterns, and it may well be that there are better ways to draw the diagrams to exemplify the properties and relationships. With a large drawing and enough colours it is possible to make a master diagram containing them all.

Why do patterns emerge at all? Why do the patterns for multiplication by 2 and by 8 have the same structure? Multiplication by 3 and by 7? $2+8=10$ and $3+7=10$. But $4+6=10$ and the patterns for multiplication by 4 and by 6 do not have the same structure. We might expect 0 to be an odd digit out, but why is 5 always apart from the main structural pattern? Because it is half of ten?

We know that the units digit of a number is also its remainder on division by 10 (see p.76). If we think of these patterns as telling us something about the remainders when we divide by something, we can at once turn to explore the behaviour of the remainders when we divide by a number other than 10. Will patterns appear? If so, will they be like those we have already found? Perhaps they will yield clues which will help us to understand the mathematics behind the earlier patterns.

A small selection is given below, without further comment. What can you find?

Remainders on division by 6

Doubling

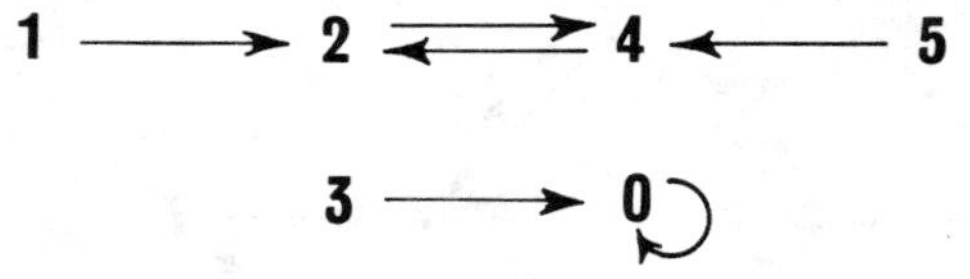

Fig.42

Trebling

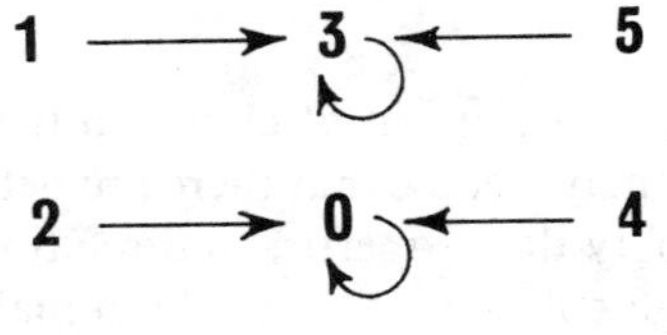

Fig.43

Multiplying by 4

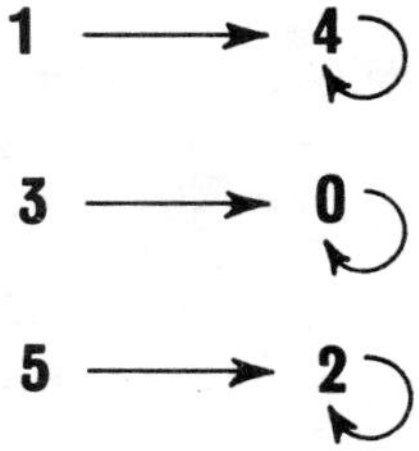

1 ⟶ 4 ↺

3 ⟶ 0 ↺

5 ⟶ 2 ↺

Fig.44

Multiplying by 5

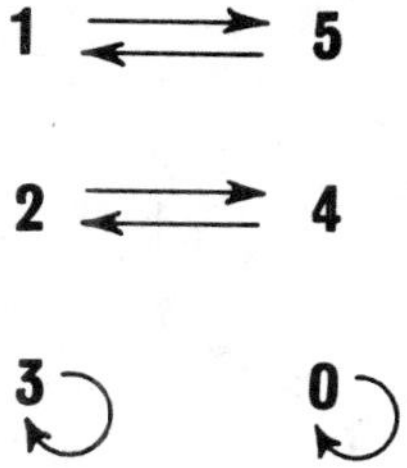

1 ⇄ 5

2 ⇄ 4

3 ↺   0 ↺

Fig.45

Remainders on division by 7

Doubling

Fig.46

Trebling

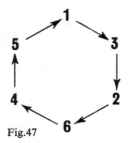

Fig.47

Multiplying by 4

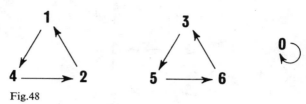

Fig.48

Multiplying by 5

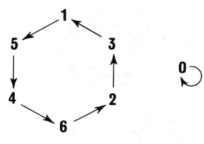

Fig.49

Multiplying by 6

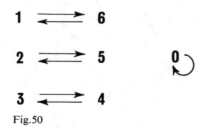

Fig.50

(by a group of six-to-seven-year-olds)

1 I went to the Botanical Gardens. I took a bag of nuts. Twenty birds each ate ten nuts. Six squirrels each had twenty-six nuts. I dropped seven nuts. I threw out eighteen. I had six nuts left. How many nuts did I start with? (Hannah)

2 One fine day, 20 spiders collected in a barn. 4 of them had lost 3 of their (eight) legs. 3 flies (who each had 6 legs) had a chat with the spiders. 3 cows came, 2 sparrows, 3 swallows, 1 swift and a tit. How many legs were there altogether? (Hannah)

3 There were 18 holes in a clearing. 3 mice came. They each had a hole. Some badgers came. They each had a hole, there were 9 holes left. 12 rats came. They each dug a hole. 7 ran away. There were some rats left. Each animal had a store house. There were 3 nuts for each. How many nuts were there? (Hannah)

4 If I had 100 boy friends and I gave away 20 and I gave away another 20 and I gave away 40 and I married one and locked him in a cupboard and married another, how many would be left? (Jane)

5 I picked 19 acorns and I dropped 12. I picked double what I had left and gave 10 away. How many acorns have I now? (Mary)

6 8 girls went to the sea-side and 4 of them each made a sand-pie. Each sand-pie had 8 shells. The other 4 built one big sand-castle and it had forty shells. How many shells were there? (Elizabeth)

7 I built 15 sand-castles and the tide washed away 10 of them and I built 7 more and I put 3 shells on them. How many shells would I need? (Jennifer)

3

Induction

This chapter is a discussion of some of the issues arising when we try to generalize and produce a mathematical result from a number of particular instances. The process is usually called induction. We use it a lot in the mathematics classroom, whether we recognize it from its name or not. It is not such a simple process as is sometimes thought, but without it very little mathematical thinking can be done. This is not the place for a very deep analysis of the activity which we call inductive; as it is, this section may seem arid to some readers. We put it here because we would like to initiate some consideration, by teachers, of the assumptions we make when we put certain situations before our pupils, and to awaken some appreciation of the range which the word 'induction' may cover – from guessing to (in Polya's [89] words) plausible reasoning.

So much of what we do with number patterns is concerned with the act of induction, an intuitive process which we often use without being aware of it. The following type of question is very familiar:

'Write down the next two numbers,

- (a) 1, 2, 3, 4, . . .
- (b) 1, 2, 4, 8, . . .
- (c) 1, 3, 6, 10, . . .'.

Very few children will hesitate before writing down

  1, 2, 3, 4, 5, 6,

and 1, 2, 4, 8, 16, 32.

Continuation of (c) requires a little more thought. How many numbers do we feel should be given before asking for the sequence to be continued? One? Of course not – anything can happen! Two? No, two wouldn't distinguish between (a) and (b), for example. Three? Four? Yes, the pattern should be clear now.

What we are really asking in questions like this is that the child shall guess *our* rule, and so we give him what we think should be enough information to find it. Of course, these are 'obvious' number patterns, the 'obviousness' depending upon the kind of analytic procedures that we have at our disposal. This 'give the next one' type of investigation probes into the techniques which the child has at his disposal. For instance, if he does not think of considering successive differences he may not see a pattern at all in (c). Why should the child select *our* rule? Admittedly, in most cases we choose an 'obvious' pattern, but it is important to recognize that there are *ways* of continuing – an infinite number of them – rather than '*the*' way. Anyone is free to choose his own. A pattern that can be detected in, say, a set of four numbers carries with it no compulsion for extension to the next one. The extension depends upon our decision. For instance, a particular rule for the continuation of the sequence 3, 6, 12, 24, 48 gives 95, 183 for the next two numbers. What is this rule?

$$\begin{array}{ccccc} 3 & 6 & 12 & 24 & 48 \end{array}$$

1st differences	3	6	12	24
2nd differences	3	6	12	
3rd differences	3	6		
4th differences	3			

The rule is that the fourth differences will be 3, 5, 7, 9, etc., so that the consequence for the first line is:

$$\begin{array}{cccccccc} 3 & 6 & 12 & 24 & 48 & 95 & 183 & 339 \\ & 3 & 6 & 12 & 24 & 47 & 88 & 156 \\ & & 3 & 6 & 12 & 23 & 41 & 68 \\ & & & 3 & 6 & 11 & 18 & 27 \\ & & & & 3 & 5 & 7 & 9 \end{array}$$

'Far-fetched', you may say, 'No-one in his senses would construct such a sequence.' Perhaps not; but it shows that it is only our naïve assumption about the likely construction ('doubling') that enables us to answer the question with 96, 192. What is more, this illustration throws up the possibility of a much more exciting question: 'What patterns can *you* put into this sequence? In how many different ways can *you* extend it?'

Let us pursue this matter of 'obviousness' a little further. Quite often we meet a type of number pattern which seems to reflect some basic property of numbers. For instance,

$$3^2 = 2^2 + (3+2)$$
$$4^2 = 3^2 + (4+3)$$
$$5^2 = 4^2 + (5+4)$$
$$6^2 = 5^2 + (6+5).$$

The pattern of the first line is repeated in the second, except that 3 and 2 have been replaced by 4 and 3, respectively. The pattern is observed again in the third and fourth lines with similar replacements of the numbers. The basic pattern which underlies the changes of the numbers might be written

$$\square^2 = \triangle^2 + (\square + \triangle).$$

Fig.1

On reflection, this pattern appears unsatisfactory since it does not reveal the relationship between the numbers in each line. We can take account of this by writing

$$\square - \triangle = 1.$$

Fig.2

which transforms our pattern into

$$(\triangle + 1)^2 = \triangle^2 + (\overline{\triangle + 1} + \triangle).$$

Fig.3

If $\triangle$ is replaced by 5, we get $6^2 = 5^2 + (6+5)$, one of the original statements. But if we replace $\triangle$ by 8, 12, 26 in turn, we have

$$9^2 = 8^2 + (9+8)$$
$$13^2 = 12^2 + (13+12)$$
$$27^2 = 26^2 + (27+26).$$

What justification have we for regarding these statements as true? In the first instance we looked at a set of four statements (did we check their truth?) and recognized a pattern common to them all. Now we have produced further statements based on the same pattern. But as things are, we have no reason to regard these statements as true *simply* because they reflect the given pattern. Verification is required.

Visual representations can often help us to see the structure behind the property.

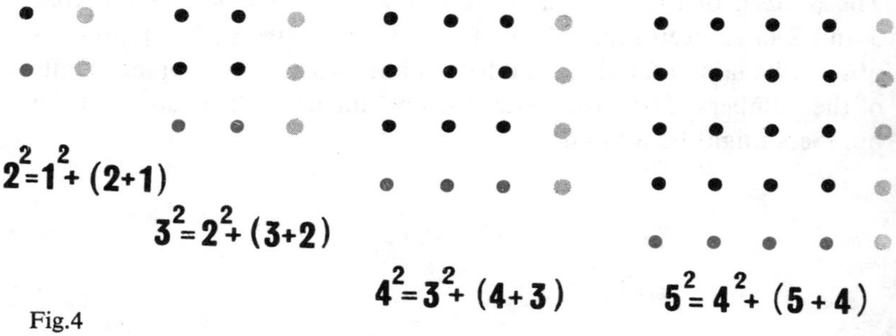

$$2^2 = 1^2 + (2+1)$$
$$3^2 = 2^2 + (3+2)$$
$$4^2 = 3^2 + (4+3) \qquad 5^2 = 4^2 + (5+4)$$

Fig.4

Take the 4×4 square. It is possible to view the dots in such a way that the equivalence of 4^2 and $3^2 + (4+3)$ is evident. Furthermore our way of looking at this particular square—a border row and column being separated from the other dots to leave the preceding square—is not peculiar to it. This pattern can be drawn from any square array, and for this reason we say that we have a general property. Thus the visual representation reveals the structure of the situation in a way which the statements themselves cannot.

Number properties of this kind lend themselves to this sort of treatment, but it may take a little time to perceive the 'appropriate' pattern in the array of dots.

Consider the pattern
$$(2 \times 2) - 1 = 3 \times 1$$
$$(3 \times 3) - 1 = 4 \times 2$$
$$(4 \times 4) - 1 = 5 \times 3$$
$$(5 \times 5) - 1 = 6 \times 4, \text{ etc.}$$
$$\text{or} \quad (\Delta \times \Delta) - 1 = (\Delta + 1) \times (\Delta - 1)$$

and take the 4×4 array as a 'representative special case' (see Polya [89], vol.1, p.25).

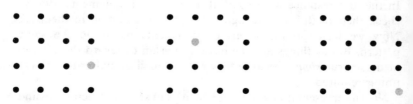

Fig.5

How can we perceive $(\Delta \times \Delta) - 1$? There are three essentially different ways of isolating the single dot. (How many in a 5×5 array?) Which is the most appropriate for this particular pattern, bearing in mind that we wish to show the equivalence of $(\Delta \times \Delta) - 1$ and $(\Delta + 1) \times (\Delta - 1)$?

Of course, we can begin by choosing a pattern which we repeat in successive arrays and then interpret our action in terms of numbers. Take for instance the following sequence, in which the action is selecting the square in the centre and the four corner dots:

Fig.6

As such this is a non-numerical activity, but we can give a numerical interpretation. We have the pattern

$$\Delta^2 = (\Delta - 2)^2 + 4(\Delta - 2) + 4.$$

For a 5×5 array, $\quad 5^2 = 3^2 + (4 \times 3) + 4.$

For a 9×9 array, $\quad 9^2 = 7^2 + (4 \times 7) + 4.$

For an 18×18 array, ...?

We do not need to check these statements by calculation, since their equivalence is recognized at the moment when we superimpose one pattern upon another. (See also the work on square and triangular numbers on p.27 and the examples at the end of this chapter.)

Patterns can be made in many ways and with different objects. Mention was made earlier (p.24) of the possibility of building up patterns of rods by means of a repetitive action. In one example a square was made with red rods and was then bordered by pink ones, giving another square, and so on.

We have a way of continuing, and this particular rule can produce the number pattern:

$$3^2 = 1^2 + (4 \times 2),$$
$$5^2 = 3^2 + (4 \times 4),$$
$$7^2 = 5^2 + (4 \times 6), \text{ etc.}$$

which is very like the one above.

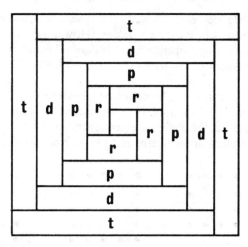

Fig.7

Partitions and regions

We can also make patterns of a somewhat different kind. In how many different ways can a length equivalent to that of the red, green, pink, yellow rod, etc. be made? (For the sake of this illustration let us consider red followed by white as being different from white followed by red.) Including the rod itself the partitions are as follows:

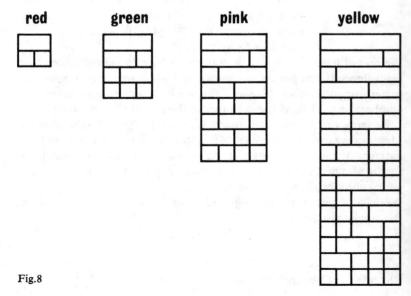

Fig.8

The number sequence we obtain is 2, 4, 8, 16. There is a strong suspicion that the next number will be 32 and the next 64. Why? We are using intuitive induction at this point; we recognize an 'obvious' pattern and feel fairly confident that we have the 'right' one. But a number sequence has no *inherent* pattern, as we saw earlier. However, in this case it is a manifestation of an activity with the rods, and if we can see what it is about the patterned activity which produces the sequence 2, 4, 8, 16, we may then be able to decide how it will continue. Of course, we can consider the partitions of the dark green rod, black rod, etc., and verify that additional numbers belong to the sequence, but this does not entitle us to assume a certain rule although it may increase the probability of its truth.

'2, 4, 8, 16' is a powerful director of one's thoughts and occurs in a variety of contexts. Suppose we are given a circle with two points on the circumference. A line joining the two divides the circle into two regions:

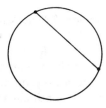

Fig.9

Add a third point and join it to the others. We then have four regions:

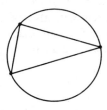

Fig.10

A fourth point then gives eight regions:

Fig.11

How about five points? 16 regions?

Fig.12

And six points? 32 regions? (Check it!)

Number of points	2	3	4	5	6
Number of regions	2	4	8	16	?

We now have two situations, each producing the numbers, 2, 4, 8, 16; but whereas it can be shown that the first example continues as a doubling sequence, the second example continues with 31 and 57 – and our intuition suffers a severe blow. (A typical reaction to the appearance of 31 is a belief that one has miscounted, so strong is the feeling that the number should be 32.)

The figure on p.87, showing the partitions of the length of the yellow rod, has been constructed to give a clue to the way that the sequence of partitions can be verified. If the clue seems too obscure, it does not matter here; there are other approaches that will solve this problem. The sequence of regions in the circle can also be derived from a general proof, but this is too involved for us to discuss. The point we are making is not dependent on our being able to give the whole story.

Line crossings

Finally, we look at a problem involving lines in a plane and their intersections. The diagrams below show the maximum possible number of intersections of a number of lines in general position. We exclude cases in which any two lines are parallel, or in which any three are concurrent, for these special cases will reduce our number of intersections. (There are other explorations which take these special cases into account. For example, given five straight lines, how many different numbers of intersections can we produce by rearranging them?)

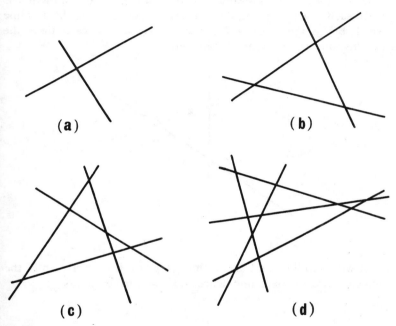

(a)   (b)   (c)   (d)

Fig.13

How many intersections with three lines? With four? Two? Five? Drawing and counting are relatively simple as long as the number of lines is small.

lines	intersections
(1)	(0)
2	1
3	3
4	6
5	10
6	?

How many intersections with six lines? There is the beginning of a familiar pattern, the triangular numbers, one of the examples given at the beginning of this chapter (p.47). We may conjecture that the next number will be fifteen. The fact that the counting verifies this strengthens our belief that we have perceived the pattern which characterizes the particular activity, but it provides no final confirmation. (Remember the circle example.)

Look, not at the completed diagrams, but rather at what happens when each new line is added to the existing set, for it is the new line which brings the additional points of intersection each time; the existing intersections remain unaltered.

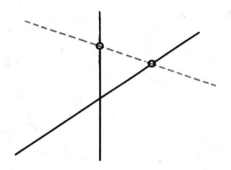

Fig.14

Start with two lines and take a third (Fig.14). It crosses each of the two lines already there, and hence adds two further points.

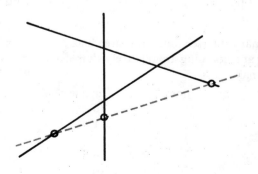

Fig.15

A fourth line crosses each of the three lines already there, and therefore adds three intersections. Any new line must cut all the previous lines. This is our general statement. The nth line cuts $(n-1)$ lines and thus adds $(n-1)$ points of intersection. So the following pattern emerges:

lines	intersections	
2	1	1
3	1+2	3
4	1+2+3	6
5	1+2+3+4	10
6	1+2+3+4+5	15

We are now in quite a different position from the beginning when we looked at the numbers 1, 3, 6, 10 and wondered whether we had chosen the correct rule for continuing. The mind has now perceived a way of proceeding derived from the activity itself.

That the actual discussion may not be so simple in the classroom, and that the question of the intersection of straight lines – as with the other examples we have taken – may not be so unambiguous as we suppose, is illustrated in the report with which we close this chapter.

We have hinted, in these few pages, at some distinctions that exist in the character and validity of the generalizations that we make on the basis of the evidence we have. In many of the number patterns of Chapter 2, for example, the induction is a direct result of the way in which our number system is constructed. In this section we have looked at some examples of 'action proofs' which develop a generalization from the activity of the situation; this may not be expressed firmly in mathematical terms, but it is a step beyond mere observation of the evidence. There are, too, inductions which are fully consummated in familiar mathematical terms. Almost any situation calling for an inductive response can be treated at levels ranging from pure hunch to a formal mathematical treatment. We have not made these distinctions clear, for they are not in reality clear. They can be artificially clarified by a theoretical discussion, perhaps; but this may not help us in a practical situation to decide just how far to press on with a demand for a rigorous proof of the generalizations that are being made. Rigour is, in any case, relative, depending on what a particular social group accepts as a proof at a particular time. A teacher may impose a demand for rigour, and make many pronouncements about the fallibility of guesses, but his pupils often will not listen because they are not ready to understand. But there are times when the situation is reversed and the teacher accepts too readily generalizations which some, at least, of his pupils are able to substantiate more strongly. Some understanding of the levels at which intuition works, and the techniques by which it can be supported, is essential equipment for the teacher of mathematics.

Lesson with class of 34 eight-year-olds (*unstreamed*)
I asked a child to come and draw a straight line on the board:

Fig.16

I asked another child to draw a straight line crossing this one:

Fig.17

How many crossings are there?
Three children said 'Two', all the rest said 'Four'. When asked to point out the crossings some children pointed to the lines (as if they were four lines meeting at a point) and some to the spaces. When asked, they recalled that two straight lines had been drawn.

There seemed to be no way out. I asked who had a toy railway. On the blackboard I drew the following diagram:

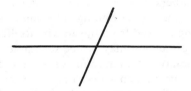

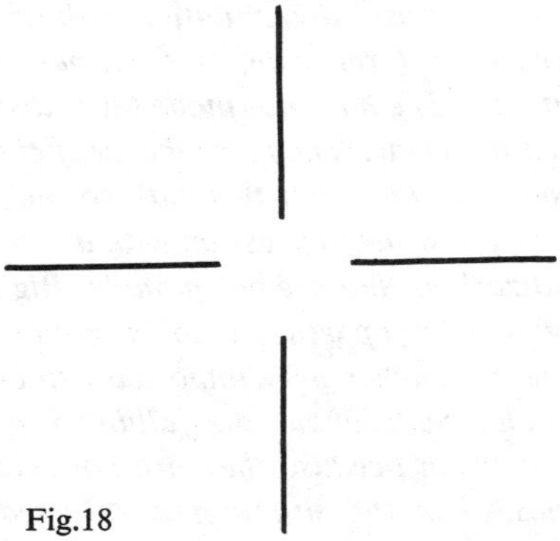

Fig.18

and asked how many crossings were needed. The boys all happily agreed 'One'. I'm not so sure about the girls.

I asked if it were possible to draw two straight lines and get more than one crossing. The children tried on paper and no-one suggested immediately that it was impossible. Eight children imitated the blackboard drawing and stopped. Some children made five or six attempts before saying it was impossible.

What happens with three straight lines?
One child drew:

Fig.19

Another continued:

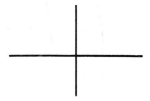

Fig.20

And a third child completed the diagram:

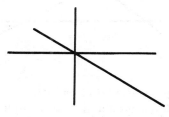

Fig.21

How many crossings are there?
Most children said 'six'. I asked three more children to draw lines:

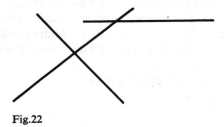

Fig.22

Is this different? Yes. *How is it different?* There are only two crossings.
How many crossings are there with three straight lines?
There was a certain tentativeness, but the children began to grasp the idea.
One child started with parallel lines:

Fig.23

All agreed that it was possible to draw a diagram with three crossings:

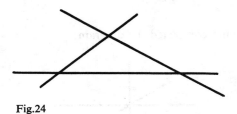

Fig.24

How many crossings are there with four straight lines?
Almost all the children produced three or four variations. Several discovered that it was possible to have a drawing with six crossings.

One of the children made a table on the blackboard:

lines	crossings
1	0
2	1
3	3
4	6

The bell went and I suggested that they might like to try five lines.
One boy immediately said 'Nine crossings'.
Two boys came to me after lunch and said there were nine.

Peter (4) counting, 'One, two, five, . . .' Older brother Ian interrupts: 'That's wrong!' Peter retorts, 'I know it is. It should be three, but I like five better.'

Peter (5) comes home from school and decides to show the family the 'sums' he has been doing. He writes down '5−5= ', then looks up brightly and says, 'What do you want me to put?' On being asked what it 'makes' (his version of 'equals'), he says, 'I don't know; I can't do it without my counters.' Ian suggests using fingers. Peter considers this and decides that he will, but that it will 'make something different'. He finally decides that the answer is 'nothing' and writes a big round O. Next he writes '2−4= '. Ian says, 'You can't do that until you're my age.' Peter retorts, 'I can! I can put another O', and does so. Ian says, 'Look, Peter, if you had two sweets and you wanted to eat four, you couldn't, could you?' 'No. But I could eat the two and have nothing left.'

Peter (6) going to school one afternoon said, 'Bye-bye, see you in two hours.' 'Oh – yes.' 'I go to school for two hours in the afternoon and three hours in the morning. That's five hours a day.' 'How much is that a week?' (Using his fingers to indicate the days) '5 hours on Monday, 5 hours on Tuesday, 5 hours on Wednesday, 5 hours on Thursday, 5 hours on Friday. 5 and 5 make 10, that's 20, and the other 5 makes 25.' On that day, the first day of term, Peter had started doing 'tens of units' sums. Six weeks later he was still doing tens and units, 'addition with no bags', and asked me to give him some sums. On one I omitted the headings 'T', 'U', and was told this was not a tens and units because 'it hasn't got those things on top'. Then he said, 'Do you know, *she's* never given us anything more than nine. I'm going to do a hard one.' And he wrote down

T	U
10	11
3	1
—	—
13	12
—	—

Place-value

Finding Hymn No.325 in the hymn-book can be quite a difficult
exercise for the young child. He may plunge about in the pages until
he comes across a number like the one he is seeking. But at an early
stage he will not necessarily be aware that No.327 is 'warmer' than
No.425. We may say that his difficulty arises because he does not
understand the place-value system that our arithmetical notation
uses. Presumably he doesn't; but does he need to know very much
about place-value to be successful in searching for a hymn number?
Finding a word in the dictionary is a difficult skill too. How far are
the mental operations comparable? Both require the repeated application of a memorized ordered sequence – of digits in one case, and of
letters in the other. But neither has much to do with place value, only
with the established routine that we start at the left in each case.
When numbers are being used as labels, as they are in the hymn-book,
the most he needs to know is the order in which they appear. He is
not concerned to do anything with the number; he just needs to be
able to locate it.

When we begin to operate with numbers, however, or to describe
their relationships in more detail, we need to understand the place-
value system that we use in our notation. It is unnecessary to deal
with this fully here as recognition of its importance is widespread
and most recent books give it good coverage. Let us merely make one
or two observations.

1. Our familiar notational system reflects just one way in which a
system of whole numbers can be constructed. To be able to build 'on
and on' and not be limited by the symbols at our disposal to the
representation of just a few numbers, we must have certain clear and
agreed rules that allow us to continue. When we write 2507 as

$(2\times1000)+(5\times100)+(0\times10)+(7\times1)$

we display the conventional rules that we are using. And if we write
$$(2\times10^3)+(5\times10^2)+(0\times10^1)+(7\times10^0)$$
the structure becomes even more apparent. Corresponding to the written form, we have the words 'two thousand, five hundred and seven' which also show the structure (if not so clearly); the verbal pattern too, can be used to speak of numbers of any size without requiring more than a fixed repertory of words.

2. When we write out 'in full' the meaning we give to '2507', as we did above, we can see the complexity underlying the simple and economical exterior. The statement of what the sign means brings in symbols for adding, multiplying and raising to a power, none of which was visible in the simple form. It also shows that the digits of '2507' are coefficients of powers of ten, the ten, too, being 'understood' but not expressed. (The ten is the base of the numeration that we normally use.) We customarily introduce the notational system long before we have treated powers of ten, or powers of any number for that matter, and it would seem very unlikely that most children appreciate the implications of the notation that we offer them. There are a number of courses that can be adopted to try to lead children to understand it. One is to take the line that the rules of notation, like the rules for counting, can be told to the child, and that when he has, at a later stage, considerable familiarity with them, he can be led to analyse them and see how they work. (This must have been the path to understanding for most teachers.) A second method is to provide the child with structured material, like the Dienes Multi-base Arithmetic Blocks, which offers a physical model of the powers of the base, so that a considerable part of the job of structuring is already done by the material. A third method is to work through with the child, from the beginning, some of the decisions that are involved in making a suitable construction. For a discussion of a way in which this might be done see Goutard [50] (pp.88 ff.).

3. The formal computational procedures that we use in arithmetic combine the place-value notation (which, as we have seen, hides a considerable part of its structure) with the operation of certain formal rules for the manipulation and combination of numbers. We can analyse out of this mixture a number of general principles relating to the acts of adding and multiplying. Let us consider, for example, a quite simple addition:

$$375$$
$$+163$$
$$\overline{538}$$

If we try to write this without benefit of place-value, we find ourselves forced into some explanation like:

$(3\times10^2+7\times10^1+5\times10^0)+(1\times10^2+6\times10^1+3\times10^0)$*

$=(3\times10^2+1\times10^2)+(7\times10^1+6\times10^1)+(5\times10^0+3\times10^0)$

$=(3+1)\times10^2+(7+6)\times10^1+(5+3)\times10^0$

$=4\times10^2+(10+3)\times10^1+8\times10^0$

$=4\times10^2+1\times10^2+3\times10^1+8\times10^0$

$=(4+1)\times10^2+3\times10^1+8\times10^0$

$=5\times10^2+3\times10^1+8\times10^0.$

Of course, a direct comparison between the two written computations is not at all fair since the second version does not suppose that anything much can be done in the head; the first assumes a good deal behind its bland exterior. And we are not recommending that the second form should be followed. What is significant is that the abandonment of the place-value notation has made apparent the presence in the computation of some principles that can be applied more generally.

We see, for example, that our second written account assumes that the terms we say we are adding in the first line can be re-grouped in the second line. The principle that asserts we can do this is called the *associative law for addition*. It says that if we have three or more numbers to add, we can group them in any way we like in order to perform the addition. (There is a similar law for multiplication.) In moving from the second line to the third line we have used the principle expressed by the *distributive law for multiplication over addition*. If we are adding multiples of the same number, we may add the coefficients together to give a single multiple of the same number. (The distributive law can be symbolized by the statement: $(a+b)\times c=a\times c+b\times c$, where a, b and c are numbers.) The fiddling about in the third, fourth and fifth lines is forced on us because we may not have a coefficient of a power of ten which is greater than 9. This corresponds to the 'borrowing' and 'carrying' that we talk about when we do the sum in the usual way.

---

* We use the convention that the multiplication sign takes precedence over the addition sign so that we can simplify the notation by omitting subsidiary brackets around terms like 3×10^2, etc.

We have said all this because it raises the matter of general principles, like the associative and distributive laws, that we may now want to look out for in other contexts. (An analysis of a multiplication sum on similar lines is an interesting exercise. See Dienes [30] p.72). These laws can be powerful tools to have to hand when doing computations. But we must not leave this example without pointing out that if we want to do computations in the routine way, as we initially did our addition, most of what we have just said is not helpful. Our standard methods of computation make it unnecessary to be aware of associativity or distributivity. The place-value notation, combined with the way the sum is written and the routine procedure of adding in columns, takes care of all that. In fact, the place-value-associativity-distributivity complex is meshed together so tightly in the standard procedure that a conscious analysis of it is likely to confuse. We may say, in short, that if routine computation procedures are wanted, they may as well be taught as routines.

4. We hope the last paragraph will not be misunderstood. We would like children to know that the standard form of a computation is merely one possible way, and to have at their command the tools to fashion their own computational procedures. Computation, as much as any part of mathematics, gives scope for invention, selection, schematization and sheer ingenuity. It is when computation is tackled in this spirit that the general principles and properties of arithmetic become generative devices, and the associative and distributive laws come into their own.

How can you multiply 34 by 17?

Keith (7): *3×17 is 51, so 30×17 is 510. Double 17 is 34 so 4×17 is 68. $510 + 68 = 578$.*

Barbara (8): *Double 34 is 68 so 20×34 is 680. This is three times 34 too many. 3×30 is 90 and 3×4 is 12, so 3×34 is 102. $680 - 102 = 578$.*

Paul (7): *4×17 is 68 so 40×17 is 680. This is 6 times 17 too many. 3 times 17 is 51 so 6 times is 102. $680 - 102$ is 578.*

5. At times it is convenient to be able to distinguish numerals (which we write) from number-names (which we speak), and distinguish both from the numbers that they represent. Numerals and number-names are conventional signs which we combine according to sets of agreed rules. The conventions can be changed and we then see that different signs can signify the same number. Nevertheless, the way we construct our system of whole numbers has its roots in the

language and symbolism we use. We know that in the absence of suitable language and symbolism, as in a primitive tribe, numbers do not exist. Furthermore, the agreed rules of combination which we apply to the number-names and numerals we use are our only means of knowing that numbers 'go on and on', and demonstrate to us a way in which the set of whole numbers can be constructed. For these reasons, it is perhaps unfortunate that mathematicians call whole numbers 'the set of *natural* numbers', as if they could be discovered, after diligent search, occurring in nature.

The development of an abacus

A description of one approach to place-value avoiding the use of pre-structured material.

The idea of a merchant wishing to record the loading and unloading of his ship in harbour is adopted. The children are encouraged to 'live' the situation: 'He might forget', 'If a lot of ships came in he might get muddled', 'He might want to show it to somebody else'. The merchant on the quayside begins then to record his counting of his cargo, and what better than to match pebbles against the boxes coming in off his ships, placing them in a straight line (because they are easier to count) beside the harbour wall in the dust?

Fig.1

This is soon seen to be an uneconomical system. The line gets awkwardly long, or he runs out of pebbles. What can be done? Use a stick to represent a certain number of pebbles. What happens when the sticks run out? Big pebbles? The pebbles already vary in size – and size and colour don't matter. One pebble to stand for two boxes. How does he record an odd number of boxes? Put a pebble in another position, in another line, to stand for so many boxes. How will he be sure it is in the new line? Mark lines in the dust or sand (the *sand abacus*).

There may be some discussion about the position of the second line relative to the first (to the right or left of it?), and the conventional nature of the decision suggested – or the historical situation described.

The children now try recording as the merchant records, using pebbles in a sand abacus. No particular 'base' has been insisted on, and naturally the children choose for themselves. Additions and subtractions (the merchant totals several cargoes and deducts those he sells) are carried out in any of the chosen bases, using the pebbles on the lines and exchanging so many pebbles in the first line for one in the second where necessary. More than two lines can be drawn in the sand.

The 'harbour wall' is now forgotten since, by familiarity, it is accepted that powers increase to the left. A form of abacus is now adopted (the merchant wants to carry his records to another place). A suitable type can be made from a piece of soft board supported at its ends. Knitting needles are driven upwards through the board to represent the 'pebble positions' and beads or rings take the place of the pebbles. The height of the knitting needles above the board can be adjusted so making it impossible to get more than a certain number of beads on them.

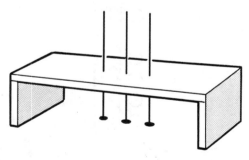

Fig.2

The next major step occurs when the recording on the abacus is transferred to symbols on paper. Children working with the abacus can transcribe directly from the beads on the needles. Some may need to have their paper pinned to the abacus in the early stages so that the direct correspondence can be seen.

No zero symbol has yet been mentioned. The need for this arises when the abacus is not there, or is recording something else, and the written record is all that remains to show what beads were used. Then it is necessary as a place-holder. (When working with various groups of children, 0 was rarely suggested as the symbol – dots, crosses, blobs and empty squares have been some of their suggestions.)

Changing the base of numeration

It is clear from the last example that the base of a workable numeration system need not be ten. We are familiar with this from our experience of the British system of measures, of course. We know that we can record any sum of money from a penny upwards in multiples of pence, shillings and pounds. It is as if we were using a three-place numeration system involving two different bases (twelve and twenty). (*These are not strictly bases, though, since their powers are not involved.*) The reasons for the choice of these numbers is historical. There is not much doubt that it is mathematically more convenient, and less of a strain on the memory, to have a single base, together with its powers, providing the structure for a place-value numeration.

In the last few years (there is no mention of the topic in the Mathematical Association's 1956 report [70]) there has been a growing belief that children gain a better understanding of our familiar place-value notation if they have experienced it working in bases other than ten. The Multibase Arithmetic Blocks were specifically designed to give this experience, but it can be given in a variety of ways.

Working with a single base and its powers, any number can be written with digits . . . $a_3a_2a_1a_0$ as a shorthand form of . . . $a_3x^3 + a_2x^2 + a_1x^1 + a_0x^0$. The base x can be any whole number; we note that $x^1 = x$ and $x^0 = 1$. The digits . . . a_3, a_2, a_1, a_0 are also whole numbers (or zero), but they cannot exceed one less than the value of x.

Exercises

1. 4203 in base five notation is short for $4 \times 5^3 + 2 \times 5^2 + 0 \times 5^1 + 3 \times 5^0$. In base ten notation, therefore, this number would be written as 553 ($4 \times 125 + 2 \times 25 + 3 = 553$). Write the same number in base nine.

2. In base four notation the written form 512 would be disallowed. 5×4^2 is the same as $1 \times 4^3 + 1 \times 4^2$ (why?) and so we should write 1112 instead.

3. We can convert a number written in base ten notation to base seven by the following procedure:

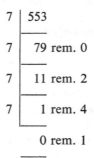

Therefore 553 in base ten is equivalent to 1420 in base seven. Explain how and why this works.

4. In what number base systems are the following true?

$7 \times 6 = 46 \qquad 41 \div 5 = 5$.

5. What does 0·11 mean in base two notation?

6. Square the number which is written 11 in base five notation and write the answer in the same notation. Repeat for the number which is written 11 in base six notation; and in base seven notation; and in base eight . . .

7. How does one test a number expressed in any base for divisibility by the base number?

8. Is the number represented by 21 in base six a prime number?

The last question raises in a very simple way the matter of what changes and what stays the same when we rewrite numbers in other systems of numeration. It is important that children should realize that the change we make is merely one of notation. Different notations can signify the same thing. We can write the same number as 49 in base ten and as 61 in base eight. The fact that the appearance of what we have written has changed should not make us think that the number has changed its spots (its properties). We know that the number we represent by 49 is a square number. It is still a square number if we write it as 61 (base eight). Of course the latter way of writing it shows that it can be thought of as $6 \times 8 + 1$, but this is not a new property that the number did not possess before. The awareness that the sign and the number signified can be distinguished is a most useful by-product of work in different bases.

The same applies to the verbal signals that we use. For instance, we can count in base three by saying, 'one, two, ten, eleven, twelve, twenty, twenty-one, twenty-two, a hundred, . . .' Thus the number that would normally be signalled with the sound 'nine' is now signalled with the sound 'a hundred'. The sounds we use are no more absolute than the written symbols. That there is a superficial ambiguity here need not really worry us, for it is we who choose the system of symbols and sounds that we are going to use, and once we have made our choice we know quite clearly what they mean.

In the classroom we must not, of course, carry on this discussion entirely in terms of sounds and symbols; this would maximize the possibility of confusion. We can base our discussion on things that we can talk or write about. A set of objects on the table, or the set of each person's fingers, can be counted aloud in different base systems. The adoption of different number-names then becomes a game in which the constancy of the number described is obvious. Cuisenaire rods can be used to make parallel rows of equivalent length which can then be written about in different notations.

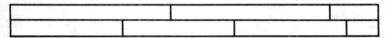

Fig.3

The same length can be expressed as, for example, 23 (base ten) and 32 (base seven), and the choice of base is reflected in the choice of rods used to measure the length. In such ways, what is arbitrary and what is absolute in a numerical situation can be discriminated easily.

Binary numeration

Fig.4

A bank of, say, four electric light switches on the classroom wall may prompt an investigation of the number of different ways in which the switches can be operated. There is, in fact, a range of possible investigations here, but to restrict ourselves to one, let us decide to concentrate only on the appearance of the bank of switches. We may have, for example, one switch on (down) and all the others off (up). But we can distinguish four different possibilities within this one.

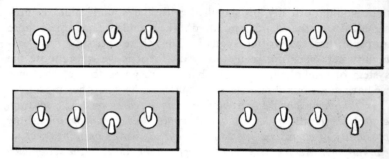

Fig.5

How many different possibilities can we distinguish if two switches are on and two are off? How many if three are on and one is off? How many altogether?

This is a fairly simple example and we may represent the different possibilities with little drawings on the lines of the one above. If we have to deal with five or six switches, or even more, we will probably want a simpler notation for recording the possibilities. All we really need are two symbols, for each switch can be on or off, and an agreed order in which to write them. We will use – while remembering that other notations would serve this problem equally well – the symbol '0' to mean off, or up; and the symbol '1' to mean on, or down. Since in the figure we supposed the switches were banked horizontally, we will just write the appropriate symbols in the same left-to-right order.

So 1010 will be taken to mean that switches A and C are on, switches B and D off.

We can now itemize our possibilities:

(a) one switch on: 1000, 0100, 0010, 0001   4 possibilities

(b) two switches on: 1100, 1010, 1001, 0110, 0101, 0011 6 possibilities

(c) three switches on: 1110, 1101, 1011, 0111   4 possibilities

(d) all on: 1111, or all off: 0000   2 possibilities

This gives us 16 possibilities altogether. (There may be some resistance to including the case in which no lights are actually on. Well, we can just take a straight decision whether to include this or not. It seems to fit the question we said we were investigating, although it would not fit other questions that we might have started from.)

The notation which has been (deliberately) introduced may now suggest to us that we are dealing with numbers in binary numeration, or, more shortly if less accurately, with binary numbers. But it is worth saying that we are so far using the symbols only as labels for certain states of the switches. We cannot (or should not) assume that *this exercise* gives us any right to treat these four-figure symbols as numbers. For one thing, they are not ordered: we do not know which comes first, which next, and so on. For another, there is no meaning that we can give to the combination of any two of these symbols.

We can, of course, import some notations from our experience and see if these symbols can be invested with the properties of an order, given an addition, etc., in some sensible way.

Putting the question, 'How many different weighings can you make with 1 oz., 2 oz., 4 oz., and 8 oz. weights if you have a set consisting of only one of each?' or 'How many different lengths can you make if you only have one white rod, one red rod, one pink and one brown?' can give rise to a similar set of symbols. For example, taking the second question, we can eventually set up a table:

Length in cm.	B	P	R	W
1				1
2			1	
3			1	1
4		1		
etc.				

The successive lengths that can be made, which run from 1 cm. to 15 cm., can be recorded in terms of the rods they require. If the blanks in the table are filled with 0's, we find we have fifteen of the sixteen four-figure symbols we encountered in the switches problem. (Which one is missing?) But this time they are in a definite order. This order has been imposed on the symbols by the already familiar order of a set of lengths.

The possible interpretation of the symbols as a way of writing numbers is obvious now. They are in order and we can add them:

$$\text{e.g.} \quad \begin{array}{r} 3 \\ +5 \\ \hline 8 \\ \hline \end{array} \qquad \begin{array}{r} 11 \\ +101 \\ \hline 1000 \\ \hline \end{array}$$

We have dropped out some 0's and just retained those that are needed for place-holding. We can now interpret the symbols comprising 0's and 1's as numbers written in a base two numeration.

Binary labels, which we can use in any 'two-state' systems (see p.222) and binary numeration, are mathematically important and widely applicable. It is a waste if they are introduced merely to make ideas of place-value more accessible. They will not in fact do so. Binary numeration is too special a case to shed much light on more familiar notation.

Computations in binary numeration *can* be as dull and restricting as any others if they are cast in formal and standard moulds. Pages of computations in base two are as deadly as pages of computations in base ten. And they do not even have the merit of being particularly useful.

References
Dienes [33], Fletcher [40] (ch.2), Gattegno [46], Goutard [50], Papy [79].

Remainders

What is the remainder when 2769 is divided by 10?
This is a very simple question. What makes it so easy?
What is the remainder when 2769 is divided by 5?
Also pretty easy. Why?
What is the remainder when 2769 is divided by 7?
This is not a very hard question, of course, and yet the answer is not so immediate as in the first two cases. Why is this? Most of us probably have to perform the division to find the answer: in the first two cases, we do not.
What is the remainder when 2769 is divided by 3?
Do we have to go through the routine division procedure? Not necessarily; we can add the digits together and divide this sum by 3 instead. We get a remainder of zero, and this tells us that 2769 divided by 3 gives a zero remainder.

This can be done with numbers of any size, and the summing of the digits can be carried out more than once if it helps. For example, we will find the remainder on dividing 2,547,962 by 3. Sum the digits: $2+5+4+7+9+6+2=35$. Sum the digits of this answer: $3+5=8$. Dividing 8 by 3 gives a remainder of 2. Therefore we can say that dividing 2,547,962 by 3 gives a remainder of 2. (Notice that dividing 35 by 3 also gives a remainder of 2.)

Why does this method work? We will write the original number a different way, making the place-value of the digits explicit. (For simplicity we will go back to our first number 2769.)

2769 can also be written as $2 \times 1000 + 7 \times 100 + 6 \times 10 + 9 \times 1$.

By using the distributive law, and dropping out the multiplication signs or writing dots instead, we may write this as

$2(999+1)+7(99+1)+6(9+1)+9$

$=(2.999+7.99+6.9)+(2+7+6+9)$.

We notice that 3 is bound to divide exactly into the whole of the first bracket since it is a factor of each term. So if we are only interested in the remainder after division by 3 we need only look at the remainder arising from the second bracket. But this bracket contains the sum of the digits of the original number, so that this number is the only one we need to test. Obviously we can repeat the procedure if we want to.

This is rather a lengthy and formal description of a proof of this remainder test. The analysis may have obscured the point: the proof hinges on the fact that every power of ten leaves a remainder of 1 when it is divided by 3. Does this property hold for division by any other number? *Yes, for division by 9*. And this was also obvious from our analysis. For any number other than 3 and 9? *No*.

The method of summing the digits successively has been called 'casting out nines'.

We notice that the nature of the numeration base affects the argument we have used. Does this mean that the test for remainders on division by 3 only holds if the number is expressed in base ten notation? In what other bases (if any) will it work?

Let us follow this idea of change of base a little further. We will write the multiples of three in different notations:

Base 4	3, 12, 21, 30, 33, 102, . . .
Base 5	3, 11, 14, 22, 30, 33, 41, . . .
Base 6	3, 10, 13, 20, 23, 30, 40, . . .
Base 7	3, 6, 12, 15, 21, 24, 30, 33, 36, . . .

We may notice that all the multiples of 3 expressed in base four 'look like' multiples of 3 as we are familiar with them, in spite of the fact that some familiar ones do not appear to be present. Does this 'looking like' tell us anything? It appears as if we could use the same remainder test for division by 3 in base four as we have already used in base ten. Is this a rational belief? We remember that the crux of the situation in base ten was that every power of 10 gave a remainder of 1 when divided by 3. Perhaps this property holds for powers of four. *Yes, it does*.

Does the same remainder test hold in any other base?

We can now free ourselves from any particular base, and from division by any particular number, and search for other cases in which a remainder test of the same kind works. Is it true that we can use the same test for remainders when numbers are expressed in base six and divided by 5?

In any base there will be at least one remainder test of this kind. (Why?) Do we know when there will be others?

Calendars

January 1967

Sun.	1	8	15	22	29
Mon.	2	9	16	23	30
Tues.	3	10	17	24	31
Wed.	4	11	18	25	
Thurs.	5	12	19	26	
Fri.	6	13	20	27	
Sat.	7	14	21	28	

When we look at the calendar for a particular month we may choose to look at it as a number array with certain properties. What do we notice? The numbers in the rows of the table increase steadily by 7 each time, and the reason for this is very obvious. (We could say that each row is the start of an arithmetic progression with common difference 7.) It may not occur to us immediately, but it is a consequence of the successive addition of 7, that the numbers in any row leave the same remainder when they are divided by 7. For example, all the dates of the Tuesdays in January 1967 leave a remainder of 3 when divided by 7. If a date in January 1967 leaves a remainder of 6 when it is divided by 7, we can say that it must be a Friday.

Because of this consistency, we can set up a number-code for the days of the week; that is, we can allocate to each day the remainder its date yields when it is divided by 7.

Sun.	1
Mon.	2
Tues.	3
Wed.	4
Thurs.	5
Fri.	6
Sat.	0

If we know a date in January 1967, we can use this table to say what day of the week it is.

But let us try to extend the idea a little further. It is clear that if we had calendar months with only 28 days our code would apply to any date in the year. What can we do to offset the irregularities in the lengths of our months? Consider the month of February 1967. 1 February is a Wednesday; 8, 15 and 22 February are also Wednesdays. If our code is to hold for February as well as January, each of these dates should give the code-number 4. We can ensure this either by adding 3 to the remainder these dates give when divided by 7, or by adding 3 to the dates and then dividing by 7 to find the remainder. Perhaps the second alternative is slightly better, because this way of doing it will make quite sure that we do not finish up with a number greater than 6, whatever date we start with.

Does this adjustment of adding 3 to the date work for all dates in February?

In a non-leap year (like 1967), we can deal with March if we can deal with February. March dates, then, will need the same adjustment as February dates. For example, consider 21 March 1967. Add 3 to the date, giving the number 24. Divide this by 7, giving a remainder 3. From the code table we see that 21 March is a Tuesday.

Can we generalize what we have done to enable us to find the day on which any date in the year falls? We have probably noticed that the adjustment we made to the February dates corresponds to the number of days in January over and above 28. It is easy to see why this should be so. We can, then, work out adjustments for all the months by keeping a running total of the days in excess of 28 in each month. This gives us the following set of adjustments:

Month	Jan.	Feb.	Mar.	Apr.	May	Jun.	Jul.	Aug.	Sept.	Oct.	Nov.	Dec.
No. of days over 28	3	0	3	2	3	2	3	3	2	3	2	3
Adjustment		3	3	6	8	11	13	16	19	21	24	26

But since we are going to divide by seven after adding the adjustment number, there is not much point in having adjustment numbers greater than 6. In fact we can 'cast out sevens' from these numbers before putting them in the table:

Jan.	Feb.	Mar.	Apr.	May	Jun.	Jul.	Aug.	Sept.	Oct.	Nov.	Dec.
0	3	3	6	1	4	6	2	5	0	3	5

Example: What day of the week is 19 April 1967? Add the adjustment number (6) to the date, giving 25. Cast out sevens, leaving **4**. Therefore 19 April falls on a Wednesday.

The steps in this argument can be developed by most children without much assistance. Those who become fascinated in the problem can turn their attention to the more difficult matter of finding the day of the week for any date whatever. Here again, provided they are given some of the relevant facts such as, for example, which centuries are counted as leap years, some children will find a workable system. A brief discussion will be found in volume 6 of 'Mathematics with Numbers in Colour' and in most encyclopaedias.

A colour game

A number of children are seated, preferably in a ring, and numbered off. The teacher gives a Cuisenaire rod to each child in turn. He uses only the first five lengths in order – white, red, green, pink and yellow – and repeats the sequence as many times as necessary until each child holds a rod. While he is doing this, he questions them: Which colour must I give you? Who holds the rod the same colour as yours? How many white rods must I give out? Do you see how I am giving out the rods?

We have already described this situation in chapter 3 of *Some Lessons in Mathematics* [40], summarizing a lesson given to some 12–13-year-old boys by Puig Adam. We suggest it again here because this simple situation can give quite profound insights into the essential properties of finite (or 'remainder') arithmetic.

The teacher asks: What colour does No.7 hold? No.12? No.13? What number has the same colour as yours? Write down all the numbers with the same colour as yourself. Will any other children have the same list as yours? Suppose there were many more of us playing this game – 50 or 100, say. Write down all the numbers between 50 and 100 which would have the same colour as you have. Write down some numbers over 100 which have the same colour as 5, 63, 21, etc. Do you notice anything about those numbers which have the same colour?

These are sample questions that might be asked: they are not models that must be followed. The questions direct the children's attention to the fact that every number can be allocated a colour, even those numbers which have no representative in the group of children. All the numbers with the same colour belong together in some way. We can see that the difference between any two numbers with the same colour must be a multiple of 5. It does not very much matter if the children do not see this at first; and it certainly does not matter that they may be unable to express it in just this way. Nevertheless if they understand the game at all, they will experience the feeling that any number can be put into one of five classes, corresponding to the five colours that are being used.

Who has the colour red? Whom shall we choose – No.7? Who has the colour pink? No.4? Supposing we add these numbers together, what is the colour of the number that we get? Is it white? Choose someone else with red and someone else with pink and add their numbers together. What colour do we get? White again? Will we always get white if we add a red number and a pink number? Try some more and see. What colour will we get if we add a white number and a yellow number? What colour will we get if we add a yellow number and a green number? What colour is twice a red number? Twice a green number? Twice a yellow number?

We can compare this with the adding game described on p.17. The constancy of the answers, whatever actual representatives of the colours are used, is at first very surprising. Some children will be able to give the reason to their own satisfaction, and should be allowed to express their findings in their own language, however informal. When they have explored a number of these 'additions', they may like to compile a list of them all. This is quite simple to do since there are only a limited number of possible additions. One way to display the collected information is in the form of a two-way table:

+	W	R	G	P	Y
W	R	G	P	Y	W
R	G	P	Y	W	R
G	P	Y	W	R	G
P	Y	W	R	G	P
Y	W	R	G	P	Y

We use the initial letters of the colours. The table can be built up gradually, starting with the known results. It will suggest, by its structure, other results which can be checked. (It is usual to read a table like this by using the first colour to pick the row of the table, and the second colour to pick the column. The result of the addition is then written where the row and column meet. Because this addition is commutative we would get the same entries if we worked the other way round.)

If the table seems too formal a device, the results can be recorded in separate symbolic statements, e.g. R+G=Y, R+Y=R. But it seems a pity not to utilize the excitement of the table's structure to provoke more exploration of the properties of this addition.

What do you notice about the table? Why does each row shift along one place compared with the row above? Why are there only five letters in the table? Why is it symmetrical about the diagonal from top left to bottom right? What do you notice about 'adding Y'? (*It leaves the colour it's added to unaltered.*)

By putting such questions as, 'What colour must be added to pink to make white?', we can introduce the idea of subtracting colours. Our question can be written symbolically as $P + ? = W$ or as $W - P = ?$ We found out how to add any pair of colours. Can we subtract any pair? (Inspection of the table tells us that we can, since every colour appears in every row.) We can introduce multiplication of colours, either by using repeated addition, or by going back to our original numbers and using those. Make up a multiplication table in the same form as the addition table already shown. Are questions of the type, 'What colour must I multiply green by to get yellow?' answerable?

Many children in the upper forms of the junior school will be able to take the story as far as this. But our discussions, and particularly the notes given below, are intended for teachers. This kind of game has its own intrinsic interest, but it may be helpful to know that the mathematics involved is by no means trivial and has an important place in mathematics.

Notes

1. We have been working in a *finite arithmetic*. It is called finite because only a finite number of elements – the five colours – are involved. Compare this with whole number arithmetic where we have an infinite set; we can go on and on constructing bigger and bigger whole numbers without coming to an end. We are entitled to call our game with colours an *arithmetic* because we have operations of adding and multiplying which strongly resemble the familiar operations of ordinary arithmetic. In fact, in this game we obtained the 'new' addition and multiplication from the usual operations in the way we have described.

2. The elements in our finite arithmetic can be thought of as *classes* of familiar numbers. For example, the colour red comprises the set of numbers 2, 7, 12, 17, 22, . . . Any whole number we like to think of can be allocated to one of the five classes, and we have *partitioned* the set of all whole numbers into five separate and distinct subsets. We

can therefore say that when we have been adding colours we have effectively been adding classes of whole numbers. This is perhaps an unnecessary piece of sophistication, though, because it only means that if we add any elements selected from each of two classes, we can forecast the class to which the answer will belong. We have seen this already in the adding game in chapter 2 as well as in this colour game.
3. Because we have used Cuisenaire rods to initiate the colour game, we may be tempted to replace the colour names with their numerical equivalents. The addition table on p.81 then becomes:

+	1	2	3	4	5
1	2	3	4	5	1
2	3	4	5	1	2
3	4	5	1	2	3
4	5	1	2	3	4
5	1	2	3	4	5

Some of the entries correspond exactly to ordinary addition, e.g. $2+3=5$, but others do not. It may occur to us that yellow makes no difference when it is added. (We may say that 'yellow is the *neutral element* for addition in the colour game'.) Yellow, therefore, behaves like zero does in ordinary arithmetic. If we write 0 instead of 5 and re-order the rows and columns, we get:

+	0	1	2	3	4
0	0	1	2	3	4
1	1	2	3	4	0
2	2	3	4	0	1
3	3	4	0	1	2
4	4	0	1	2	3

If we add a number which gives a remainder of 2 when we divide it by 5 (say 27) to a number which gives a remainder of 4 when we divide it by 5 (say 74), we obtain a number which gives a remainder of 1 when divided by 5 ($27+74=101$; cast out fives; remainder 1). The above table summarizes this if we interpret the numbers as remainders on division by 5. This is why this kind of arithmetic is sometimes referred to as *remainder arithmetic*. In more technical

3. Make a circular slide-rule to illustrate addition modulo 7 using two concentric circles of card. (Multiplication modulo 7 can also be illustrated in this way. For hints see [40], p.66).

4. Play the colour game using the first *six* sizes of Cuisenaire rods and find any significant differences from the game described above.

5. The simplest finite arithmetic is the arithmetic of odd and even numbers, i.e. the residue classes modulo 2. Write down its addition and multiplication tables, and try to find some applications of its properties. ('She loves me; she loves me not.')

6. Put the thumbs of each hand on white keys on a piano keyboard. Keeping the two hands in step, play a scale upwards with the right hand on the white notes and a scale downwards with the left hand on the white notes. Do the two hands strike keys with the same name simultaneously? The answer may be Yes or No. Distinguish the possibilities. If the answer is Yes, will the coincidence occur again if the two hands continue? Does it make any difference if the left hand moves up the keyboard while the right hand moves down?

Make up a problem about days of the week suggested by the above exercise.

7. Can you find any points of contact between the ideas of place-value and the arithmetic of remainders?

8. (a) *Tinker, tailor, soldier, sailor; rich man, poor man, beggar man, thief.* What mathematics can you read into counting 'cherry-stones'?

(b) Take any familiar 'counting-out' jingle which children use to eliminate one of their number. Develop some strategies for using it ruthlessly.

References
Fletcher [40] (ch.3), Gattegno [46] (vol.6).

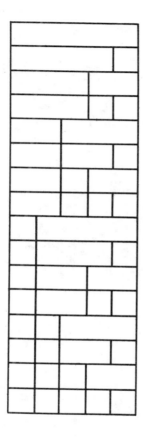

5

Visual representation

1

A group of first-year infants ran to tell me about their graph, and took me to see it. 'Our graph' had one red and one blue column.

'Look, the red is longer than the blue, and this means . . . You won't understand properly if I don't tell you properly.'

I was taken to another part of the room and shown some pictures of boys and girls.

'Josephine made the girls and Martin made the boys.'

Here Martin joined in, and the two children told me that everyone had been comparing sets, using one-to-one correspondence. After a lot of this work with apparatus, the children lined up for play, each boy taking a girl by the hand. Four girls had no partners, and they told the teacher after play that there were four more girls than boys in class because when each boy had a girl partner there were four girls without a partner. They wanted to record this, and set to work drawing and cutting out pictures of little girls. Martin wanted to help, and began making pictures of boys.

As the piles of cut-outs grew, Sally and Martin went round giving a 'girl' to each girl and a 'boy' to each boy. Martin said, 'This was to make sure we were right.' Then the figures were pasted on to paper to show the partners in line, and the four girls alone. On this sheet Leslie had written. 'This shows there are four more girls than boys.' I asked how he knew and was told the whole story again. They thought this picture looked untidy, so they made two 'models' with two pieces of string, each threaded with beads – red for girls and blue for boys. These were hung up with their story pinned above them. Below was a piece of pegboard with coloured counters, and coloured rods, both displaying the same information. Josephine said, 'But we couldn't carry those about to show people so we made a picture we could carry. We made it on squared paper because it was easier to crayon.'

which was more than the permitted variation of 5%. They requested that these figures be put right, so the Head called in four children who were told that in future they would be responsible for the number of meals that were to be ordered. The relevant past figures were obtained from the Auditors and the children then drew a graph of the ordering and accounting figures, using coloured lines to differentiate between them. From this graph they were able to anticipate the trends and were able to forecast the numbers of meals that needed to be ordered. The graph was then kept up to date week by week and a remarkable convergence between the ordering and accounting lines began to appear.

A graph is only one way of looking at data. If the children keep a record of the number of letters delivered to their houses on each day of the week, and enter them on a large chart, it gives an array of numbers:

	Mon.	Tues.	Wed.	Thurs.	Fri.	Sat.	Sun.
ANN	2	0	1	2	5	3	0

(This is, of course, not the only situation which would provide data that can be represented in this way. This is only taken as an example for discussion, and data of more immediate interest to the children would be used in the classroom.)

What sort of things can we do with this table now that it has been made?

We can simply look at the numbers that are there. *Do the numbers lie between 1 and 5? Have we all the numbers between 1 and 5?*

We can add the rows of numbers. What does the total tell us?

We can add the columns.

If we add the totals of the rows and the totals of the columns what do we notice?

Is there any column that has only 0's in it? Will this always happen?

Because of the way in which these numbers were collected these totals have a meaning and we can get further information from the table.

How many letters were delivered to all the children on a certain day of the week? How many letters were delivered to each individual child?

And there are other questions. Some of the information could be put in the form of a block graph, but this gives us no more information than we already have by looking at the original array of numbers.

We can ask questions about the frequency of numbers in the array.

How many times does 2 appear in the array?

How many times does 3 appear in the first column?

How many times does 1 appear in the second row?

Because of the way the information was obtained we can give a meaning to these questions. 'How many times did 2 appear in the first column?' can be interpreted, 'How many children had two letters delivered on Monday?'

We can ask questions about the frequency of the totals and what significance these have. We can draw a frequency distribution diagram of some of these results, but again this will tell us no more than we already know from our questions about the numbers in the array, although it may provide a useful visual representation of the information.

Graphs

We do not give very much attention in this book to the drawing of graphs – not as much as the importance of the subject seems to call for. But as we said in the introduction, we are not particularly concerned to say what has already been said, and the primary school teacher can now find a wealth of advice and practical help in the Schools Council Curriculum Bulletin No.1 and a number of recent text-books.

Like much else that is elementary enough to be taught in the primary school, the drawing of graphs *can* degenerate into a meaningless routine. The stories at the beginning of the chapter, and the experience of our readers, confirm the enjoyment that children often find in making block graphs, for example, but it is no denial of the importance of this feeling of pleasure and achievement to point out that the mathematical return for many hours of work is sometimes very slight.

This is expressed in too purist a form – we do not want to suggest that any classroom activity should be judged in terms of its productivity rating. The physical act of making a graph, the pleasure in its form, the appreciation of its compactness, are valuable aspects even if the mathematical content of these feelings seems low. But these values are not really cumulative: they do not increase with the number of times they are experienced. It seems to us quite wrong to suppose that every situation that *can* be graphed *should* be, or that because one kind of situation has been graphed once it should always be graphed when it reappears. We are only saying, in other words, that when the activity becomes a habit its mathematical and other merits fall to zero.

It is easy to give negative advice on the basis of this attitude; to say, for example, that the purpose of a graph should be clearly in mind before it is drawn, or that no graph should be drawn if its characteristics are not to be studied. This may be sound advice, but we would rather stress that graph-drawing is only one kind of mathematical schematization, that there are other kinds worth examining, and that the choice of representation is in itself a mathematical exercise. Moreover – and perhaps this is the most important thing to be said – drawing, and therefore graphing, is a dynamic activity. It has a life of its own and a pleasure peculiar to itself. It often starts with familiar material and then develops from within itself to produce results that could not have been foreseen. Most of us do not experience this kind of activity in the classroom because our drawings and graphs have become fossilized into conventional forms. Perhaps the nearest we get to it is when we scribble at a problem on a scrap of paper and the marks we make seem to reorganize themselves into a solution. If we could free ourselves from the restrictions of habit, who knows in what directions our drawings might lead then?

Let us begin by re-defining the word 'graph' so that it is not tied to the conventional squared-paper rectangular-axes usage. A not-too-large step is to allow it to cover the arrow-graphs of the next section (see also Fletcher [47], ch.6, and Papy [79]). Then we may notice that other drawings in this book also have some claim to the name if we stretch it a little further still.

An arrow game

A group of backward girls watched expectantly whilst the numbers 1 to 40 were written on the blackboard in a random manner. Two arrows were drawn, linking 3 with 6, and 7 with 10 (using the relationship $x \rightarrow x+3$). The girls giggled rather self-consciously. Asked if anyone would like to draw in another arrow, three of them volunteered. They each drew a short arrow linking two adjacent numbers, without apparently considering the actual numbers chosen. These arrows were rubbed out by the teacher but the next attempt, $9 \rightarrow 12$, was a 'correct' one and was left on the board. After this there was a succession of short arrows, with the numbers apparently chosen at random. (Both the arrows that had been drawn were short ones, and this had perhaps led the girls to think that the length of the arrow was the important point rather than the numbers linked by it.) Then Christina, who had sat quietly watching the proceedings, put in a correct arrow at her first attempt. (Having done this, she took no further interest.)

This second success inspired others who had not yet ventured to make an attempt. By now almost all the possible short arrows had been tried, and there were some puzzled murmurs about long arrows. Then someone asked 'Can you do one as long as you want?' 'You could find out by trying one.' But still no-one tried. There were many more wrong arrows, then a third correct one, followed by great excitement, and a series of correct attempts, now including longer and longer arrows. By the time twenty correct arrows had been drawn it was almost impossible to see the numbers clearly, so we started a new game.

For the second game the relationship $x \rightarrow 2x$ was chosen by the teacher and one short and one long arrow were drawn. The short one was $6 \rightarrow 12$, and this took everyone's attention. The girls all thought they knew the secret this time, and the first four attempts were all based on the relationship $x \rightarrow x+6$. Then came a few random attempts, followed by more of the type $x \rightarrow x+6$. There were at least thirty wrongly drawn arrows before anyone had even considered the second arrow, $19 \rightarrow 38$. Then Veronica got out her notebook and began to make calculations. Two others followed her example, but it was a different girl who drew $9 \rightarrow 18$, the first correct arrow. It was quite a long time before a second correct arrow was drawn and then more girls began to get them right.

When the children were invited to make up 'arrow games' for themselves, almost all of them wrote their numbers and arrows in horizontal sequence across the page:

$3 \rightarrow 6 \rightarrow 9 \rightarrow 12 \rightarrow 15 \rightarrow 18 \rightarrow 21 \rightarrow 24 \rightarrow$ etc.

This arrangement leaves out two thirds of the numbers entirely, and there seemed to be no apparent connection in the children's minds between this and the two related sequences $1\rightarrow4\rightarrow7\rightarrow10\rightarrow$ . . . and $2\rightarrow5\rightarrow8\rightarrow11\rightarrow14\rightarrow$ . . . To show this connection a more systematic presentation seemed called for.

We wrote $1\rightarrow8\rightarrow15\rightarrow22\rightarrow$ and this line was soon completed by the children up to the number 50. What next? Was the whole arrow pattern there? Why not? We considered the numbers left out. What about 2? They began a new line with 2, placing it below and just to the right of the 1. When this line was completed an exciting discovery was made: all the numbers in the second line were one more than the numbers in the first line. Eagerly the girls started a new line with 3, and were delighted to find the same thing again. Now they could complete the sequence without actually adding 7 at all. When they had finished they discovered that all the numbers from 1 to 50 had been written. The girls repeated the procedure, but this time began $3\rightarrow9\rightarrow15$. The next three lines, beginning with 4, 5 and 6 were completed without difficulty. At the next line, beginning with 7, the teacher stopped them and asked them to consider whether any numbers were going to be left out. It was a long time before the girls realized that 1 should precede the 7. It seemed very difficult for them to work backwards by subtraction.

After more work on this type of presentation, including multiplicative relationships, the class discussed how to find a still better way to make the pattern clear. Eventually the idea of a number-line emerged, with the numbers written in order first, and the arrows put in afterwards. Again they were excited to find that the displacement in an addition pattern was constant, and thus the length of the arrows was always the same.

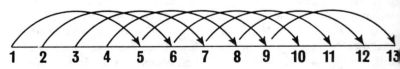

1   2   3   4   5   6   7   8   9   10   11   12   13

Fig.2. Adding on 4.

This pattern suggested a row of hills or clouds. Later, the girls were struck by the shape of the pattern of a relationship of the type $x+y\rightarrow$constant ('adding on to make . . .' was their name for it). This was described as 'like a tunnel'.

In multiplicative relationships, the pattern of arrows was con-

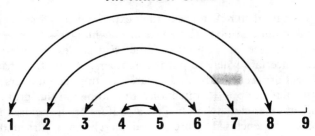

Fig.3. Adding on to make 9.

fused by the repeated crossing of lines, and various ideas were put forward to make the presentation clearer.

'Put one arrow above the line and the next one under it.'

'Make the arrows bigger' (this was explained as making them come up higher).

'Make them come up to a point and down.'

'Make them up and along and down.'

All these were tried out and it became clear that altering the shape of the arrows did not help. 'If you wanted an arrow from 3 to 5 you could draw the arrow up from 3, put a 5 at the top and cross out the 5 at the bottom.'

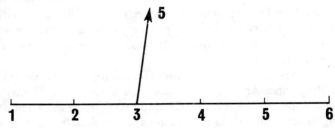

Fig.4. Susan's invention.

'That seems a good idea. What do we do next?'

'4 to 6 and cross out the 6.'

'What next?'

'5 to 7.'

'But I've crossed out the 5.'

So they had to put the 5 back on the line, and soon a second line of numbers was written across the blackboard above the first. Several girls soon discovered that a ruler could be used for drawing the arrows and that the lines followed each other in regular pattern.

There was a marked reluctance in their experiments at first to use any relationship but addition. There was more willingness to experiment with lines in different positions. Some tried circles or semi-circles, but were uncertain where to put the numbers. Others tried triangles (the subject of recent study) and squares, writing the numbers round the perimeters in opposite directions. But no-one in this group tried two lines at an angle; always two parallel lines or an enclosed figure. Sometimes the enclosed figure served merely as a surround, two parallel lines being drawn neatly within it for the numbers.

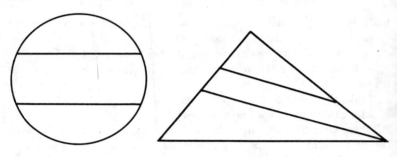

Fig.5

An interesting development was a series of parallel lines with an arrow pattern between each pair. One of these showed $x \rightarrow x+4$ followed by $x \rightarrow x-4$, a useful illustration of subtraction as the inverse of addition.

They also experimented with larger sheets of paper, the girls working in small groups. Again all the lines were parallel but by this time multiplication had become the dominant interest. There was, throughout, an interest in the numbers which were 'left out' in each pattern – those which had no arrows to or from them – and a realization that in some cases this was due to the limitations on length of line imposed by the paper. There were many pictorial descriptions of the types of patterns, as each operation was seen to have its own type. 'Zebra crossing' for addition and subtraction; 'fan' and 'duck's foot' for multiplication. Various names were suggested for the method of representation as a whole, of which the most popular was 'dot to dot'. Other more original suggestions were:

Doodledots	Dianas (a play on the word diagonal)
Puzzledots	Dotty arithmetic
Spots and dots	Arrowbone

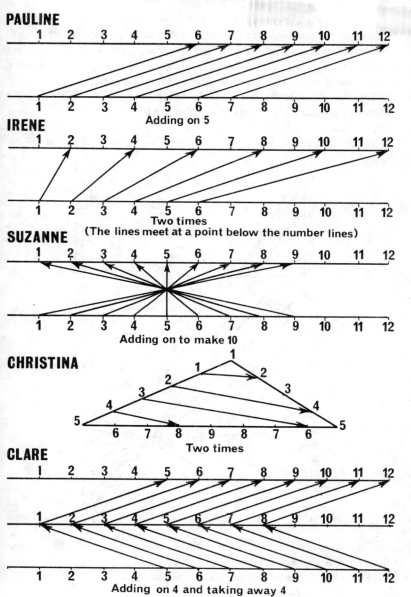

PAULINE

Adding on 5

IRENE

Two times
(The lines meet at a point below the number lines)

SUZANNE

Adding on to make 10

CHRISTINA

Two times

CLARE

Adding on 4 and taking away 4

Fig.6

Consider the representation by arrows and a number-line of the processes of doubling and trebling. What does the development look like when one 'jump' starts from the end of a previous one? What does such a chain of linked nodes show? What does it signify if two or more chains have nodes at the same point? Multiples? Factors? L.C.M.? What else? Look at Pauline's and Irene's drawings (Fig.6). The interest shown in the numbers left out gives promise of work with fractions and with negative numbers.

What happens if we reverse the order of numbering along one of the lines?

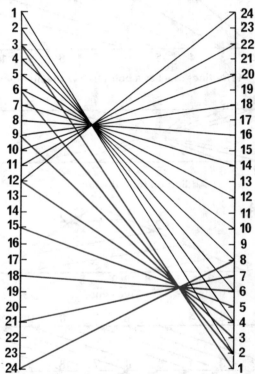

Fig.7

In the figure, black lines are 'tracing' the relationship n→2n and purple lines represent the relationships n→⅓n.

Where are the resulting nodes (crossing points)?

Why are they just there?

What happens if we join from n on one side through the mid-point between the scales? Or through some other point? If we choose two points and draw the line through them to cut our number-lines, what does it tell us?

What happens if we join n to 24/n? How does this compare with the patterns that Irene obtained when the number-lines were numbered in the same directions?

What happens if we draw one line on a background and the other on a slide, so that we can move one of the number-lines? What can we do with this 'machine'?

Suppose we put two geoboards side by side, perhaps with a numbered scale over the edge rows of pins, and put rubber bands to join the appropriate pins instead of drawing the lines as we did on paper. What happens now if we turn one of the 'axes' (edge of boards) round, still lying on the table? Or twist it up and out of the plane of the table? Is it possible to put a piece of paper so that it touches all the rubber bands (lines)? Can this be done with a pencil (or lollipop stick, etc.)? In what positions?

Again, what happens if a number-line is 'wrapped' round the circumference of a circle?

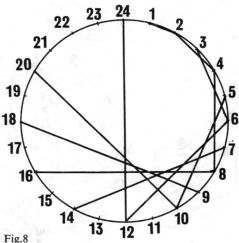

Fig.8

What happens if we wrap number-lines round two concentric circles? What if the circles are different sizes? Or numbered in opposite directions? (Fig. 9).
Would we have a zero mark?

Suppose the circles are pivoted (on separate cards) at their common centre, what effect does turning have? What 'machines' have we now?

The patterns from number-lines can be used as inspiration for curve stitching. Figure 10 shows exploratory patterns stitched to 'rules', with number-lines marked on squares and semi-circles.

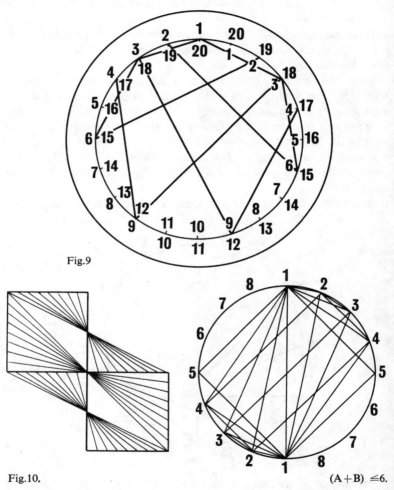

Fig.9

Fig.10.   (A+B) ≤6.

The pattern of the diagonals of a regular octagon is easily obtained from stitching on a number-line round a circle. This was drawn on their maps by mediaeval navigators, all parallel lines being in the same colour. The bearing required to sail between any two places was easily read from the direction of the nearest line parallel to the route.

A query

Do we represent numbers as points on a line? Or lines through a point?

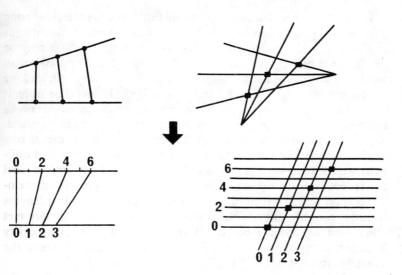

Fig.11

We join points by lines	OR	lines by points.
Ah-ha! The lines meet in a point		... the points lie on a line.
The graph of $y=2x$ is a point		... is a line.
		'We discovered a linear relationship.'(I made sure you did.)
The arrow graph labels points.		The cartesian graph labels lines. But the scales are marked as for an arrow graph and it seems as if we are labelling points.

Confusion.

Position fixing and co-ordinates

Several methods of position fixing in two and three dimensions are possible with juniors (see Piaget [87] and Lovell [67]). In work on plans and maps a position is fixed by means of a direction angle and a distance in that direction. Position fixing on the surface of a sphere uses longitude and latitude.

In this section we consider the method of fixing position by giving two distances measured from fixed axes. When the axes are at right angles this yields the usual cartesian co-ordinates. The idea may be encountered first of all in the game of battleships and cruisers, or in locating a portion of a street map having a label like D3, or in looking at the way in which theatre seats are coded. If the classroom is arranged with the desks in tidy rows and columns, particular desks can be indicated by counting from the wall and from the blackboard, say. In the above cases the label-pair indicates a region rather than a point. This may be part of the rea
culty with simple work involving c
the spaces between the gradations
selves, and find a surprising amou
directly from the axes. Most chil
and solved this problem before in l
have had to transfer their attentio
symbols attached to the gradation

The following treatment is one
see the locations as the intersectio

Each child had a sheet of paper ru
represents a map of a town in the year 2
and between the streets are buildings. We wan
road from another – what shall we call them?'

As a result of the children's suggestions the vertica
referred to by letters and the horizontal lines by numbers. The
where the roads cross can now be named B1, B2, C3, etc.
(i) 'You live at B1, and are going to have tea with an aunt who is meeting you at F5. Draw on the squared paper a way of getting from B1 to F5 and write directions for someone else to follow the journey.' (Is it necessary to put in all the road crossings or only the ones at the beginning and end of a straight portion?)

Two children drew their journeys on a large squared sheet.
'If they both walked at about the same speed, who got there first, Ann or Robert? Or did they both arrive at the same time?'

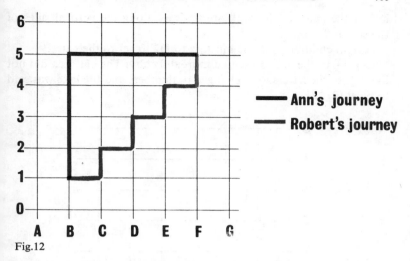

Fig.12

(Most children settled for Robert. They were then asked how many sides of a square all had walked along.) 'Did any children go along more than 8 sides?' Two had drawn:

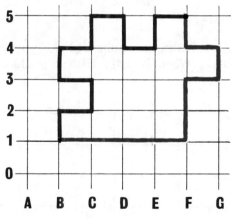

Fig.13

After discussion the children suggested that any path within the rectangle B1, B5, F5, F1, was a 'shortest' path provided one kept moving from left to right and bottom to top (see also p.249).

(ii) 'In the middle of this town there is one square that has been kept as a park with a lake in the middle. Can you direct someone to the lake if the gates of the park are halfway along the vertical sides of the square?'

Several children said one must go to D2 to get to the gates.

Getting to the lake presented more difficulty. The children did not like C$\frac{1}{2}$, so the letters were changed to numbers and the lake was said to be at $(2\frac{1}{2}, 2\frac{1}{2})$.

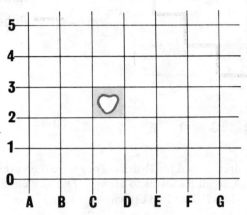

Fig.14

If a piece of squared paper is numbered along both axes, and the children are asked, 'Where is (3,4)?' this can produce two different answers.

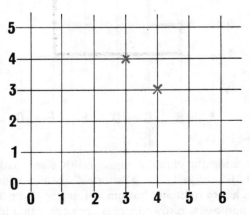

Fig.15

It is necessary to have an agreement to count along the horizontal first and then up the vertical every time.

Position fixing can also be explored with pegs and pegboard.

(i) One pupil is asked to turn his back on the class and another to decide what instructions to give to the first so that he can place a peg in a particular hole without it being pointed out. Usually the counting of holes across and up is chosen and discussion follows about the recording of such instructions in an unambiguous way, leading to the usual notation.

(ii) Using a pegboard, limiting it to a 6×6 grid, and two dice, one to give the horizontal co-ordinate and one to give the vertical co-ordinate of a point, play games to see who is the first to get, say,

3 points in a line (horizontal, vertical, sloping);

4 points in a line;

points at the corners of a square;

points at the corners of a rectangle.

Exercises

1. Join (2,2) to (2,5) to (5,5) to (5,2) to (2,2). What shape have you made? (A square.)

On the same piece of paper draw any other square, and write the pair of numbers for each corner.

If the pairs of numbers for each corner are written down is there any pattern?

(2,2)	(3,3)	(1,1)
(2,5)	(3,4)	(1,6)
(5,5)	(4,4)	(6,6)
(5,2)	(4,3)	(6,1)
(2,2)	(3,3)	(1,1)

Can you write the numbers for the corners of another square without drawing it first? What would be the pattern if we had been drawing a rectangle?

2. Using $\frac{1}{4}$ in. squared paper, plot the star constellations.

   (a) *Orion* (10,4) (13,6) (12,9) (14,10) (16,11) (18,14) (16,4) (12,16). Which points give the belt?

   (b) *Casseopaeia* (5,7) (8,9) (9,5) (12,4) (13,6).

   (c) *The plough* (48,15) (51,23) (44,28) (51,7) (9,23) (48,19) (48,29) (49,11). Which point is the pole star?

3. Put pegs in a board at the corners of a square and note the co-

ordinates; then experiment with transformations of the co-ordinates and see what happens to the square, e.g.

(a) add 3 to the horizontal co-ordinate of each corner and 2 to the vertical co-ordinate;

(b) double both the co-ordinates of each corner of the square.

Make up some more transformations and try them on other shapes.

4. (i) Put pegs at (1,2), (2,4), (3,6), (4,8), etc. What do you notice? Why?

(ii) Now put in pegs at (1,3), (2,6), (3,9), (4,12), etc. What do you notice? Why?

Can you symbolize the relationship between the horizontal co-ordinate (H) and the vertical co-ordinate (V) in the above cases?

Try the following in the same way:

(iii) (1,9), (2,8), (3,7), (4,6), etc.

(iv) (2,36), (2,18), (3,12), (4,9), (6,6), (9,4), (12,3), (18,2), (36,1).

(v) (1,1), (2,4), (3,9), (4,16), (5,25), etc.

(vi) (1,2), (2,4), (3,8), (4,16), (5,32), etc.

Keith (9) had been performing the experiment of dropping a ball from various heights and recording the height of the bounce. He dropped the ball from 6 ft. and found it bounced to 4 ft. He then drew a straight line on his graph paper from the origin through the point (6,4). When I asked him why he had done this without dropping the ball from the other heights, he said that every other graph they had done had been a straight line and he expected this one would be too.

The kind of work suggested by Exercise 4 above seems to bring out very clearly the fact that a definite relationship between the co-ordinates of the sets of points is associated with a definite pattern on the graph. When graphs are constructed from experimental data, rather than from sets of given number-pairs, similar patterns often emerge – in an approximate way, at least. These similarities may lead us to say that the quantities we are graphing bear certain precise mathematical relationships; for example, we may say that the load carried by a spring is directly proportional to the extension of its length, and that its 'true' graph is a straight line. But it is important to note the way in which the characteristic graphs of mathematical relationships are actually used in science and engineering. If experimental results are plotted and approximate closely enough to the graph of a particular relationship, we may be able to use our precise knowledge of the form of the mathematical graph to make predictions about further experimental values. We say, in effect, that for certain practical purposes the behaviour of the spring can be described in this way.

The mathematical graph is being used here as a 'model' of the experimental situation; it is not being 'discovered' from the data. This is a perfectly sensible thing to do, provided we remember that all models are accurate representations only within certain limits. A lot depends on what we may regard as 'a reasonable approximation to' and there are no absolutely valid rules for deciding this criterion. But we must not let an assumption about the mathematical law we want to use blind us to the experimental results as they really are. It is quite common to see children experimenting with loading a spring and being led to draw a straight line graph when, for the particular spring they are using, such a graph is manifestly a very poor model. The experiment can be a valuable one because it enables the children to calibrate their springs in order to use them as weighing instruments but it should not be thought that the experiment provides sufficient grounds for the discovery of a completely general 'law'.

A similar situation will arise with graphs obtained by plotting the length of a pendulum against its time of swing, or the height of rebound of a dropped ball, since it is only under very restricted conditions that the physical data are even approximately related to the simple linear mathematical relation. There is the further difficulty that even when the mathematical relationship does approximate closely to the physical situation being explored, junior children's inaccuracies in measurement may be such that it could not be said that the graph produced is very close to a simple mathematical relationship. These problems have to be dealt with when they are met, but it is obviously unwise to insist on the experiment illustrating the

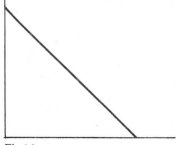

Fig.16

presence of a particular relationship when all the evidence makes the claim look absurd.

There are some physical situations where the chance of producing data which approximate well to a simple relationship exists, and where the children can argue for the existence of such a relationship. Consideration of the pressures on the supports of a plank, for example, as a painter walks along it may lead to an experiment with a small plank, two spring balances and a brick. Here the children can see that the total weight of plank and brick must be shared by the two supports, and the graph becomes illuminating. (Fig.16)

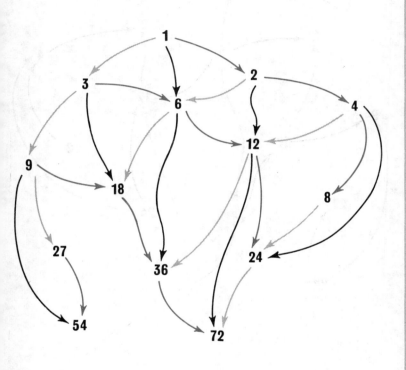

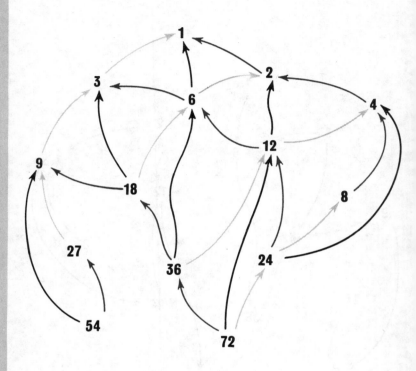

Measurement

In this first section of this chapter we give some reports from a number of classrooms of children engaged in measuring and of children thinking about measuring. We do not think these reports need comment, and we do not give any.

1

An assignment card for a group of seven-year-old children said, 'How many dried peas are there in a pound?' They were given a handful of peas. 'There aren't enough peas. Can we have some more?' 'I haven't any more; you'll have to manage with what you have.'

One group proceeded as follows: they weighed the peas and found there were $1\frac{3}{4}$ oz. They played around with this for some time and then gave it up. Next they weighed out 1 oz., counted the peas and multiplied by 16 'in the way we learnt yesterday'.

One group weighed out 1 oz. straight away, counted them and doubled the answer. They doubled again, then again, and yet again to get the answer.

Another group weighed $1\frac{3}{4}$ oz. and counted them, doubled this to find the number in $3\frac{1}{2}$ oz., doubled again for 7 oz. and again for 14 oz. They then added on the number of peas in $1\frac{3}{4}$ oz., and weighed out $\frac{1}{4}$ oz. and added on this number. (During the process of doubling, one girl had to double 988. She worked from left to right, doubling the 9 first, but wrote down 19; then wrote down 7 followed by 6, finishing with 1976.)

2

Mary (9) completed an assignment card of personal measurements.
My height is 3 ft 9 in.
My span is $5\frac{1}{2}$ inches.

My stride is 34 inches long.
My wrist is 5½ inches.
My waist is 18 inches.
My foot is 7 inches long.
My chest is 25 inches.
My hips are 27 inches.
My arm is 13 inches long.
I am not very big.

3

An intelligent eight-year-old who carries out operations with parcels
and scales and then writes

'The green parcel

> weighs more than 12 oz.
> weighs less than 1 lb.

I guess it weighs 10 oz.'

seems to me to have gained very little from her mathematics. When
she deals with quantities she shelves her common sense and starts to
go through motions like a circus horse. She has no difficulty with
12×3 lb.12 oz. The class discussed this; many children could see
nothing funny. I decided to try and help them to think about what
they were doing by asking them to write down exactly what they
were doing, and making deductions from their observations.

Apparatus used: jars of different capacities

> cards of different lengths
> parcels of different weights
> scales, rulers, capacity measures.

Example: 'The brown jar

> holds less than 1 qt.
> holds more than 1 pt.

I guess 1 pt. 1 gill.

I measured it and it holds more than 1 pt. 1 gill.

I guess 1 pt. and ⅓ of a pt.

It holds nearly 1 pt. and ⅓ pt.'

(The fact that the child here finds out that ⅓ pt. is more than 1 gill
is incidental.)

Much of the work for half a term proceeded on these lines. I was
surprised to get things like:

'The red parcel weighs more than 2 lbs.

The red parcel weighs more than 1 lb.'

However, this work had its compensations. I quote one verbatim and in full.

'1. 3 school milk bottles can fill 1 pt. bottle.

I poured a school milk bottle in a pt. bottle and another and another till it was full and it came to 3 school milk bottles.

2. Our school milk bottle holds a $\frac{1}{3}$ pt. I poured a school milk bottle into $\frac{1}{3}$ pt. measure so that's how we know 3 $\frac{1}{3}$ pt.=1 pt.

3. If I drink 3 school milk bottles I would have drunk a pt. of milk because the school milk bottle holds a $\frac{1}{3}$ pt.

4. I drink 1$\frac{2}{3}$ pt. in 5 days. I poured 5 $\frac{1}{3}$ pt. into 1 pt. and $\frac{2}{3}$ bottles and it came to 1$\frac{2}{3}$ pt.

5. 32 children drink milk every day. I counted the children who have milk and it came to 32. Every day the class drinks 10 pt. $\frac{2}{3}$. I said my 3 times table and it came to 10 pt. $\frac{2}{3}$.

If it was 6d. a bottle it would come to 5s. 4d. because 10 comes to 5s. so a $\frac{1}{3}$ would come to 2d. because 3 $\frac{1}{3}$ come to a pt.'

There may be very little actual mathematics used here but it seems to me that this child was truly involved in the work she was doing. Mathematical investigation had given her the opportunity to write precise, logical and in its way exciting English.

4

Class: Second year Junior – mixed ability – 'culturally under-privileged.'

Situation: discussion with average ability group on results arising from two tasks:

1. Draw round penny on graph paper; count the number of little squares it covers.

   Repeat with halfpenny, halfcrown, etc.

2. Put these in order of *size:*

   halfcrown, shilling piece, halfpenny, *square inch.*

Most could not see which was bigger, halfpenny or square inch. How do we find out? I began to question them to see what they meant by 'bigger'. Almost invariably they equated size with length.

I cut two pieces of thin card, A and B.

Q. *Which is bigger?*

A. *A.* (The minority who said 'B' could not tell me why they thought so; they were just being contrary!)

Fig.1

I then cut B in half, along bb_1, making sure that they saw I was neither taking away from nor adding to it. I put the two halves in position (ii).

Q. *Which is bigger?*

A. *B.*

'But you said "A" before and I haven't added any.' Pause.

I then cut A along aa_1, and repeated the procedure. A was now biggest. I cut each half of B into halves and repeated. B was now biggest.

After several attempts one child said, 'Ah, but you don't know because one's thicker.'

The pieces looked something like this by then:

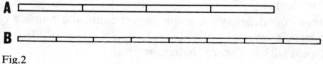

Fig.2

Q. *Well, how do we find what is bigger?*

A. *You have to measure the thickness as well.*

This led us into a discussion of how you could tell the difference between two cards 8 in. × 3 in. and 6 in. × 4 in. since you could measure the height and 'thickness': but so what?

In the course of the discussion I asked Trudy and Joan to stand next to one another, and asked 'Who is bigger?' (Trudy is about 2 in. taller than Joan, but Joan is fat, and about 1 st. heavier. The kids appreciate this because earlier they had done height and weight graphs, using the school weighing machine.)

Only one or two said 'It depends what you mean . . .'.

We began to get somewhere near when one child suggested, 'cover one card up with the other and cut off the bits left over and fill up the spaces with it'.

So far, no-one had suggested using a 'unit' of measurement, the *square inch*, and in fact I had to implant this suggestion.

5

I had asked a group of children to find out how many halfpennies it would take to stretch the length of the classroom. They had measured the length of the classroom and found it was 32 ft. I asked them what they were going to do next. Wendy (7) said, 'Multiply by 2.' When I asked her why she was going to do this, she said, 'Because two half-pennies make a penny.'

6

Ann (9) was weighing her collection of conkers. She found the group of weights on the pan too light, so added another ounce weight (the smallest available). The weights pan was now too heavy. She removed the last ounce added; the pan holding the conkers went down. Ann moved across to the conkers pan and carefully pushed the conkers closer together. She looked expectantly at the still not-balancing pans; abandoned the whole affair.

David (backward 10) in a similar situation retained a collection of weights which was just too light and added a coloured bead. Recorded the weight of conkers as '13 ounces+bead'.

Linda (backward 10) also experienced difficulty. With the weights pan just too heavy she removed the offending one-ounce weight and placed it on the balance arm between the fulcrum and the pan. The scales balanced. Linda appeared satisfied, but unfortunately did not record what she had done.

Alison (6½) faced with the same problem assisted the balance with a finger under the pan; smiled with satisfaction.

Michael (a non-reader at 11) weighing a brick, repeatedly removed the brick and watched the weights crashing down on the other side.

7

A group of seven-year-old children were asked to measure how much water came out of the tap in one minute. Five minutes later they were found with the tap full on, hopefully holding a ruler under the tap.

8

Alison: Your answer is different, Gail. You have got it wrong because there are sixteen ounces in a pound.
Gail: Oh my god! I thought there were four.

9

A group of eight-year-olds were given three pieces of material, in this case, brick, concrete and flint, of roughly the same size, and they were asked how they would find out which was the largest.

After some consideration David said, 'You could cover each piece carefully with plasticine, then take it off and see which piece needed the most plasticine.'

Philip objected to this on the grounds that it would be impossible to make sure that the plasticine was spread evenly. He suggested that each piece could be covered with plasticine, which could be split down the middle to provide two halves of the mould of the stone. More plasticine could be squeezed into the mould and then taken out to provide the shape of the original stone. If this were done for the three pieces, the plasticine could be rolled up into three balls, and it would be easy to see which was the largest.

David pointed out that this was a good idea except that the new plasticine squeezed in would stick to the mould and you wouldn't be able to get it out. He said that it would be a lot better to use plaster.

Melanie said that you would finish up with just the three shapes you started with.

Paul suggested using sand in the mould but it was pointed out by Sandra that this too would stick to the plasticine.

Brian, who had been scratching at the brick with his penknife, said you could grind up the three pieces to powder and see which was the biggest.

This was largely ignored, except by Melanie, who said that the three plaster casts suggested by David could be ground up easily and compared.

Philip suddenly jumped up and said, 'If you fill each half of each mould with water, you could measure the amount of water in a jar.'

This was acceptable to the whole group, and this is what they did.

10

Pauline (7) as part of an assignment, had been asked to measure the length and width of a 9 pin geoboard. She measured one side and wrote it down. She picked up the board again, measured the side, looked at her book, measured the side again, looked at her book, measured all four sides of the board, looked at her book, and finally put down the ruler and board and sat. Suddenly she smiled, picked up the ruler and board, measured the thickness of the board, and wrote down, 'width $\frac{1}{4}$ inch'.

11

A group of children were given an assignment to find out how many tiles there were on the floor of the school hall. They knew exactly how they were going to do this. The hall was rectangular and the tiles were 9 in. square, so they told me they were going to measure the hall, find the area, and because there were 16 tiles to a square yard it would be easy. They were gone a long time, and eventually one returned and asked me if I would come and move the piano. When I arrived, I found they had measured the width, but they said they couldn't measure the length, because there was a cupboard on one side and a piano on the other. These were intelligent children in the 9+ range.

12

I had in mind that Peter and Michael should explore the different rectangles that could be made with an area of 36 square inches and possibly plot the graph of length against breadth. On a whim I told Peter to take 24 squares so that he would have a different situation from Michael's.

After a short time I was called over because Peter said he couldn't make a square with his square inches and Michael could! Surely there is a square with an area of 24 sq. in. ? What would the side have to be? Looking at his squares he said 'Less than five, bigger than four. Can I have some squared paper?' On $\frac{1}{4}$ in. squared paper he tried $4\frac{1}{2}$ in. and $4\frac{3}{4}$ in. squares, working out the area by counting and making up parts into square inches, and was satisfied that it was somewhere between $4\frac{3}{4}$ in. and 5 in.

The following week I suggested he drew a graph to show how the area of squares changes as the side increases. He started constructing squares out of the square inches but complained that it would be boring when the side of the square was large. I said he might find a

pattern after making a few squares, and shortly afterwards he cam‹
and said 'I've found a pattern', showing me his paper:

2 in.	4 sq. in.	5	
3 in.	9 sq. in.	7	'It goes up 5, then 7, then 9, then 11.'
4 in.	16 sq. in.	9	
5 in.	25 sq. in.	11	
6 in.	36 sq. in.		

Not the pattern I expected him to find! From his graph I asked if he
could find a more accurate answer to his problem from the previous
week. This he did, after suggesting adding some extra points for
$4\frac{1}{2}$ in., $5\frac{1}{2}$ in., $6\frac{1}{2}$ in. squares. While drawing these he asked 'Can you
calculate the area when its got a fraction in it instead of drawing it?'
We looked again at the $4\frac{3}{4}$ in. square and saw there would be 19×19
small squares each $\frac{1}{16}$ sq. in. in area. Further experiments followed
with the $4\frac{1}{2}$ in. square and then a rectangle $4\frac{1}{2}$ in. $\times 4\frac{3}{4}$ in., and it then
seemed reasonable to set out the calculation as $\dfrac{9 \times 19}{2 \times 4}$ so that 'multiplying' fractions took on meaning.

13

Lynn recorded as her answer after a weighing exercise that there were
more peas than beans to a pound because they were *smaller*.

14

A group of seven-year-old children were each given three pieces of
paper about the same size. From these pieces of paper they were
asked to cut out three shapes as large as they could, the first shape
to be made up of straight lines, the second of curved lines, and the
third any shape they liked. When these were cut out, they were asked
if they could say which of their shapes contained the most paper.
Although some said they thought they could do it, they all agreed
that they could not be definitely sure. Discussion then took place as
to possible ways of dealing with the problem.

    Andrew suggested that we might weigh the pieces, but when the
most sensitive scales were produced, it was quite evident that no
difference in weight could be registered. Several unacceptable solutions were offered, and it was some time before two possible ways
were put forward. The first came from Janet who suggested that if
the pieces were cut into strips of equal width and placed end to end,
it would be possible to measure them. The second suggestion developed from this and came from Michael who said that you could cut

he strips into squares and count the squares. When it was hinted that his would be a rather long and tedious business, they thought it could be made easier by drawing round the shapes on a piece of squared paper and then cutting them out.

They did this for each shape, but before they reached the cutting out stage, many of them had realized that they were in a position to count the number of squares and so compare the amount of paper in each shape. The squared paper had $\frac{1}{4}$ in. squares, but no attempt was made to look for actual magnitude; all we were interested in at this stage was comparison.

The following discussion then took place:

Teacher If you wanted to find out which was the taller of two children, how would you do it?

Pauline I would stand them back to back and then I would be able to see.

T And if you wanted to say how much taller one was than the other, how would you do it?

Ian You could measure them both.

Alison You could stand them both up against a cupboard and put a ruler on the head of the smallest one and see how many inches it was to the top of the head of the other.

T Suppose you wanted to find out how much heavier one stone was than another, how would you do it?

Jennifer I would weigh them both and see how many ounces more one was.

T If you wanted to know how much more water there was in the sink than in the bucket, how would you do it?

Denise I would use a pint bottle and see how many times I could fill t from each one.

T Suppose I asked you how much bigger the top of my desk was than your desk, what would you do?

Alan I would measure your desk and mine and then I could say.

T How would you measure it?

Alan I would measure how long it is.

T Would that be enough?

Melanie He would have to measure how wide it is too, because it's bigger that way as well.

T Suppose you wanted to say how much bigger the sand pit (rectangular) is than the pond (circular), how would you do it?

Gail I know it's bigger.

T But could you say how much bigger?

Gail We could measure it.

T How would you measure it?

Philip I know how big the sand pit is, because I did it last week. It's 9 feet wide and 13 feet long.

Alan And I know that the pond is 5 feet across and 16 feet all round.

Philip (who has been busy with pencil and paper), Well, its 44 feet all round the sand pit and 16 feet all round the pond, so its 28 feet bigger.

Three dimensions

Much of the young child's activity is directed to exploring the three-dimensional space in which he lives. A ball is out of reach yet can be seen; the rattle is out of sight, yet can be felt somewhere down there. Objects are grasped and bumped against. Some objects can be held in the hands and squeezed or crushed; others are so big that they must be crawled round. Is it too heavy to lift? Can it be filled with something?

Out of the multitude of activities spring various classifications of objects by, say, colour, texture, shape, rigidity, elasticity, size, weight. Classifications by shape are the beginnings of geometry. In school these classifications can be supported by activities of building with bricks, packing things in containers, painting the surfaces, and so on. Gradually a collection of objects is made, and the teacher can call attention to their surfaces, to the edges that separate parts of the surfaces, and to the corners which appear where edges meet.

1. Which of the shapes have no corners (vertices)?

2. Which have only one corner? Two corners? etc.

3. Which have no edges? One edge? Two edges? etc.

4. Which have only straight edges? Only curved edges? Some of each?

5. Which have only one face? Two? Three? etc.

6. Which have only curved surfaces? Which have only flat (plane) surfaces?

7. Which objects stand on the table? Which of them will roll? Which roll in a straight line? Can we find any which will roll in a curve? A circle?

8. Which of them make contact with the table over a surface? Which make contact along a line (curved or straight)? Which make contact only at 'a point'?

The handling and discussion of the properties of objects can be supplemented by constructional activities. Building three-dimensional objects from three-dimensional bricks is familiar experience to all children. But three-dimensional objects can be constructed in other ways.

(a) What kinds of shape must we draw on paper or cardboard to be able to fold the material into a 'solid'? Simple solids can be made from patterns of squares or rectangles or triangles. The *net* of a cube is a suitable arrangement of six squares which can be folded and glued (if flaps are left) into the shape of a cube. The usual arrangement of squares is shown in the figure.

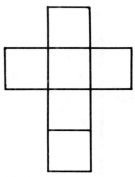

Fig.3

Is this the only possible arrangement that will fold up in the right way? How many of the hexominoes (p.157–160) will be suitable?

Can we forecast what kind of solid a particular net will make? Can we design a net to make a particular solid?

The net is quite a sophisticated preparation for making a solid. Is it not better to start with a set of squares and some Sellotape? Or with a set of equilateral triangles (p. 131)?

If we omit the last face of the solid, or hinge it so that it does not get in the way, we can pour plaster into the container and obtain a *real* solid.

We can obtain various cardboard containers, sweet-boxes, for example, and see if the cardboard can be flattened. Can we flatten it in different ways to obtain different shapes?

(b) Making solids from nets concentrates attention on the faces of the solids. Making skeleton models from milk straws threaded with cotton or fixed with pipe-cleaners makes us conscious of the edges of the solids. How many squares do we need to make a cube? How many milk-straws do we need to make a skeleton cube? How many pipe-cleaners do we need?

Is a skeleton cube rigid? A triangle is the only plane shape which is fully determined by the three sides (a triangle of three pieces of wood or three Meccano strips cannot be deformed by reasonable pressure). What is the simplest three-dimensional rigid skeleton?

Why is a skeleton octahedron not rigid? Its eight faces are all triangular.

(c) If we sellotape a milk-straw to the edge of a cardboard triangle and rotate the triangle by twirling the straw, we say we *generate* a cone.

Fig.4

We do not produce a 'real' cone, but the movement makes us think of a cone – if we know what one is like already. If we have a solid cone we can twirl that in the same way. What do we notice? The cone appears the same if it is stopped in any position. Can we find other shapes which look the same when twirled? Can we describe the shapes generated by twirling the following plane shapes about the milk-straw? (Fig.5)

Can we generate a cube by twirling a flat shape in the same kind of way? A square? But doesn't a square generate a cylinder when it is twirled? Only if we twirl it in one particular way. What other solids can we generate by twirling a square?

If we twirl a cube it does not look the same in every position, but there are some positions in which it does look the same. How many of these positions are there?

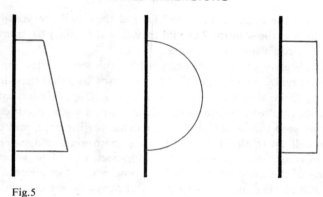

Fig.5

Let us look at a number of solids turned half-way round, a quarter way round, and so on. Do any of them look the same? What does this tell us about their symmetries?

Representing shapes

The main topic of the class had been 'Furniture', and this led naturally to wood and to the cutting down of trees. In the logging picture the circular ends of the logs could be seen and the saw was cutting the log from end to end. 'What would be the shape of the surface of the cut?' Most drew rectangles or rectangles with semicircles on one end; one boy (was he just fascinated by the large saw?) drew a zig-zag line. The teacher suggested that the men might make a slanting cut across the log. 'What would be the shape of the surface of the cut now?' Only Linda, a very backward 10, drew an ellipse. Although Linda seemed to know she was right it was apparent that the rest of the class, whose drawings ranged from semi-circles to figures of eight, were unbelievers. The teacher promised to find a saw at break and cut a dowel rod to settle the point. Then a large tin can was noticed in the room and a boy sent to part-fill it with water. Linda was already bouncing excitedly in her desk and as the boy bearing the tin entered the room she dashed out with a cry of 'I'll show them', grabbed the tin, violently tilted it, shooting most of the water over the desk, and pointed authoritatively at the now elliptical surface of the water.

Linda's success at this particular task is certainly striking, but perhaps the point of the story is that all the other children failed to give the hoped-for answer. Why was this? It is obviously impossible to say: we do not have enough information. Did the children fail to understand the original question? Or did they lack the visualizing power to 'see' the solution? Or did they lack the ability to 'translate' this image into a suitable drawing?

It is indicative of the complexity behind this simple situation that we cannot really disentangle these three causes, and that they do not represent three successive stages of understanding. 'Understanding the question' already presupposes some store of visual experience – of having seen things cut or sliced or sawn, for instance, and being able to call up to the mind's eye some appropriate image. This is fairly obvious, and no teacher would expect a child to know the meaning of the question if he lacked some relevant experience. But this is not all. Having seen an object cut across is not enough. It is no good asking the child to 'look' and draw what he 'sees'. Until he has met *some* conventional representations or symbolizations of the kind of thing he is to look at, he has no idea how to select what he should attend to, and no idea how this could be described or represented.

Children have to learn how to look, how to select what to look at, and how to look at it. In this learning process symbols play an essential part; they may be gestures, or words, or signs or drawings. The child acquires them by seeing and hearing them used in appropriate contexts, and at any stage the 'vocabulary' of symbols that he knows is growing and developing, increasing his ability to comprehend. It is not just that the extent of his 'vocabulary' determines how much he understands of what is 'said', although that is part of it; nor that his 'vocabulary' determines how much he can communicate of what he understands, although that is another part of it. But the words and signs at his disposal have a more dynamic life; they are the tools he needs for his explorations.

Every teacher knows that this is true in the case of language. Words are not solely for talking with. They are part of the process of structuring experience and giving it meaning. The same is true for any other system of symbols, and in particular for the system of conventions that we use to describe shapes: the models we make and the diagrams we draw. Certainly the figures we draw are not merely copies of nature. Squares and rectangles and circles are as much abstractions as numbers are, and we would never arrive at them by simple observation of things around us. Yet it is true that the kind of civilized environment we live in has itself been influenced by the existence of these abstractions and it is much easier for us to acquire our familiar geometrical 'vocabulary' than it is for a member of a different civilization. Our culture makes these conventions accessible to us. A child's post-box toy is a trivial example of geometry influencing a bit of the environment, which then in turn offers back a particular kind of geometrical experience to children who have not yet learnt the conventions. But this experience, polarized as it is, would come to nothing if it were not for the fact that it can immediately be linked with language and with symbolic representation. The child's parents will ask him to post the 'oblong' piece; 'Is the square piece inside?' Father will show him how to draw a square, and will point to drawings in the newspaper.

Gradually the child begins to 'make sense' of this complex situation. As he does so, he is able to apply the words and symbols he has learned to new situations – they 'tell' him what to look for and enable him to express what he 'recognizes'. And he starts simultaneously to master the reverse action of stringing words together and organizing new graphic symbols to refer to other things about him. This process is subject all the time to social checks. Can the child make himself understood? Can he understand what is said or shown to him? It seems to be one of the tasks of the teacher in the classroom to try to bring the state of this communication into focus.

We know from the story that the other children had graphic symbols at their disposal – rectangles with semicircular ends, the zig-zag line – and that these were not meaningless scribbles made by children who had no idea at all what was required of them. Their drawings made a good deal of sense, even if it were not the sense that Linda shared with her teacher. The only resolution of their disagreements will come from further 'conversations' at other times. We cannot feel confident that Linda's demonstration will have converted them all in an instant.

It is quite common to find children who have learnt the graphic symbol for a cube. (Fig.6) A parent or teacher may have shown a child how to draw this, but at some early stages the 'conversation' will not have continued long enough. The symbol may then be a relatively useless piece of geometrical lumber, even though it is an achievement of which the child is proud. 'I can draw a cube!' But this ability guarantees no operational control over the symbol and the process of developing it into a usable model may have hardly begun.

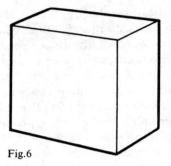

Fig.6

Let us look briefly at the process the other way round.

Three boys: Derek (11), Leslie (10) and David (11).

We had a large cube on the table and were discussing the number of corners, edges and sides. I was trying to get the boys to tell me about the cube without giving them the vocabulary.

We started with corners. Only Derek counted the corners he could not see. The others had to be prompted and encouraged to count the corners by touching them physically.

I asked them to draw the cube.

Derek drew:

Leslie drew:

David drew:

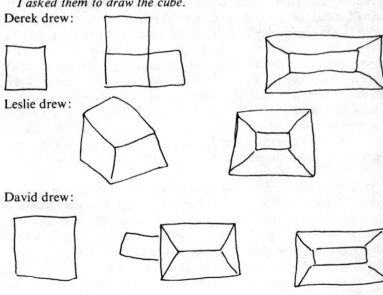

Fig.7

John (5), who had just started school, was heard to say, 'What is two and four?' A voice behind him said, 'That's six'. 'Oh no,' said John, 'it can't be. Three and three are six.'

A four-year-old boy with a drawing and arrows on it which his father does not understand. Father asks if he can put one in and puts one from a car to the house.
'Oh no, Daddy. You can't put the car in the house.'

Working with a group of five-year-olds, I took two green Cuisenaire rods and said, 'This one is Mary, and this is John'. I then shook them up in my hands and put them on the table. I asked Angela to tell me which was which. Without hesitation she pointed to one and said, 'That one is Mary'. When I asked her how she knew, she said, 'Well, Mary's a girl isn't she?'

Question in a well-known textbook: 'When you divide a number by 7 there is a remainder of 1. What is the number?' Kevin (9) wrote, '8, 15, 22, 29, 36, 43, 50, 64, 71, 78 and a lot more. Take your pick'.

Question in a well-known textbook: 'A piece of paper has an area of 96 square inches. It is 12 inches long; how wide is it?' Howard (9): 'It all depends on the shape of the paper'.

Tessellations

This is a record of a series of lessons with some ten-year-olds. Similar work has been done with younger children.

I held up a small equilateral triangle in front of the class and waited for them to speak. 'It looks like a tent or a road sign' someone said. 'It's called a triang', came from another. (This last seemed to be associated with Triang toys.) 'What else about it?' I asked. 'It has three edges.' 'Show me what you mean by an edge.' Most of the children pointed to the corners of their desks. We went on to discuss phrases like 'edge of the sea', 'edge of a desert', 'edge of a field', which helped to make clear that what they had called edges I called corners. I told them this shape was called a triangle.

They were each given a copy of this triangle, a sheet of thin cardboard and some scissors. They were told they were to cut out triangles the same shape and the same size, and try to get as many as possible from their cardboard.

They drew round the edges first and then cut. A few did.

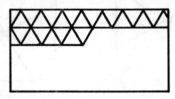

Fig.1

The others had many versions varying right up to random cutting. (Fig.2)

When they had about twenty triangles each they were asked to make shapes by placing triangles together on their desks. This produced a large range. Some made shapes by placing the sides of the triangles

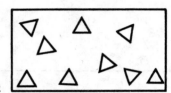

Fig.2

together, coinciding exactly; for example

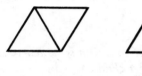

Fig.3

Others put sides together, but without coincidence.

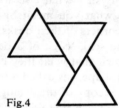

Fig.4

Others made shapes by placing vertices together

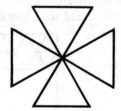

Fig.5

and others by placing triangles on top of others.

Fig.6

When we had seen what a rich crop could be had by using our
riangle as the unit, we decided to bring in some limitation and
xamine for a while only the first type. We found four more basic
hapes.

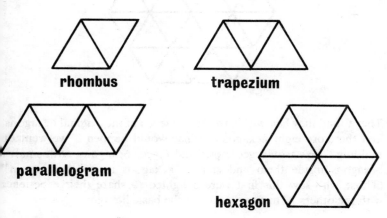

hey then went on trying to discover others. Some made a star,

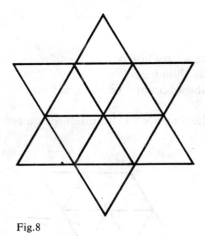

Fig.8

and, adding to this, made a larger hexagon. (Fig.9)

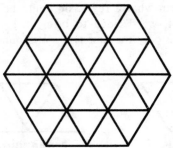

Fig.9

They found they had within this figure seven of the original hexagons, and therefore eight hexagons. 'What would happen if we went on building?' 'We would get bigger and bigger hexagons, with smaller hexagons inside them and smaller hexagons inside them again!' (Those who saw this first were delighted to share their experience with the others.) Then we looked at the basic hexagon.

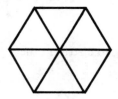

Fig.10

'What shapes have we got inside this?'
'Well, we've got six rhombuses!'
'How many rhombuses could it be separated into?'
'Three!'
'In how many different ways?' (This produced quite a long and fruit-ful discussion.)
And so on . . .

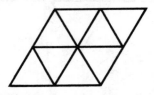

Fig.11

'We've got six different trapeziums!'

And so on . . .

'Can we build a bigger rhombus than the basic one?'

'Yes'.

We studied this in the same way as before. Then we continued building it up and saw we had rhombuses within rhombuses within rhombuses. We were also back with our hexagons within the rhombuses and, of course, trapeziums inside those.

We did similar things with the trapezium, parallelogram and triangle.

By this time the children seemed to feel the way these shapes were tied together. They also gave every evidence of a growing awareness of the infinite repetition as the triangles were added. 'We could go on as long as we liked and we would always come back to these shapes!'

The children next took their triangles and spread them together on the floor as if they were tiling it (*tessellating the plane*). They were asked to have a good look and see what shapes they could pick out. Then they were asked, 'Could we go on and cover the whole floor with these triangles without leaving any spaces?'

Eventually most of the children decided it was possible, but were not so sure about the edges of the classroom. By spreading the triangles near an edge it was decided that here they would have to be cut.

'Could we carry on past the walls and cover the whole playground?'

'Yes! Except that we would be in trouble at the edges again!'

'What shape would the playground have to be so that there would be no trouble at the edges?'

Only one or two at first, but gradually more saw that it might have to be a triangle of the same shape. (What about a rhombus, trapezium or hexagon?)

'Could we go on and on covering the ground with these triangles and leaving no space?'

'Well, as long as the ground was flat.'

It seemed we were in a bit of a difficulty with the earth being a sphere; but a flat space, however big, could be covered in this way, they thought.

Now I pinned on the wall a large sheet of cardboard, tessellated with triangles. The children came out and painted in the different shapes they could see. They found the five basic shapes and bigger versions of them. They were then given sheets of paper tessellated with triangles and with their coloured crayons asked to design the plan of a tiled floor.

First I suggested they use only hexagonal tiles. It was interesting that only about half the class were able to do this successfully,

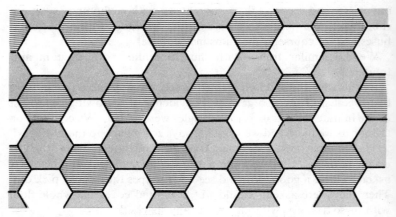

Fig.12

the other half leaving triangular and rhombic spaces between their hexagons.

Next they tiled a floor with trapeziums. By now they were more able to fit them together without leaving spaces and they produced some very interesting and attractive patterns. Again, only about half got away from what might be called a 'ribbon development' of colouring.

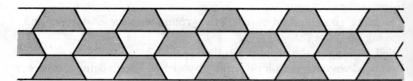

Fig.13

We did the same thing with rhombuses and then they were free to use a mixture of any tiles. They seemed to enjoy this thoroughly and produced some attractive designs.

Fig.14

Notes

A plane can be tiled with other shapes besides the four shown so far.
Perhaps the most productive geometrically is the scalene triangle:

Fig.15

The children can see that all the lines are parallel. Now take a cardboard triangle (shown shaded) and slide and rotate it to cover other
triangles in the tessellation. In this way all the angles can be marked,

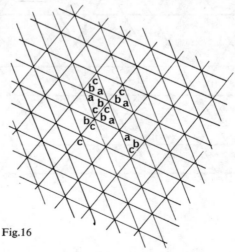

Fig.16

and at any point (vertex) in the diagram it is clearly seen that $a+b+c=180°$ (i.e. the sum of the angles of a triangle is $180°$).

Take any two of the parallel lines and a transversal,

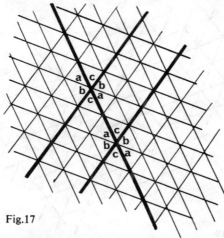

Fig.17

and we see that 'alternate angles are equal', 'corresponding angles are equal' and 'interior angles on the same side of the transversal add up to $180°$'.

Take any set of parallel lines and two transversals:

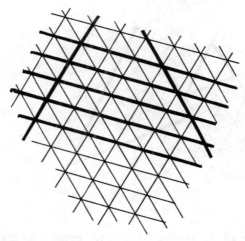

Fig.18

This demonstrates the equal intercept theorem.
Consider a triangle such as

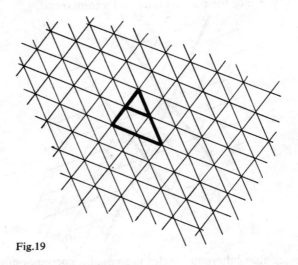

Fig.19

and we have the mid-point theorem.
Take two triangles such as

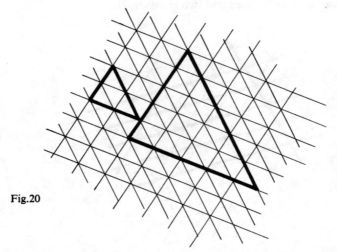

Fig.20

and we have all the similar triangle theorems. (See the section on similarity, p.149.)

Any quadrilateral will tessellate the plane,

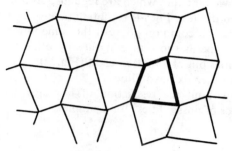

Fig.21

and from this we have 'the sum of the angles of a quadrilateral is 360°'. And there is, in particular, the well-known square tessellation which is seen all around us (chessboards, floors, etc.).

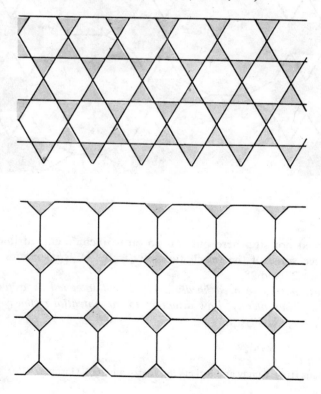

Fig.22

In all of these we have been restricted to one shape and size of tile. Suppose now we take tiles which are regular polygons and mix them as the children did (see Fig.14) to obtain *homogeneous* tessellations, i.e. each vertex is a common point of the same number of polygons of the same shape as those meeting at any other vertex. We have these possibilities out of a total of eight (Fig.22).

(What are the other six possibilities?)

Mixing tiles without the restriction of homogeneity, we have an infinite number of possibilities; for example:

Fig.23

We need not stop here but can go on to include curved lines and produce some of the tessellations illustrated in *Mathematics teaching*, Nos.27 and 28.

These notes, we need hardly say, are not intended as a teaching scheme. They merely draw attention to the potential richness of the tessellating activity.

References
Steinhaus [109], Cundy and Rollet [26], Lietzmann [66], Gardner [42].

Out of the plane

When the children were asked to make shapes by fitting the triangles together, some children had already started to prop triangles up against each other and make solid shapes. Now they were given Sellotape and told: 'See what shapes you can make by fitting the triangles together, and you don't have to confine yourselves to laying them flat on the desk.' Some children very quickly got the tetrahedron. We found whichever way you turned it and looked at it you saw the same shape, and here it seemed to have a similarity with the triangle we were using. Now we really had something we could call edges; we still had corners; and we had a new thing which we could call a face.

To go any further with new solids was difficult, but we obtained all sorts of irregular ones by adding tetrahedrons. I then asked: 'How many triangles have we got meeting at each corner of the tetrahedron?' 'Three'. 'Is it possible to make a solid with four triangles meeting at each corner?' This caused great interest and investigation and eventually some children produced the octahedron. We studied this in the same way as we had the tetrahedron, and saw it too was regular.

By now, one or two children were trying to make a solid with five triangles meeting at each corner. The word soon got around and they were all after a solution. This, of course, was a tough one, but eventually most of them managed. We found it too was regular.
'Sir, you can't make one with six, can you?'
'Can't you? What do the rest of the class think?'
'Of course you can!' 'No, you can't.'
'Well, will you all try?' I said. Soon, we saw that it was not possible. 'Because what you get is flat!'

As a last little thing, we counted up the faces, vertices and edges, and after a few hints they saw that the numbers had quite an interesting relationship.

Symmetry

Most of the learning about symmetry will take place outside the set mathematics lessons, and this is as it should be, for this topic permeates the whole of the child's life, and opportunities for discussion will arise with great frequency, and at times when thoughts of mathematics are very much in the background. The most important thing is that the teacher should be sensitive enough to mathematical ideas to seize upon this gratuitous presentation of opportunity as it arises.

The first ideas of symmetry which a young child demonstrates is that of the human body. Even in the first scribblings, when an attempt is being made to represent people, the child's awareness of the symmetrical properties of the human body is made clear. It is interesting to note that although a young child may draw a figure very much lacking in proportion, there will be an attempt to reproduce the symmetry of the body, e.g. the arms may be much too short or too long, but they will be of the same size, and the same applies to legs, ears, eyes, etc. There is, too, a natural desire for symmetry in the drawings of animals, houses, trees, flowers, and birds.

It is interesting to watch the development of young children during the period of their first acquaintance with material such as Cuisenaire rods. The first play usually takes the form of flat arrangements of rods to form the ground plan of houses, or the layout of gardens and farms, and, more usually with boys, intricate patterns of roads and railways. There seems to be no attempt at symmetrical arrangement here, which seems to suggest that although the children may look upon the stylized representation of a house as being symmetrical, they are well aware that the inside layout of rooms is certainly not. Following on the vertical building stage, a further pattern-making period develops, particularly among girls, when far more intricate patterns are produced, often in three dimensions. These patterns are usually built up by deliberately adding rods of the same colour to each side of the pattern. A particular instance of this is the response of slightly older children to the request to make a staircase. They will very often start with the longest rod and continue in both directions. Further examples of pattern making may be seen when children are using geoboards or mosaic shapes.

The fundamental concept of bilateral symmetry will probably be well established at the infant level through art and craft work, as the children will quickly realize that this is a useful tool which can be used to enhance the quality of their work. If you want to paint a large butterfly, you can fold the paper in two, draw one half of the butterfly in charcoal, fold and press, and the other half, perfectly symmetrical, is produced for you, providing a far better result than you would otherwise have obtained. The children are quick to seize upon this method for use in a variety of ways using charcoal, paint, ink, or by folding and cutting. It is very useful for the children to have a large mirror available which can be placed on the fold in the paper so that the reflection can be compared. By experiment in this way the children will discover for themselves which shapes are symmetrical and which are not, where the lines of symmetry lie and how many of them there are.

All these things have been happening for many years in the education of young children, but hitherto the mathematical implications have not been fully exploited by giving the children an opportunity to discuss among themselves, and with the teacher, the full significance of the concepts involved in the empirical methods they are using. The wise teacher will seize upon the developing interest to encourage further investigation and discovery along the same lines. This applies, of course, throughout the whole range of education and one teacher reports the following situations where ideas of symmetry have developed in the course of other activities.

'A group of eleven-year-old children were allowed to take upon themselves the decoration of the school for Christmas. As part of the decoration they had decided to cut out letters from coloured paper and stick them on the windows to read A MERRY CHRISTMAS AND A HAPPY NEW YEAR. Their first attempts were pretty poor and permission to stick the letters on the window was refused until some uniformity of style and size was achieved. After discussion it was decided that the first essential was to cut the letters from uniform pieces of paper, and a large quantity of four-inch squares was provided and the children left to experiment. Resulting from this they found that by folding the paper they could cut most of the letters, that some letters could be cut by folding the paper twice, but some letters had to be cut straight out as no method of folding would produce the desired result. When the actual task on hand was completed, the children went on to discover how many letters of the alphabet had one line of bilateral symmetry, how many had two lines, how many had no line of symmetry, how many possessed rotational symmetry, and the case of O with an infinite number of lines of symmetry.

An instance of the way in which previous experience can manifest itself unexpectedly was provided by a group of children who were making pentominoes, i.e. they were trying to find out all the possible arrangements of five squares. These were eight-year-olds, and although they had had no set lessons on symmetry, the topic had been raised whenever opportunity offered. When the full complement of possible pentominoes had been collected (Fig. 24) they readily classified them into the ones without any line of symmetry, the ones with one line, the one with two and the ones with rotational symmetry. They also, incidentally, represented this classification by Venn diagrams, and then went on to find out which of the pentominoes would tessellate.'

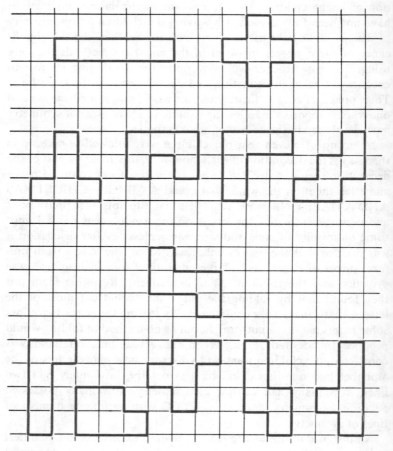

Fig.24

Hole-filling

An assortment of geometrical shapes is carefully cut from a large piece of card. (Fig.25) The pieces are retained, and the sheet of card is pinned to a board or stuck on a backing-sheet of a contrasting colour.

Fig.25

The discussion may begin with the teacher asking for any observations. Some of the shapes will be familiar to the children and can be named; some may be known but not recognized because they are placed in an unfamiliar orientation. The children may offer, or ask for, names of the shapes that they do not know very well. It is probably better for the teacher not to insist on giving names for all the shapes unless the children want them. In their observations, the children may start to classify the shapes in some way, or the teacher may prompt them with a question. A likely reaction is for the children to classify the shapes according to the number of sides they have. The lesson may then go on to suggest another classification, based on the symmetries of the figures.

Margaret, will you please choose one of the pieces that has been cut out. Where was it cut from? Is she right? Oh, you are not sure which way round it should go? Can you put it back in any other way, Margaret? Is she right? There are other ways, are there? All right, come and show us, Peter. Is that all the possible ways that he can do it? How many ways has Peter put it in?

Perhaps Margaret chose the equilateral triangle. This triangle can be replaced in its hole in six different ways. (It may be necessary to mark the piece in some way to keep track of all the possibilities.) Other shapes are selected and the same question asked. The children can be asked to guess how many before the piece is tried. (The parallelogram often proves difficult: it seems to ask to be turned over.)

The shapes can be classified now by the number of ways each will go into its hole. In this classification, the rectangle and rhombus go together, each having four positions. The isosceles triangle, isosceles trapezium and parallelogram each have two positions. The parallelogram does not seem to belong with the others and the children can discuss significant differences. They may say that the parallelogram is 'the same way up' in both its positions, but that the isosceles triangle and trapezium need to be 'turned over'. It is worth looking to see how each shape can be moved to fit a second time when it has been fitted in once. With several of the shapes it is possible to start from a fitting-position and turn the piece over or turn it round to get it back in the hole again. The parallelogram can only be turned round, and the isosceles triangle has to be turned over.

Note

The shapes that can be turned over to fit are said to have line (*or* axial) symmetry. *We can imagine rotating the shape through two right angles about a line in the plane. Such a line is called an axis of symmetry; several of the shapes have more than one. The rectangle, for example, has two axes of symmetry (shown by dotted lines in Fig.26).*

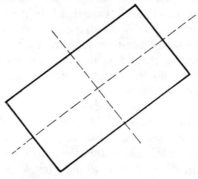

Fig.26

The shapes that will fit again after being turned round in the plane, provided the angle of turn is less than a complete revolution, are said to have rotational (*or* central) symmetry. *The single point of the shape that remains in the same position is called the centre of symmetry. Which shapes have both kinds of symmetry? One kind? Neither?*

These symmetry types can be studied later, probably in the secondary school, from another point of view. Shapes with line symmetry are transformed into themselves by reflection *in an axis; shapes with central symmetry can often be transformed into themselves by rotation about the centre through a* half-turn. *This leads to the idea of geometrical transformations and the study of symmetry groups.*

The children can be asked to draw other shapes having the same symmetry properties as the shapes on the board, or to pick out capital letters (idealized a little) which would 'go into their holes' in various numbers of ways. It seems appropriate to use the hole-filling activity to see if some of the simple geometrical properties will emerge. For example, the fact that the parallelogram can be given a half-turn and will fit again shows that the opposite sides are of equal length (because they change places), that the opposite angles are equal (for the same reason), and that the diagonals bisect each other (because the two parts of each diagonal change places).

It is not suggested that these results should be treated at all formally, or even stated in the words used here. Nor is it necessary to press the children to find all the properties. In fact it is not possible to discover all the geometrical properties of the figures by this kind of exploration. We have already seen that the rhombus and the rectangle have the same symmetry properties, so a study of the symmetry alone cannot account for the differences between the two shapes.

The hole-filling activity on which this work is based seems to have a strong appeal and can lead to very powerful insights into geometrical properties. It is perhaps worth remembering that children have had many experiences of this kind of activity in other contexts, and that some toys for pre-school children are based on this principle.

Similarity

The junior school child who is provided with a rich geometrical experience will meet situations which can be described in terms of mathematical similarity. Tiling flat surfaces and building solid constructions provide the principal raw material for the discovery of similar shapes. Scale drawing and modelling, making maps, finding heights and distances, enlarging diagrams, projecting pictures on to a screen, changing the scales of a graph, making and using a pantograph, are some of the other activities that can lead to ideas of similarity. But although all these things can conveniently be put together under this heading, it is not always easy for children to perceive that they are connected. Although primary school children should be encouraged to take the study of similar shapes as far as they are able, it is unwise for the teacher to attempt a premature unification and formalization of their experiences. It is not likely that any definition of similarity in the usual text-book language will be appropriate. 'Corresponding sides are proportional' is, for instance, a deceptively easy phrase to communicate. It is a summary, however, of a range of quite complex ideas, and should be avoided until it becomes absolutely necessary.

Some of Piaget's work (see particularly [86]) suggests that the ability to operate with equivalent proportions does not develop in most children until the age of eleven or so. Even if these researches are not the last word, they indicate that the mental operations involved in the manipulative aspects of similarity are considerably more sophisticated than might be supposed. A reasonable degree of facility in handling fractions is by no means enough. We suggest, then, that the primary school is the place for an exploration of similarity in a variety of concrete instances, but that no attempt should be made to force the various experiences into a single abstract idea.

From an early stage, the teacher can explore his pupils' use of the word 'similar'. He will almost certainly find that they use it, as he often does himself, to mean 'rather alike' or 'very nearly the same'. As we have discussed elsewhere (p.279), the word 'same' is a crucial word in mathematics and is always used in the sense of 'the same in certain respects' (which may not necessarily be explicit). As we would expect, 'similar' is sometimes used interchangeably with 'same', although in ordinary usage it generally implies that the 'differences' are more noticeable. A child comparing two shapes, say two triangles, may call them 'similar' if they are both right-angled but are manifestly not congruent. The same two triangles may be described as the 'same' if he is only concerned with the fact that they have right angles, and is discriminating them from triangles which have not.

Since these uses of the word can be a hindrance when we want to talk about mathematical similarity, should we proscribe these loose uses and insist that children only call geometrical shapes 'similar' when these are mathematically similar in the strict sense? The question hardly needs asking; the answer is obvious. We cannot manage without the word 'similar' in a large number of situations which have nothing to do with strict mathematical similarity. We have to accept that a word belonging to everyday language has been adopted by mathematics and given a highly specialized meaning. The two kinds of use exist side-by-side and all we can do is to be aware of the inherent ambiguity. We have mentioned this point because we are interested in the language that children spontaneously use, and because we think that the teacher should know that here is the possibility of confusion. He can resolve it in a number of ways. Perhaps all that he needs to use in the junior school is the phrase 'having the same shape', and concern himself with the various meanings this can have.

Exercises

1. Look at some of the common tessellations based on a single shape and see which contain larger editions of the same shape.

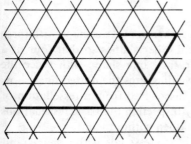 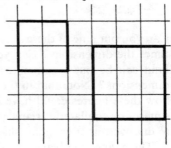

Fig.27

2. Try any less well-known tessellations, e.g. the hexomino tessellations on p.157.

3. It is possible to build larger equilateral triangles out of a supply of congruent equilateral triangles:

  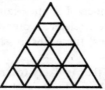 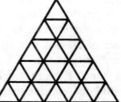

Fig.28

Is the same kind of construction possible with squares, rectangles, rhombuses (diamonds), parallelograms, scalene (i.e. non-special) triangles, trapezia?

4. The first three explorations may suggest that when a larger similar shape can be made, *four* of the unit shapes are needed to make a larger one with twice the dimensions, nine will make a shape with three times the dimensions, and so on. Is this the case in all the examples tried so far?

In the following diagrams, four congruent pieces have been put together to make shapes of the same kind with twice the dimensions.

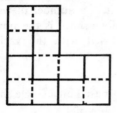   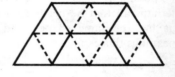

Fig.29

Can you put nine of these shapes together to make a shape with three times the dimensions? Can you find other shapes so that four of a kind can be put together to make the same shape with twice the dimensions? (Note that in the above diagrams the dotted lines show how these figures could have been discovered from a tessellation of squares or equilateral triangles. Try inspecting the basic tessellations to discover other irregular shapes hidden within them.)

5. The connection between being able to tessellate with a shape, and being able to build larger similar shapes from it, seems close; but it is not by any means perfect. Find some shapes which will tessellate, but which cannot be put together to make larger editions of themselves. Contrariwise, find some shapes which can be put together to make similar shapes, but which will not tessellate. (We must not forget that a large number of shapes cannot be tessellated or built into similar shapes. The circle is an obvious case. If we think of the set of all possible shapes, these unruly shapes are obviously in the majority.)

One of the problems that is likely to arise at an early stage in the study of 'similar shapes' (or 'the same shapes') is again related to the use of words, although it has roots in specific properties as well. For the child, shapes may be similar if they are called by the same name. In one sense this is of course true or they would not have been given that name. But we are here thinking of 'similarity' in a special way, and the kind of similarity that makes us classify shapes together and give them the same name is not necessarily the similarity that we are now talking about. Squares, for instance, are always similar to each other in the strict mathematical sense. The collection of properties that entitles a shape to the name 'square' automatically ensures that it is similar to any other square. But rectangles, although they have a number of properties that entitle them to the same name, are not necessarily similar in the mathematical sense.

The rectangle is a particularly tricky case because any number of congruent rectangles can be put together to make another rectangle:

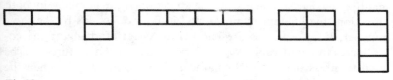

Fig.30

A discussion of the similarity of two rectangles, therefore, carries problems that the discussion of the similarity of two squares does not. An attempt to settle the matter by talk about corresponding proportions is, as we have already said, better postponed. But it is possible to direct children's attention in other cases to the fact that enlarging a shape to a similar one doubles (say) *all* the dimensions. This may be sufficient to indicate to them that it is this requirement, rather than a looser one, which it will be best to use.

6. If we have two cardboard triangles and wish to demonstrate that they are similar, we may put the smaller one on top of the larger so that it fits each corner in turn. Effectively, this verifies the equality of the pairs of angles. Can we do the same with two cardboard rectangles? We can do it, but it will not prove anything since all the angles of both are right angles anyway. What additional check can we use to verify practically that they are similar? Devise 'practical' checks for other pairs of similar shapes. Estimate the degree of conviction that your tests carry.

7. Only plane shapes have been mentioned so far. Extend some of the ideas to three dimensions.

8. From the tessellating and constructional activity with plane shapes, and from the three-dimensional constructions implied by Ex.7, some simple conclusions about the areas and volumes of similar shapes will emerge. What are they?

Enlargement

1. The standard way of obtaining the enlargement of a map, drawing, blueprint, etc., is by superimposition of a squared grid on the original, noticing where the grid lines are crossed, and reproducing the situation on a grid of a different size. This technique can be refined by supplementing it with careful measurement.

Two maps of the same area with different scales can provide an exercise in comparing the sizes of suitable grids.

2. Shapes drawn on squared paper can be studied for the effect of multiplying measurements in one direction by a number, in both directions by different numbers, and in both directions by the same number. If co-ordinates are known, the effect of changing the co-ordinates in comparable ways can be looked at. Caricatures can be used to stress that a 'true' enlargement is produced only when the multiplying factor in both directions is the same.

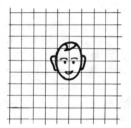  

Fig.31

3. The study of some basic tessellations *may* throw up cases in which two similar shapes in the tessellations have a 'centre'. In Fig.32 O is the centre of similarity of the two triangles.

The same centre, or any other point in the tessellation, can be used to enlarge or diminish other shapes hidden in the tessellation.

4. A pantograph is a simple mechanical device for enlarging irregular shapes. It can be made from Meccano or strips of stout card. In Fig.33, ABCD is a parallelogram and O, B, and E are in a straight line. O is fixed to the paper when an enlargement is being made. As B is moved to trace the outline of the figure, E copies the figure on a

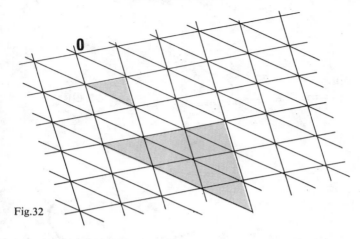

Fig.32

larger scale. Obviously the same device can be used for diminishing
the size of a drawing.

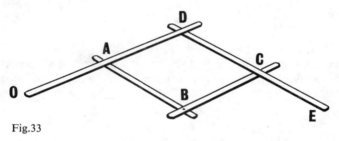

Fig.33

What determines the scale of the enlargement? What effect has the
position of O on the enlarged figure?

5. A simpler device is an 'elastic pantograph'. Two (or more) elastic
bands of the same size are knotted together. A drawing pin in the
loop of one of the bands acts as the enlarging centre. A pencil in the
loop of the other will now draw the enlargement if the knot is made
to follow the outline of a figure. (Fig.34)

Experiment with three bands, tracing the outline with either knot.
Experiment with the position of the drawing pin.

6. Enlargement can be produced more statically by the 'spider'
method. A point is chosen on the paper and a number of lines drawn
from it to points of the figure to be copied. These lines are then
extended to twice the length, say, and their ends joined 'by eye'. (Fig.35)

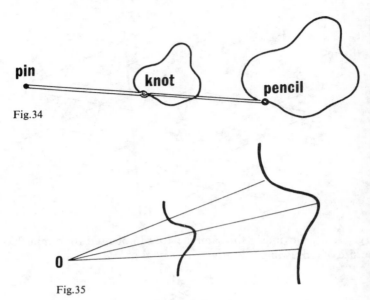

Fig.34

Fig.35

If the figure to be copied is a polygon of some kind, and if the enlarging centre is taken inside it, the resulting figure can be related to previous discoveries to show that its area is now four times as great as it was.

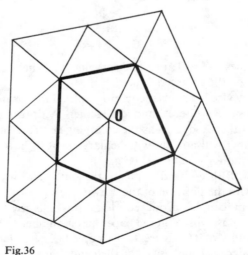

Fig.36

Tessellation patterns with hexominoes by eight-year-olds

Valerie

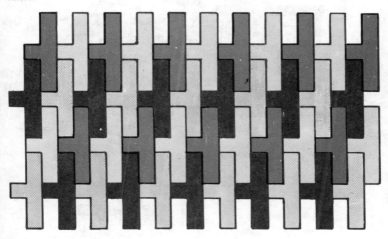

Valerie

Hexominoes

Andrea

Timothy

Susan

Zena

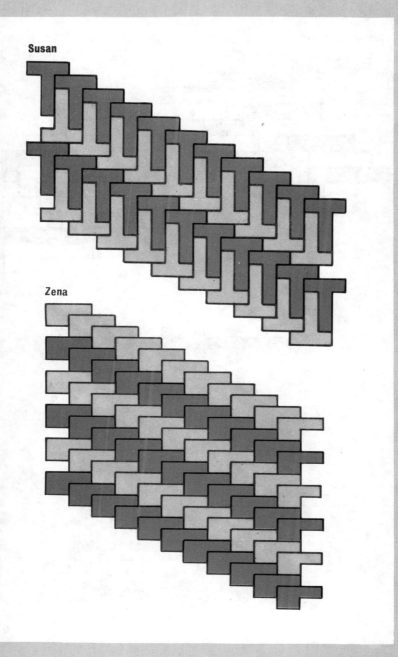

Hexominoes

Pauline

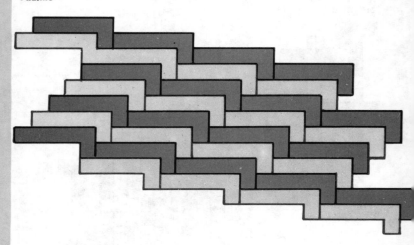

Alexandra

Geoboards

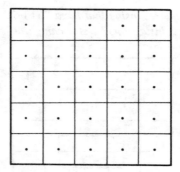

Fig.1

'What do you do with this?'

'This' is usually a square piece of plywood with a square arrangement of pins. Coloured rubber bands are stretched on it and a box of bands lies to hand.

The reply, 'Anything you like', though true, is received with suspicion.

'But whoever thought of it must have had something in mind?'

'Oh! yes . . . but that's not what you asked.'

At this point the conversation may well cease, the questioner having no further patience with such a pedant. Or it may go on, not necessarily in words, for the questioner may then take a rubber band and stretch it across the pegs – and another – and another. And he is doing what he likes!

'But what can you do with it?' 'Well, I saw two boys do this the other day.'

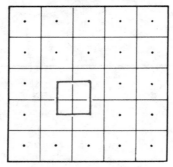

Fig.2

'*How many small squares inside that band?*' (Fig.2) '*Four!*' *They both agreed.* '*How many inside this?*', *stretching the same band to that shown in Fig.3.*

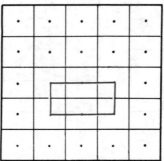

Fig.3

'*Eight*', said one. '*Four*', said the other. *One explained that the two small individual rectangles were the same as two squares each, while the other insisted that until you put another band across the rectangle you only had the four – two at each end.*

I left them arguing.

A piece of apparatus like this can do many things and those who have seen children active with such material know that even if there was a set task in the first place, this will often give way to questions that have occurred as the stuff is employed.

It is a contrived situation but with an enormous number of degrees of freedom. 'Why not use graph paper?' Curiously enough, the simple answer that graph paper with a pencil is not the same as pinboards with rubber bands does not satisfy people. And again, 'I think peg-board is better – you know, with plastic coloured pegs and shir-ring elastic.' What has 'better' got to do with it? Each of these examples is a piece of material rich in the uses to which a human being can put it. Perhaps later we shall look at this troublous feeling that materials are only there to teach *other* things.

Children can do things with graph paper and pencil, with pin-boards, with peg-boards . . .

But they will just play!

In the first instance it is always relevant to the future that we are patient with children playing, especially when we are aware of the potential situations lying round the corner. The play, the associated words, the arguments, the questions, are grist to the teacher alongside. He has in his possession a wider breadth of knowledge; he has an awareness of his own ignorance and, in his relation to the children, knows that both these facets of himself have to be balanced. The children are to develop a confidence in their own ability to find out, and they can only be *told* in very special circumstances. That is, told in such a way that they are likely to be able to make the piece of information their own.

A work-card:

'*Make a closed polygon on the board. What other closed shapes can you make by translating the sides?*'

Questions pour out . . . What shape? What does he mean? What are we intended to do? Is this right?

And then – though these questions are still there – the fingers are busy, the bands go on the board, stretched, rearranged.

'*Well, translate means this!*'

'*Oh! but if you do that those other sides are increased and you aren't translating them.*'

'*That can't be right.*'

'*Is this what he means by translate?*'

'*Well, you can't make any other figure by translating the sides because if one goes they all go . . .*'

'*Is that right?*'

Two teachers investigated a geoboard and a work-card and this was the beginning of their discussion. They reflected conversations of children at similar tasks; except that the younger the person the less frequent are the comments about, 'Is this what we are expected to do?'

The fascinating thing about this particular situation was that the exploration, which continued long after the reported snippet, was not what the writer of the card had in mind. Does this matter?

Teaching and learning is a dialogue and the dialogue goes on. The task stimulates to action – the children learn, the teacher learns – the teacher may 'interpose' an altered question, this time based both on his new knowledge of the children and his old knowledge, taken together. He may well have moved on already in the light of his new experience to acquire a new way of talking which will cause him never to ask the same thing again. But there is no dogma here.

For one teacher seeing this situation happen, it started a whole different train of events when he next saw a class of ten-year-olds:

'How many ways can you put bands on the board?'

'I hook it on one peg and pull it to another.'

'I do that, but then I may pull one to one side onto another peg.'

'I stretch it on my fingers first.'

'I put it on two pegs at the same time with my thumbs.'

Why did the teacher ask the question? Because he had realized from the previous episode that the response to the original card had depended very much on how those teachers had put the bands on the boards when they made a closed polygon.

A closed polygon made with one band is a different structure from a closed polygon made with a separate band for each side – even though exactly the same pegs are used.

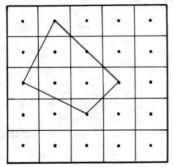 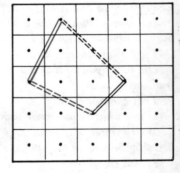

Fig.4

The task can thus give rise to different activities each with a potential realization, but dependent on the dialogues that arise. Some may lead to a blank wall while others may give rise to further satisfying work.

But the boards. What are they? How are they made? Why are the pins in the middle of the squares that are drawn?

The size of a board depends on the ease of manipulation between the spaced pins. Thus with an inch between pins, the board gets cluttered pretty quickly and the pins get in the way. The most comfortable distance between pins seems to be about 2 inches. A $\frac{3}{8}$ in. plywood board 1 ft. square makes an excellent 25-pin board. Smaller boards for 16 pins and 9 pins can be constructed in corresponding sizes. It is important that no embellishments such as bevelled borders, mitred corners, etc. are tried, as there is often something to be gained from working with several boards put together.

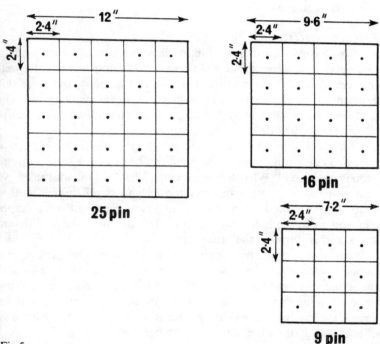

Fig.5

Instructions

1. The $\frac{3}{8}$ in. plywood should be ordered cut to size.
2. A square grid should be carefully drawn. Some may prefer a gouged line instead of a pencil line.

3. The pins are placed centrally in each square and though this can be done simply by finding the centre of each – for instance, by marking where the diagonals cross – a template is useful if a number of boards are to be made: that is, a piece of card of exactly the same dimensions as the required board with holes constructed at points where pins are required. Rapid and accurate marking of pin positions on the board is then possible. Different kinds of pins may be used: $\frac{5}{8}$ in. panel pins or brass-headed pins. This means that when driven well home, $\frac{3}{8}$ in. of the pin should be left projecting.

4. It is best if the boards are painted.

5. The rubber bands should be purchased with care as many packets on sale do not have the variety of sizes and colours appropriate to the work required of them.

Practice exercises

1. Take a small board, say 9-pin, or choose a part of a larger board and make all the recognizable shapes you can. You may be interpreting 'recognizable' as meaning that you can name it, but does this exhaust all the shapes you can make? List all the names you know that describe shapes you have made, and then try to find, or make up, names for all the others.

2. Start with one band making one shape on the board, say a triangle. Put a finger inside the band, pull one of the sides out and loop it over a nail. What have you made? Reverse the movement so that you return to your original triangle. Can you make another shape by the same kind of movement? How many different shapes can you make with this movement? Try starting with a different shape and go through the procedure again.

When you perform the looping or the releasing movement certain things change or are transformed. Do not be content just to look at the initial and final positions; *watch* the changes taking place. What happens to the number of sides, the number of angles, the sizes of the angles, the lengths of the sides, the directions of the sides, the number of nails inside or on the perimeter, the perimeter, the area?

3. When you have made some shapes on the board, turn the board round and look at the shapes from a variety of positions.

4. With a single movement – looping over a nail or releasing the band from a nail – can you make a parallelogram into a triangle, into a pentagon, into a rectangle? Can you make a triangle into a square, into a rhombus (diamond), into a parallelogram, into a quadri-

lateral? Notice when you can, and why you can; when you cannot, and why you cannot. Develop some more complicated movements – looping over two nails at once, or performing a loop followed by a release, for example – and study the effect of these.

5. Make a rectangle on any board and decide what area it has. You have two choices (at least) in deciding what basic unit of area you will use. It does not matter which you make – but you can, of course, trace the consequences of both choices.

Put a band along a diagonal. What are the areas of the two parts you have made? What shape are they? Make a right-angled triangle on the board with its two shorter sides parallel to edges of the board. What is its area? Do you need to know the formula 'half the base times the height' to be able to say? (No!) Make some more right-angled triangles in comparable positions until you can say the area at a glance.

6. Make a right-angled triangle with its shorter sides parallel to edges of the board. You know its area. Take the band at the top corner (vertex) and shift it along the line of nails parallel to the base of the triangle. Stop on a nail. What is the area of the triangle you have made? You may know a geometrical theorem about the areas of triangles 'on the same base and between the same parallels.' Do you need to know it to answer this question? (No!) *Hint:* Enclose the triangle in a rectangle.

Make any triangle in any position on the board. Can you say what its area is? Experiment with different ways of arriving at its area – by adding bits to it to make it into a square or a rectangle, by dividing it up into suitable pieces, or by a combination of these two general methods.

7. On a small board, say 9- or 16-pin, make all the triangles you can which have an area of 1 sq. unit, 2 sq. units, $\frac{1}{2}$ sq. unit, $1\frac{1}{2}$ sq. units, etc. What is the (a) largest, (b) smallest area you can enclose with a triangle on your board?

Explore similar questions in relation to other shapes. Include some irregular shapes.

8. Put a band on a board so that it is held in position by exactly four nails – that is, it would remain in position if all but these four nails were removed from the board. What have you made? A square, rectangle, parallelogram, kite, rhombus, trapezium, quadrilateral? A shape without a name? How many different kinds of shapes can you produce? Do you allow the band to cross itself? (Why not?) Do

you allow one of the nails to be inside the triangle formed by the other three? (Why not?) Examine the diagonals of the shapes you have made. Distinguish some possibilities.

But we said earlier that the teacher comes to the class with some knowledge. What may this be?

There are two distinct characteristics of such material. One is that it has been prepared to illustrate some definite mathematical point and the other is that the material itself, through being handled, throws up other possibilities.

One has heard people say on meeting it, 'Oh yes! Areas', or possibly, 'Fractions'. One may also see that if we can put shapes on the lattice of pins we have a very simple way of constructing figures of great variety. What is more they can be made quickly, renewed quickly, altered quickly. (The rapid transformations possible have an unexpectedly soothing consequence. The gentle sound of bands being moved about the boards in a class occupied in some problem is typical – even with the boy who is intent on stretching as many green bands between two pins as he can without one of the pins bending!).

As adults, with some knowledge, our approach to these kinds of things is abstract. We readily ignore some characteristics in order to be satisfied that the remaining properties will do something for us. Hence the suggestion that graph paper and pencil would be better . . . Children do not ignore the different characteristics of materials so readily. In fact, we could say that the ignoring of different characteristics is directly proportional to the degree of knowledge one already has or is expected to have. This means that for any given situation which may seem to be a reasonable starting-point for a discussion, the attention the teacher pays it and the attention the children pay it will be different and this can give rise to difficulties in comprehension – each misunderstanding the other (see Ch.12 p.282).

Classification of shapes

The reader should have a geoboard at hand and use it to follow our discussions.

In the early stages the 9-pin board provides a great deal of scope for exploration. But the number of different shapes is limited and discussion as to whether shapes are the 'same' or not is kept reasonably within bounds.

'*Let's make shapes with the bands.*' One of the things to do is to look at the number of sides and start discussing which have 3, 4, 5, 6, 7 sides.

Questions

'Can you have a two-sided shape?'

'Is this a shape 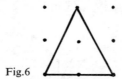 ?'

'He says this has four sides

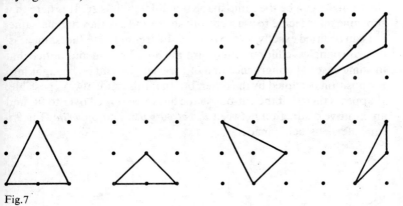

Fig.6

and it hasn't, has it?' (Or has it? What are the grounds for a boy saying it has?)

Fig.7

The example of triangles (Fig.7) and quadrilaterals (Fig.8) show the different types. (Are they all shown? How do we know? At least one is missing from Fig.8) It is interesting to see how children readily make re-entrant polygons but most adults are conditioned to produce only convex polygons. Discussion wanders over 'different shapes' in the sense that triangles of equal size and the same shape can be made in several positions on the board, and even that two of

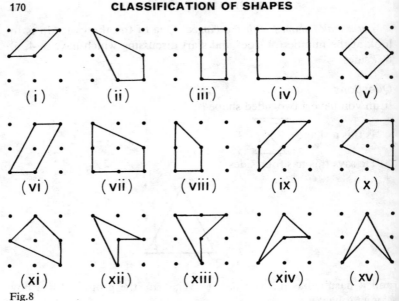

(i) (ii) (iii) (iv) (v)

(vi) (vii) (viii) (ix) (x)

(xi) (xii) (xiii) (xiv) (xv)

Fig.8

the triangles can be the same shape but different in size. It is here that someone may decide to use a cut-out shape and say they are the 'same' if it can be fitted exactly on top of each. In arguing as to the 'sameness' of two triangles, children often turn the board round and notice that in some cases of congruence one of the triangles can be brought into the position occupied by the other, but that this is not always possible. It appears then that the cut-out shape has to be turned over to fit, and an intuitive distinction between *direct* (Fig.9a) and *opposite* (Fig.9b) equivalence is being made.

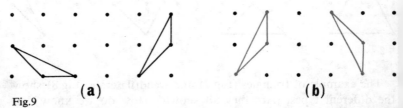

(a) (b)

Fig.9

Further elements in classification begin to arise. Triangles (called *isosceles*) are found which have two sides of equal length; but none is *equilateral*, that is, has three sides equal. It is profitable here to consider the five possible lengths for sides of figures formed on the board.

Other triangles are found which have corners of the same kind as those of a square. Can a triangle be made which has two corners of this kind? A paper set-square can be made by making a crease in any piece of paper and then making a second fold along this crease, and used for testing various objects in the room for this kind of corner. At this stage children do not distinguish between the angle at a corner and the vertex or actual corner-point, and it seems wise to defer the use of 'right angle' until the notion of angle as turning is being introduced.

If the shapes made are recorded on squared paper (on at least 1 in. square grid for clarity), larger cut-out copies may later be folded and examined for symmetry. This is experience in a form of abstraction.

Other questions develop:

  (i) Put in as many squares as you can.

 (ii) How many kites can you put in?

(iii) Put lines (diagonals) across the shapes in Fig.8. In which shapes are they the same length?

Areas

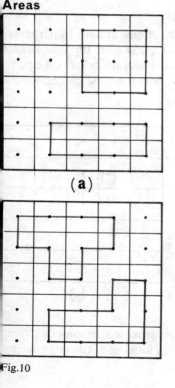

(a)

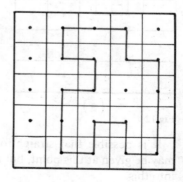

Fig.10   **(b)**

It is interesting to notice that though these (Fig.10) are simple figures for drawing on graph paper, they are not the simplest for putting on pinboards. Thus, after squares and rectangles oblique stretching is easiest, rather than stretching alternately clockwise and anti-clockwise as required for those in Fig.10b.

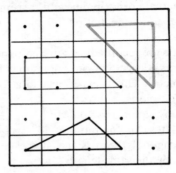

Fig.11

There are several choices open for the choice of unit. In particular the unit square made by four pins – Fig.12a – or the unit square revealed when the bands and the grid lines are taken together – Fig.12b. In most of the subsequent work the second choice will be made.

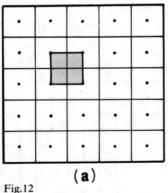

(a)

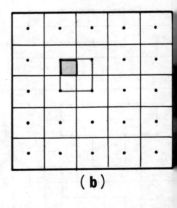

(b)

Fig.12

It is possible that straightforward information lessons on 'area' may be given at this point, but it is worth looking a little more deeply into this.

The area of a surface is a measure. Hence a comparison is involved and a unit must be used if a common measure is required for different surfaces. This no doubt will have been developed through other activities, but the board does allow action at a number of different levels of complexity or abstraction.

Make as many shapes as you can which have six squares.

Make as many shapes as you can with six squares.

Make as many shapes as you can which are six times as big as one square.

Make as many shapes as you can which have the same area as a rectangle 2 squares by 3 squares.

It is important to recognize different awarenesses of abstraction in these questions. Children react to them in different ways.

How many squares?

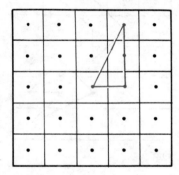

Fig.13

'One . . . no, that's one', indicating:

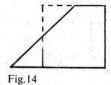

Fig.14

Then after a long pause, 'Those bits make another.'

A six-year-old is abstracting from this situation some kind of statement about the number of squares and the triangular shape.

From finding shapes which have properties in common, it is a short step to investigating particular shapes in order to find the number of squares to which they are equivalent. How complicated the shapes are that have been discovered in the previous activity depends on what the children produce.

If a child decides that.

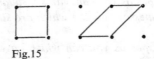

Fig.15

are equal in area for one reason or another, he may produce quite complex shapes which have six squares.

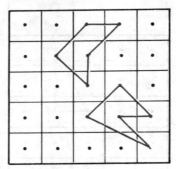

Fig.16

But if not, then shapes of this kind are there for the investigation. *How many squares?*

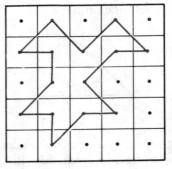

Fig.17

We are now in a better position to explain why the pins are in the middle of the ruled squares. This is best seen in terms of what happens if the pins are at the junctions.

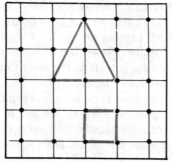

Fig.18

There are no 'small' squares.

The bands coincide in many cases with the ruled lines, making for a degree of superfluity.

The opportunities for recognizing abstract equivalences are reduced.

It is difficult to use the pins independently of the grid with this arrangement.

The wish to see this arrangement arises out of too close an association with the graph paper and pencil situation.

Rotations of the board

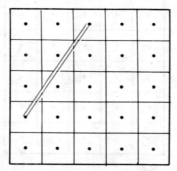

Fig.19

'Each of you take one rubber band and put it on your board to look exactly like mine. Now, keeping your board on the table, will you turn it completely round. How do you know when it has turned right round? Because it looks the same? Suppose I am not watching you very carefully; can I tell, by looking at your board before you start to move it and again when you have finished moving it, just how you have turned it? Let's see: all put your boards ready in the starting position; now I am turning my back – I want you to move your boards in some way. Right? Now I will look again – yes, everybody's board looks the same; did you all do the same things? No? What did you do, Elizabeth? Michael? Janet?

Now I want you to move your boards, keeping them flat on the table, and as far as possible keeping the pin in the centre of your board still. Right: turn your board round *once*: I see that some of you turned one way and some the other. Does it matter which way you turn the board?

Starting positions again. This time turn your board *half*-way round. Look at the other boards near you. Do they look the same? Does it matter which way you turn the board?

Now look at my board. Take the band off your board; I want you to put it back on your board, without moving your board, so that it looks like mine will when I turn it half-way round. Look at each other's. If you are not quite sure, you can move your board to make sure.

Do the same thing again now I have changed the position of the band on my board. And again. Do you think you could do it each time wherever I put my band? Try it again with this:'

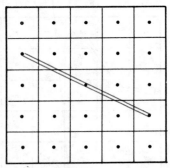

Fig.20

(Chuckles from some children.)

We notice that this action of turning the board through two right angles generates a line parallel to the original line. If we want perfect consistency here, we shall have to allow that a line can be parallel to itself – see Fig.20. At this stage it doesn't much matter whether our definition of parallelism includes the identity case or not, but it is a good idea to sow the seed so that our pupils are not too alarmed or resistant when they meet parallelism as an equivalence relation.

Of course, this is only one way – and not perhaps the most 'natural' – of generating parallel lines. A 'slide' or 'shift' is another operation which will generate parallels. It is certainly not suggested that primary school children should be confined to any one form of experience or any single definition of parallels. The case for examining the effect of turning a line through two right angles is that it adds a dimension to one's appreciation of parallelism.

'Now I have put two bands on my board: will you copy them, please, and, without turning your board, put on two more bands to show where these two will move to when I turn my board half-way round.

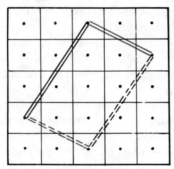

Fig.21

Can you tell me anything about the bands on your board now? They make a shape? Have you met the shape before? Can you tell me anything about the shape?

Now will you each put two bands on your board, in different positions from last time, and then put two more to show where they will move if you turn the board half-way round? What sort of things have you found? Check whether you have done it correctly by turning your board and watching it closely to see what happens.'

A variety of possibilities: the children may restrict themselves to making 'four-sided' shapes. But undoubtedly some will find some surprises – lines which don't 'join up'; figures with two or all of their sides produced; two parallels with a transversal; two intersecting lines.

Fig.22

In general, the rotation will produce (if the board is big enough) a four-sided figure with its opposite sides parallel. The exceptions should be discussed. All the children should be invited to produce a rhombus by this method, a rectangle, a square, a parallelogram (as in the teacher's example). If they can do this, they can be asked to say how they can forecast what sort of shape the turning will make.

At a subsequent lesson, it can be suggested to the class that it explores what happens if the board is turned a quarter of a complete turn. This time, the direction of rotation (clockwise or anti-clockwise) will probably arise spontaneously as they try to decide whether they each obtain the same situation.

Making a quarter-turn generates a line perpendicular to the original one (are there any marginal cases this time?). Starting with a single band, and making successive quarter-turns, generates – what? What are the exceptional cases?

This lesson is just one example using the movability of the geo-board. Anything which encourages the children to *move* their boards, and to study attentively the appearance of their figures as the board moves, is worth doing. Blackboards are generally fixed; boards need not be.

Transformations

There was the beginning of an argument a little earlier in this chapter as to whether a particular triangle had four sides. There were four pins involved. If the boy had decided that, for him, a 'side' was the segment between pins, then four was correct.

How many other such 'four-sided' figures are there? It turns out that this is the same as the number of shapes made with four and only four pins, provided the band does not cross itself.

Some have pins completely enclosed; some have no pins other than on the perimeter.

What is the area of the shapes in Fig.23*a*? And in 23*b*? What do you notice?

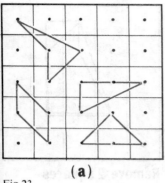 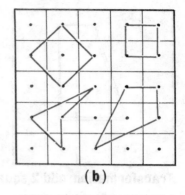

| **(a)** | **(b)** |

Fig.23

Do all the shapes that can be made with four pins on the boundary and no pins inside have the same area?

What about those that can be made with five pins? What about those with six pins in the boundary and two inside? Here are two examples:

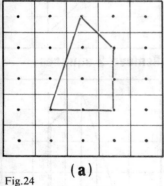 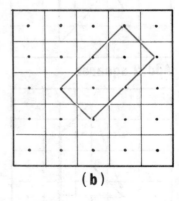

| **(a)** | **(b)** |

Fig.24

What are their areas? Are there any other shapes with the same area?

A *transformation* of rubber bands on pins is a stretching to another peg or a release. Each time this happens we can study the effect and draw appropriate conclusions. We shall be able to decide what transformations to make to produce an effect we want. Let us transform the shape in Fig.24a. The transformed shape is shown in the new colour.

The identifying of shapes by the number of pins used on the

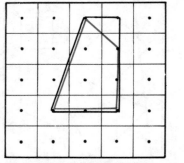

Transformation: add 2 squares

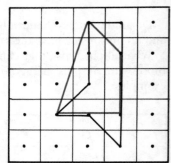

Remove 2 squares

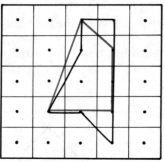

Add 2 squares

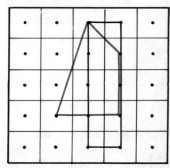

Remove 2 squares

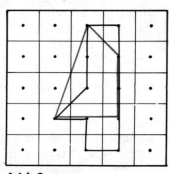

Add 2 squares

Fig. 25

Remove 2 squares

boundary and the number of pins contained inside leads to an interesting conclusion about the area. It can be stated as follows: if *m* is the number of pins on the boundary and *n* is the number of pins enclosed, then any shape whatever has an *m* and an *n* (although *n* may be 0). We can write (*m*, *n*) to categorize the various shapes. We can say generally that shapes with the same (*m*, *n*) have the same area. This can be checked with actual examples and some general statements can be found. A discussion will be found in Coxeter [25], pp.208–9. The area in *large* squares of a simple shape is given by

$$\tfrac{1}{2}m+n-1.$$

What is the corresponding rule for the area measured in small squares? With this knowledge a number of variations can be made on the transformation tasks and games.

There are transformations where the area of a shape is preserved, or changed by definite amounts; transformations in which a transfer from one pin to another is made, or where a transfer from a pair of pins to another pair is made. All these can be investigated with differently shaped figures and their effects examined.

What transformations take these shapes from one to the other? Are the shapes of equal area? Can you find transformations to take them into a rectangle of the same area?

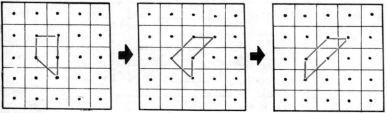

Fig.26

Later we describe other transformation games.

How many?

On any square lattice geoboard:
    how many squares?
              rectangles?
              right-angled triangles?
              isosceles triangles?
              triangles?
              segments of straight lines?
    how many different squares?
                   rectangles?
                   right-angled triangles?

how many different *isosceles triangles?*
                        triangles?
                        lengths of lines?
                        directions of lines?

And so on.

In chapter 12 we describe the value of 'How many?' situations and in the geoboard and its bands there is a plentiful source of problems of this kind. We have referred to the 9-pin geoboard and the different triangles that can be drawn. It cannot be overemphasized that the decisions as to which are or are not the same are important ones to be made by the children. So usually 'How many?' questions also involve discussions of definitions, though these need not be pedantic.

How many squares can be made on the board? It is interesting to observe the stages through which the investigation goes.

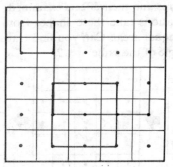

Fig.27

The patterns of squares when once completed may fail to stimulate the explorer to go further: a child may arrive at this pattern:

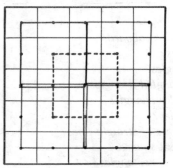

Fig.28

and perhaps miss this:

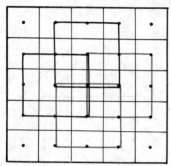

Fig.29

This is a typical feature of this kind of investigation. A group of teachers were finding out how many shapes could be made using four pins only. After a few minutes somebody said 'five', somebody else 'eight', and so on. The five were just straightforward separate discoveries, while the greater numbers were produced by recognizing a way of extending one of the shapes through successive transformations: that is, discovering and using a pattern.

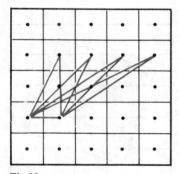

Fig.30

The trap lies in the assumption that the successful completion of a pattern solves the problem. In time one recognizes that the real solution of the problem lies in being able to justify that a pattern has *in fact* solved the problem. But before that stage is reached there is a rich variety of patterns to find.

After all, did we find all the squares? Someone is certain to have turned the board round:

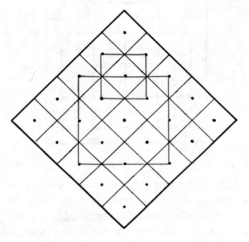

Fig.31

How many have found others?

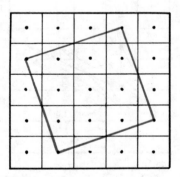

Fig.32

How many are there altogether? And then: *how do you know?*

How many different lengths can be made? How many different ways of classifying the lengths are there?

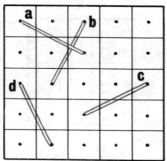

Fig.33

These segments are the same length, but a child may insist they are different, and not only because they are in different positions.

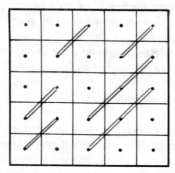

Fig.34

A ten-year-old insisted that there were only two parallel lines here: he was seeing all the single segments as one and all the double segments as another.

All this experience leads to a knowledge of the properties that it is possible to investigate on a lattice.

Some shapes are quite difficult to sort out, especially those that we mentioned earlier which may have no symmetry. Are the shapes in Fig.35 the 'same'?

Do the uncertainties we describe about the meanings of words – What is a side? What are equal lengths? Which are the same? – seem disturbing? It is natural to find them so and we would be less than honest if we did not admit to our own perplexities when misunderstandings over words arise. Yet what we are trying to say is that it is much

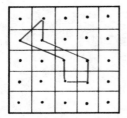 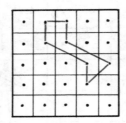 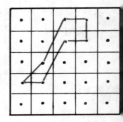

Fig.35

too naïve to suppose that communication between teacher and children can rest only on a perfectly agreed vocabulary, with the corollary that all misunderstandings can be resolved if the teacher always defines and uses words precisely and unambiguously.

Can we always define the words we need unambiguously?

Can we always confine ourselves to using these words in these precisely formulated senses?

Can we always be sure a child understands our definitions?

Can we always give him enough examples to be sure that he will know our meanings?

Surely not, in any absolute sense, although all these aims can be partially achieved.

But any discrepancies between the ideal and what actually happens are not our main point. We believe that precision cannot be imposed from without but can only be adopted from within. Being precise, being able to say what one means, comes from a decision to concentrate on some features to the exclusion of others. It involves choosing to delimit the boundaries of one's words. These choices must be made so that words and meanings can become common currency between people. We want the child to experience this process for himself, to make his own choices on the evidence he has, and to test them by finding someone he can talk to.

A shearing game

The use of numbers to represent either the points or the segments is a development which may come early or late. Children can understand a simple co-ordinate system very soon. They can plot and record shapes from simple instructions in terms of co-ordinates. An instance of this is the shearing transformation game.

We start with a 25-pin board:

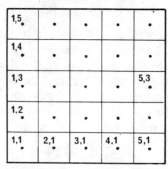

Fig.36

and give to each pin a pair of numbers as shown in the diagram. The first number in each pair indicates the column and the second the row.

Place two bands round the following nails: (1,3) (2,1) (2,3).

Change one of the bands to (1,3) (4,1) (2,3),
    then to (3,1) (4,1) (2,3),
   and then to (3,1) (4,1) (5,3),
   and then to (5,5) (4,1) (5,3).

Can you describe the transformations? Is there a common characteristic? Such a transformation is called a *shear*. Make a triangular shape of your own and carry out some shears.

See if you can transform the following shape (4,3) (5,3) (3,5)
          into (4,5) (5,3) (5,5).

Now try this one: (1,1) (2,2) (1,4)
   into (4,2) (4,5) (3,2).

What about this one? (1,4) (2,2) (2,3)
   to (4,3) (4,5) (3,5).

Did you expect that this would be possible?

Make up a triangular shape for yourself. Choose another triangle to which the first one can be transformed by shearing. How do you know it is possible? Make up several for yourself and see if you can find out what is the best way of choosing the separate shears.

Note: (a) This game may be extended to the transformation of parallelograms. In this case the shearing will involve the shift of one side along its line of pins.

(b) Any arbitrarily defined movement can give rise to similar kinds of games; for instance, a sequence of transformations on a triangle which alternately doubles a side and then halves one. What can be said about the class of figures which can be so transformed?

Segments

Another use of numbers is to describe a line segment. In Fig.33
(p.185), all the four segments can be described by one number if
only their lengths are taken into account. But if we describe them in
terms of the number of steps 'along' and the number of steps 'up',
then *a* and *c* are both (2,1) and *b* and *d* are both (1,2).

If we now introduce a second direction – 'left' and 'right', 'up'
and 'down' – by the use of positive and negative numbers, then all
four have different labels:

$a:$ $(-2, +1)$, $b:$ $(+1, +2)$, $c:$ $(+2, +1)$, $d:$ $(-1, +2)$.

In different ways and at different times these different conventions
may be used. To go a step further and distinguish between the two
directions of a segment: for instance

$a:$ $(-2, +1)$ and $a_R:$ $(+2, -1)$ (where a_R is the segment a taken in
the reverse direction)

is impossible without making an abstraction from the board. Nevertheless at some stage this can be done. Segments drawn on paper can
be given an arrow-head to fix their orientation. This, or some comparable experience, may suggest that we can, if we want to, think of
the bands on a geoboard as possessing orientation too.

Let us look back at the work-card that the teachers were discussing
(p.163) and the ways of making closed polygons on the board.

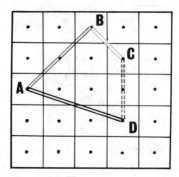

Fig.37

We suppose the sides are made with different bands. We follow them
round the polygon:

AB:$(+2, +2)$; BC: $(+1, -1)$; CD: $(0, -2)$; DA: $(-3, +1)$
(purple)   (grey)   (light purple) (black)
What do we notice?

If the corresponding numbers are added together we get zero.

$(+2+1+0-3, +2-1-2+1)=(0,0)$

What can this mean?

Does it matter in which order we add them? Does it matter in which order we put them on the board? How many ways can these segments be followed round?

Let's try. With coloured bands it is easier and more vivid. Having decided to trace the purple band in the same direction each time, difficulties with the signs are reduced.

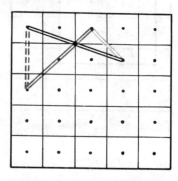

Fig.38 Purple, grey, black, light purple.

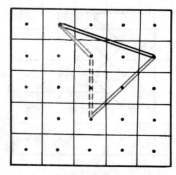

Fig.39 Purple, light purple, grey, black.

We had to move the purple to another part of the board. Does this matter?

How many other orders are there?

What is the tie-up between the numbers adding to (0,0) and what we see on the board?

Suppose we had three bands end-to-end on the board with numbers which when added came to (2,1). What could we say about them?

Fractions

Make a square and show quarters of it.

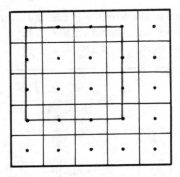

Fig.40

How many ways can it be done? Did anybody get this?

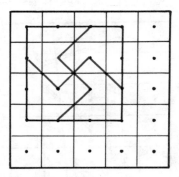

Fig.41

Any ways of making 'cuts' in a shape by putting bands across can produce fractions if we choose to think about the activity in this way The areas show us the relative sizes of the fractions. Here are some drawings made by some eight- to nine-year-olds with their own comments:

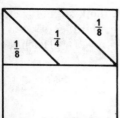

'In this drawing the quarter and the other two eighths go into the oblong once.'

Andrew (8)

$\frac{1}{8}+\frac{1}{4}+\frac{1}{8}=\frac{1}{2}$

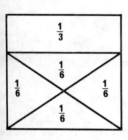

'The shapes marked 1/12 will go into the shapes marked 1/6 twice.'

Margaret (8)

$\frac{1}{6}\div\frac{1}{12}=2$

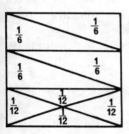

'The drawing shows that $4\times 1/6$ makes 2/3.'

Joan (9)

$4\times\frac{1}{6}=\frac{2}{3}$

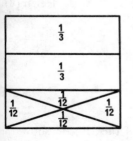

'The drawing proves that $4/12=1/3$.'

Nigel (9)

$4\times\frac{1}{12}=\frac{1}{3}$

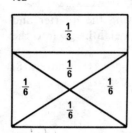

'You mite not think so, but there is 2 sixths in the third.'

Helen (8)

$\frac{1}{3} \div \frac{1}{6} = 2$

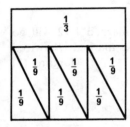

'I worked it out when there is 6/9 in 2/3 and when you cut the third into 1/9s, there is 3.'

Morag (9)

$\frac{1}{3} \div \frac{1}{9} = 3$

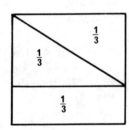

'The two triangles are thirds.'

Andrew (8)

$\frac{1}{2} \times \frac{2}{3} = \frac{1}{3}$

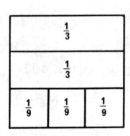

'The shapes marked 1/3 are made up of 3/9.'

Helen (8)

$\frac{3}{9} = \frac{1}{3}$

Fig.42

Without going deeper into the geometry of this, Fig.43 shows a method of finding an area which is 2/7 of the square.

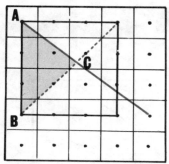

Fig.43

ABC is 2/7 of the 16-pin square. Can you see why?
What other fractions can be constructed?

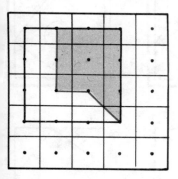 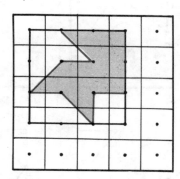

Fig.44

Both shaded areas in Fig.44 are half the square.
Do two halves make a whole?

We have still not exhausted all that can be done. Bands can be used to dissect the plane, making different numbers of regions. How many? Diagonals can be drawn on polygons. How many? The board can be filled in all sorts of different ways. Experiments can be made with tessellations (tilings). What shapes cannot be made? What shapes are produced by overlapping similar shapes?

The geoboard is a flexible material – it is something to experience, to investigate. One can learn precise things or one can stop and speculate. In any case the activity is vital.

Geoboards

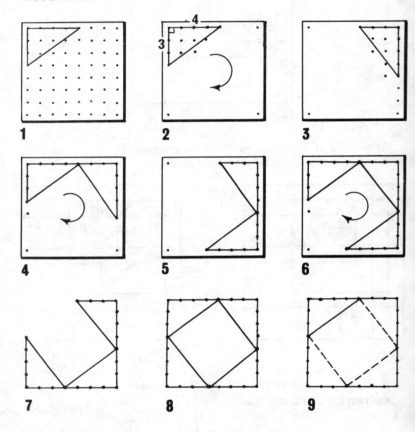

1   **2**   **3**

4   **5**   **6**

7   **8**   **9**

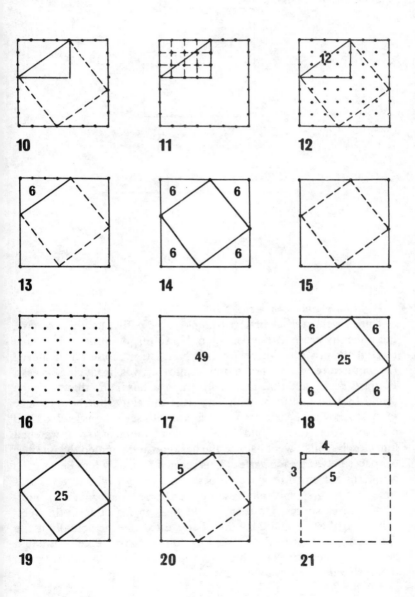

10

11

12

13

14

15

16

17

18

19

20

21

Tailpiece

On a circular 24-pin geoboard make all the regular figures you can Tabulate your results.

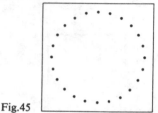

Fig.45

Sides	Yes	No
3		
4		
5		
6		
.		
.		

What have you discovered?

Things went well at first; a triangle came easily, as did a square, but difficulty arose with a pentagon. Up to this point he had worked by trial and error, moving the elastic bands around until he achieved the required result, but no amount of moving was producing success. I suggested he left that and went on to a hexagon; this again he found by trial and error with very little difficulty, but he was once more stuck when he tried to find a figure with seven equal sides. I had estimated that this should be the crucial moment, so I watched him closely. Philip went back to the hexagon and counted the number of spaces between each vertex. This seemed to satisfy him because he went straight on to produce an octagon, not by trial and error this time, but by systematically placing the elastic bands round at intervals of three spaces. He then placed ticks in his table in the 'Yes' column against 12 and 24. When I suggested that he actually made the figures, he said he didn't need to do it because he knew it could be done. Underneath his table he wrote '*You can make all the figures that have sides that divide into 24*'.

I

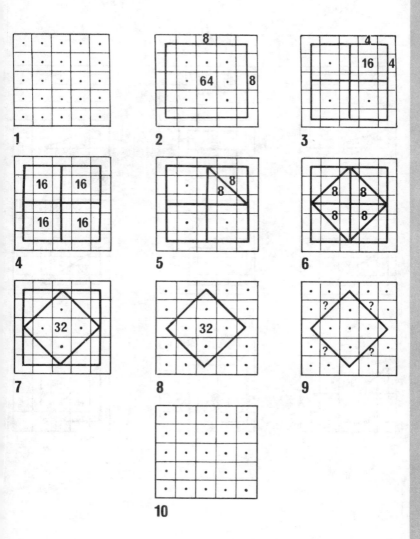

1
2
3
4
5
6
7
8
9
10

II

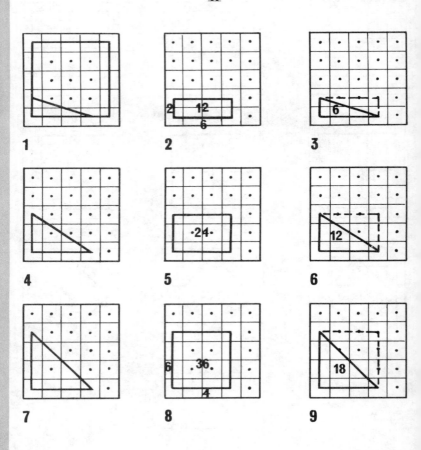

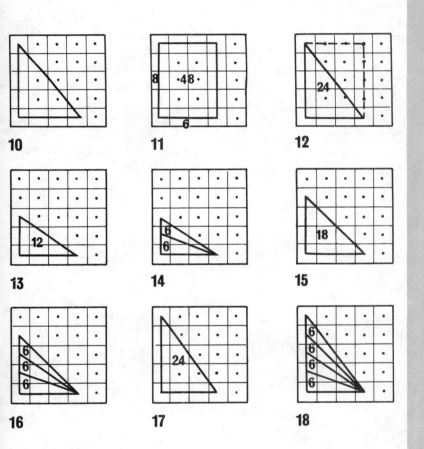

10 **11** **12**

13 **14** **15**

16 **17** **18**

Partitions

In this chapter we take up again some themes from other parts of this book, together with some new ones, and show that they have connections with a particularly important mathematical structure. We do not go into all the mathematical details of the structure: anyone who wants this can find it in a text-book of algebra. Our purpose is to demonstrate that aspects of this structure are available to primary school pupils. By putting a number of illustrations in one place we hope to convey something of the excitement that can come from the recognition that one has met the essentials of a situation before in another context. We must again declare that we have no intention of providing a teaching sequence, and we recognize that some of our examples may be inappropriate material for some children.

When children or adults are engaged in the activity of finding all the partitions of a particular rod (see p.52) it is interesting to observe the various strategies they evolve for completing the action. When the length of the rod is small, it is easy enough for the eye to take in the whole picture at a glance and detect any omissions. But when one is working on the set of partitions of the yellow rod, which as we have seen has sixteen rows, it is difficult to discover merely by scanning the pattern which possibilities one has missed. Most people develop some kind of system for dealing with this difficulty.

Some systems deal only with parts of the pattern. For example, when a row has been made with one red and three white rods, one sub-system says, 'Make all the other rows you can with the same collection of rods'. Even with this rule in common children may act differently. One may put down any new arrangement, checking that it looks different from the others already placed. Another will use the visual appearance of the rows to produce a pattern which he knows will exhaust the possibilities (Fig.1).

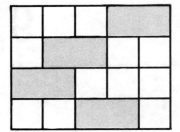 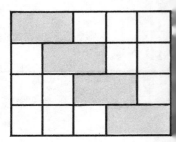

Fig.1

More general strategies may be adopted. A child may begin each row with the same coloured rod and complete them in as many ways as he can before changing the colour of the starting rod. Another may make all the rows he can containing five rods, then four rods, then three rods, and so on, exhausting the situation in this way. In most groups of children a range of reactions will be displayed, from those relying exclusively on scanning to those with an overall strategy. The majority usually employ a mixture of scanning and sub-systems.

No value-judgment is implied in what has been said. It is too simple to say that the child who uses an overall system is the one who is thinking mathematically and that the rest are not. It is not always easy to know precisely what thinking is being done from the actions the child performs, although there is usually a connection. But some children clearly capable of evolving a 'good' strategy do not always do so, perhaps because they enjoy the challenge of the scanning procedure. The teacher is, of course, interested in the more general strategies and wants to foster them. Direct instruction is usually pointless and unnecessary. The children will improve their strategies as they meet more complicated situations, helped by their observation of each other's actions and by discussions with the teacher.

Suppose that the strategy that has been adopted in making the partition of the yellow rod is based on the number of rods in each row. What can be discovered in the pattern in Fig.2?

We see that there is one row of one rod, four rows of two rods, six rows of three rods, four rows of four rods and one row of five rods. If this sequence of numbers interests us – and it is only one of many observations that can be made about the pattern – we will probably want to analyse other partition patterns in the same kind of way. The sets of numbers that we obtain for each pattern have some obvious properties: the numbers in each set increase and then decrease,

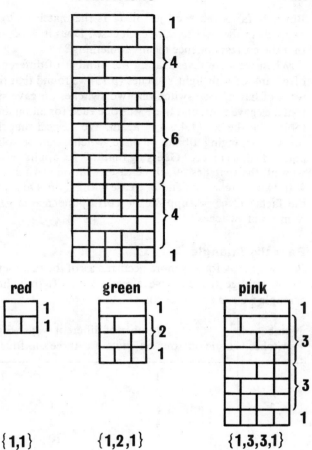

Fig.3

each set starts and finishes with 1, in each set the numbers appear symmetrically, the sum of each set is a power of 2.

We may have encountered these sets of numbers elsewhere. Calculate 11×11, $11 \times 11 \times 11$, $11 \times 11 \times 11 \times 11$, etc. We obtain the answers 121, 1331, 14641, etc. There is sufficient correspondence here for us to feel that we are meeting the same sets as before. The first two sets (corresponding to the partitions of the white rod and the red rod) seem to be missing. But if we think of 'powers of 11' we see that we can make the match exact:

$11^0 = 1$, $11^1 = 11$, $11^2 = 121$, $11^3 = 1331$, $11^4 = 14641$, etc.

But how far is the 'etc.' justified? Is the match *really* exact? What happens to the next term in each case? Does it shake our conviction that the correspondence means something?

When we were investigating the number of different appearances of a bank of four light switches (p.73) we found that there were four ways of having one switch on, two switches on gave six ways, three switches gave four, and there was one each for all on and all off. This looks like the set {1,4,6,4,1} again. We suspect that the number of ways of arranging a bank of three switches can be split into 1, 3, 3, and 1. Is this correct? Guessing that this set applies gives us one case with all the switches off, three cases with one switch on, three cases with two switches on, and one case with all on. Does this check with the facts? Can we suppose the correspondence is general for any number of switches?

Pascal's Triangle

Before we look for any more occurrences of the same sets of numbers, let us arrange the data we already have. Taking the light switch example we can set up a table:

| Number of switches | Number of different ways with | | | | | |
	none on	one on	two on	three on	four on	five on
1	1	1				
2	1	2	1			
3	1	3	3	1		
4	1	4	6	4	1	
5	1	5	10	10	5	1

The partitions yield a similar table:

| Length of rod | Number of rows in partition with | | | | |
	one rod	two rods	three rods	four rods	five rods
1	1				
2	1	1			
3	1	2	1		
4	1	3	3	1	
5	1	4	6	4	1

We can probably infer certain properties that will help us extend either table. The sequences in the first and second columns look obvious enough. Perhaps we notice that the third column seems to be giving us the triangular numbers (p. 27). We can use the symmetry of each row, and the total for all the entries in each row to take us further still.

Detaching the pattern of numbers from the table – the second table looks a slightly better starting-point – and continuing the pattern by using the properties we have noticed, we get an array, usually called *Pascal's Triangle*. We show it in three forms; it is manifestly the same array in each case.

1										1	1	1	1	1	1	1	1
1	1									1	2	3	4	5	6	7	8
1	2	1		(a)						1	3	6	10	15	21	28	(b)
1	3	3	1							1	4	10	20	35	56		
1	4	6	4	1						1	5	15	35	70			
1	5	10	10	5	1					1	6	21	56				
1	6	15	20	15	6	1				1	7	28					
1	7	21	35	35	21	7	1			1	8						
1	8	28	56	70	56	28	8	1		1							

```
                    1
                  1   1
                1   2   1
              1   3   3   1
            1   4   6   4   1
          1   5   10  10  5   1
        1   6   15  20  15  6   1
      1   7   21  35  35  21  7   1
    1   8   28  56  70  56  28  8   1
                   (c)
```

The third way of displaying it makes full use of the symmetry of the rows and is perhaps the most satisfying pattern. It is not usually very long after seeing the pattern in this form that children notice a relation between the numbers that can be used as a rule to continue the pattern. Looking at the numbers we have, it appears as if each entry – with the exception of the bordering 1's – can be obtained by adding the two numbers immediately above. Assuming this to hold we can find the next row:

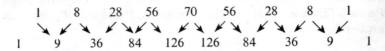

The same rule can now be read into the other two patterns, of course, but these variants can be looked at for other relationships. Diagram (b) shows a particularly interesting property: each row is made up of the running totals of the row immediately above. The fifth row, for example, has 5 ($=1+4$), 15 ($=1+4+10$), 35 ($=1+4+10+20$), etc. This way of writing the array, then, can be derived by writing a string of 1's, writing underneath the running totals, underneath that writing the running totals of the second row, and so on.

As we mentioned earlier, the triangular numbers appear in the array. Notice that, like any other sequence, they appear twice because of the symmetry.

Exercises

1. Make a triangular number with marbles or ball bearings on a flat surface touching each other. (It may help to keep the balls from rolling to contain the triangle with three books or some other frame.) Make a second layer on top of the first so that each marble in the second layer touches three marbles in the bottom layer. How many marbles are in the second layer? Now make a third layer in the same way and go on, finishing with just one marble. How many marbles are in the pyramid you have made? We will call the answer a *pyramidal number*. What are the first few pyramidal numbers? Can you find them in the Pascal Triangle, and can you account for their presence?

2. Look at the figure on p.55 which illustrates the number of intersections of lines in a plane and count the number of triangles you can see in each figure. Count *all* the triangles, including those that overlap.

3. You have four cups in a row. Take one marble. It must go in a
cup. How many choices have you? Start again with two marbles
which cannot be distinguished from each other. Each marble must be
put in a cup. In how many ways can you dispose of both of them?
(Hint: both marbles may be put into the same cup; how many ways
can that be done? On the other hand, each can be put in different
cups; how many ways can this be done?) Repeat the experiment with
three marbles, four marbles, etc.

Zig-zags

Version (c) of the triangle seems to demand the insertion of links
between the numbers. These might arise as the vestigial remains of
the arrows we used above to show how the tenth row could be
obtained.

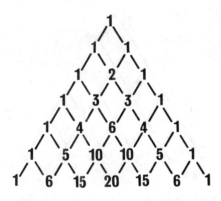

Fig.4

The numbers now appear at the intersections of a square or rhombic
lattice. Let us remove the numbers temporarily. We call the top point
S and one of the other points of the lattice F (Fig.5). Suppose that the
lattice is made by cutting grooves or channels, shown by the straight
lines, on a wooden board. We put a ball-bearing at S and tilt the
board so that the ball-bearing runs down the board.

Will the ball-bearing pass through the intersection F? We do not
know. But we can at least say that it *may* do so; the physical situation
will permit it. It is clear that the ball-bearing which starts from S *may*
pass through any of the intersections of the lattice. None of them is
inaccessible to it.

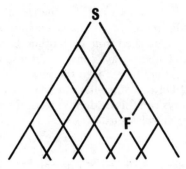

Fig.5

One of the routes which the ball-bearing may take is shown in the diagram. Are there any other routes by which it may reach F?

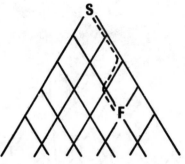

Fig.6

How many different routes may the ball-bearing take that go through F? How many routes go through G? How many through H?

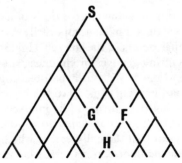

Fig.7

We may notice that if the ball-bearing passes through H on its journey it must have passed through F *or* through G. This supports the relation we find between the numbers of routes that go through F, G and H. In this case we have 4 routes which pass through F, 6 routes which pass through G and 10 (=4+6) routes through H.

Is there any general truth in this argument? Will it apply to any three intersections related in this way? Although the actual numbers of routes will be different, the argument should apply to any region of the lattice.

If we start again with the ball-bearing at S we see that it can reach the nearest intersections of the lattice in only one way for each.

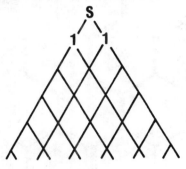

Fig.8

Applying the (F,G,H) argument repeatedly and filling in the numbers of routes which the ball-bearing can take to each intersection, we find the Pascal numbers reappearing on the diagram.

This illustration anchors the Pascal Triangle to a physical situation and we see how the structure of the physical situation gives an insight into the way in which the Pascal pattern can be built up. But we are certainly not deriving the Pascal numbers from an experiment. *In practice the board would be unlikely to behave as precisely as we want it to: the 'experiment' has taken place entirely in our minds. Nevertheless, the existence of the board may have made us curious and set us thinking, so launching us on the above exploration.*

The essence of the lattice situation is that the ball-bearing has a two-way choice at each intersection – it may roll to the left or to the right – and there is no reason to prefer one choice rather than the other – the alternative paths slope to the same extent. As we see again later, it is this underlying structure that makes the Pascal Triangle appear.

In our study of this situation we may notice that all the zig-zag paths starting from S that take a ball-bearing through a particular point of the lattice are of the same length; moreover these paths are the shortest possible lines from S to the point. See p.249 for the development of this.

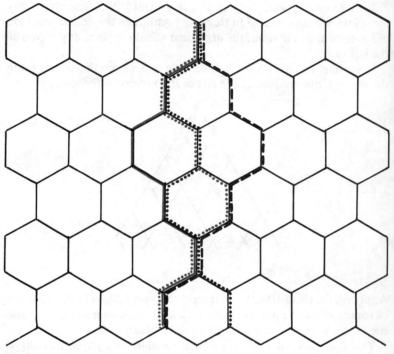

Fig.9

Exercises

1. We imagine that the board is flat and we put a counter at S. The counter can be given instructions to move by successive throws of a coin. We suppose that a head means 'move one unit forward to the left' and a tail 'one unit forward to the right'. Thus the throw of a head, then a tail, then another tail, would take the counter to A (Fig.10). We code the finishing point of the above three-stage move with the symbol HTT. What rules can be derived for determining whether two code-names describe the same point?

2. In the rolling ball-bearing situation, it is clear that the ball-bearing

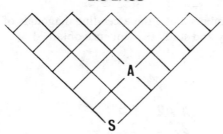

Fig.10

must pass through one and only one of the set of intersections on any horizontal line. What is the probability that it will pass through F rather than any other intersection in the same row?

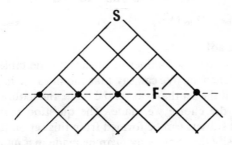

Fig.11

3. Invent a situation which will produce the following number pattern:

6	3	1	3	6
3	2	1	2	3
1	1	▨	1	1
3	2	1	2	3
6	3	1	3	6

Fig.12

4. Sum the numbers along the ascending diagonals of version (a) of the Pascal array and study the sequence obtained.

Fig.13

Subsets of a set

Suppose that we have a number of objects on the table and that we pick up some of them. We can say that the ones we have picked up form a subset of the set that was on the table, the nature of the subset depending on the choice we made. The question may arise 'How many different subsets can be formed from this set on the table?'

We can classify the choices that can be made in a number of ways. We may do this by considering the number of objects we have picked up. If there are five objects on the table there are several possible choices of subsets containing two of these objects. How many? If the objects are labelled in some way, say A, B, C, D, and E, we can represent the possibilities as {A,B}, {A,C}, {A,D}, {A,E}, {B,C}, {B,D}, {B,E}, {C,D}, {C,E}, {D,E}. So there are ten possible subsets of two objects. How many subsets are there each containing three objects? Four objects?

Shall we include the subsets comprising just a single object? We did say 'pick up some of them'. The words used may suggest we exclude this case, but the system of classification we are using suggests that we include it. It is certainly possible to 'pick up one at a time' and we will therefore count this as covered by the original question. How many subsets can be made with a single object?

Shall we include the subset containing *all* the objects? The case can again be argued either way, but it seems a reasonable decision to count this case as well.

If we arrange the information we have collected, we obtain:

	Number of subsets containing				
	1 object	2 objects	3 objects	4 objects	5 objects
5 objects	5	10	10	5	1

This seems to exhaust the number of different ways for an original set of five objects. If we are interested in trying to discover a pattern (supposing we are not already alerted by what we have discovered), we will examine other cases starting with a different number of objects.

The reader should verify some of these for himself. Here we merely give a summary table of the results for a few cases.

Number of objects	Number of subsets containing					
	1 object	2 objects	3 objects	4 objects	5 objects	6 objects
1	1					
2	2	1				
3	3	3	1			
4	4	6	4	1		
5	5	10	10	5	1	
6	6	15	20	15	6	1

The similarity this array bears to the Pascal array can hardly be coincidental. But we notice one difference: the table does not begin with a column of 1's. We can make it do so if we wish. In order to have this column in the table we shall need an additional column, and this will obviously have to be headed 'no objects'. This step may arouse a good deal of resistance (rightly, in this context), but from other mathematical arguments which we do not go into here, it is 'convenient' to have a fictitious entity called *the empty set* which is contained in any set whatever. However, *this* exercise gives no convincing reason for including it, and the desirability of the empty set must be supported from other quarters.

We spoke earlier of the 'two-way choice' underlying the structure of the Pascal numbers. Perhaps this can be brought out again if we consider a set – say one with four elements, {A,B,C,D} – and imagine someone pointing to each element in turn and taking a decision about whether to include it in a particular subset. If we tabulate all the possible combinations of decisions we can take, we should have a method of counting all the subsets that can be made.

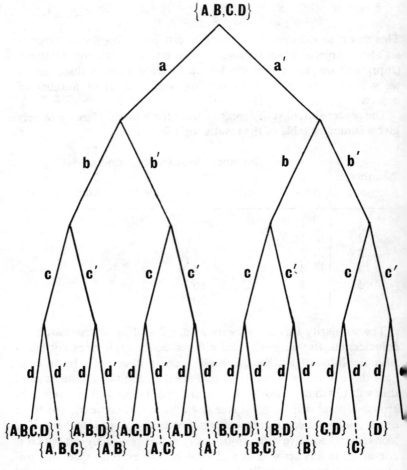

Fig.14

The diagram (called a *tree*) is read from the top downwards. It shows first the two decisions that can be made about the element A: the left branch represents a decision to include A, and the right branch represents a rejection of A. (These branches are labelled a and a' respectively.) The tree forks again on the base of the possible decision to take about B ('include' labelled b, 'reject' labelled b'). Two further sets of forks deal with the decisions about C and D.

At the end of each branch we show the subset selected by the sequence of choices. We notice that the branch on the extreme right represents the successive rejection of each element. This branch *could* then be said to yield the empty set. The number of branches in the diagram is 16. The number of subsets obtainable from a set of four elements is therefore 15 (or 16 if the empty set is included). How many branches would there be in the corresponding tree showing the subsets of a set of five elements? How many for a set of six elements?

The sequence of numbers we obtain can surely be generalized. Behind the pattern is the fact that (a) each tree has a set of forks (decisions) for each element in the original set, and (b) each new set of forks doubles the total number of branches.

Ancestors

Mary has two parents and they, in turn, each have two parents, so that Mary has four grandparents. In the generation before that she had eight great-grandparents. As we delve further back into her ancestry the doubling process continues. Starting with Mary herself, the generations number 1, 2, 4, 8, 16 and so on. This doubling process soon reaches very large numbers indeed. A well-known illustration starts with a grain of rice on a square of a chessboard, two grains on the next, four on the next and so on. The number of grains that would be required for the sixty-fourth square turns out to be larger than the total world production of rice since it was first grown.

A paradoxical version of this idea appears if the doubling process is naïvely used to calculate Mary's ancestors in, say, the year 2000 B.C. It seems as if there would have to have been at least 10,000 ancestors living on every square foot of the earth's land surface. The problem is often raised quite naturally by young children, who, without detailed calculations, argue from a doubling ancestry that the population of the world must be decreasing.

Some extracts from a taped discussion between a group of nine- and ten-year-olds: '. . . it was all one family long ago. If everybody had 64 great-great-great-great-grandparents, there must have been more . . .

Yes, but it's all in different sorts of years isn't it? ... They are not all alive in the same year, because if they are dead they can't be alive ... How do you know you've had great-great-great-grandparents? ... You have to or you wouldn't have had a grandparent ... When the world began there was only one person ... Two – Adam and Eve ... So it was less than there are now ... Some people only have a mother ... divorcements ... Some fathers marry twice ... Also there's a man who was already married and went out with another lady ... Adam and Eve had children who had children who had children who had children .. It means I must be related to her, her, him, him ... Adam and Eve must be our very great-great-grandparents ... Very, very, very great ... Who is Adam and Eve's grandparents? ... God ... Adam and Eve are my two very, very great-grandparents ... There would have to be an even number. How could it be bigger backwards than forwards? ... It can't be ... Can't have more than 1,000 very great-grandparents ... It's nuts ... It's 1965. It will go up to a high number and then it will get smaller ... I'd have about a million grandparents ... Some people die, my dear ... Two ladies and one man could have children ... They found out he was married ... What if great-grandparents died before their children were born? ... You're saying we're all related to Adam and Eve ... Your mother's very great-grandmother got married to your father's very great-grandfather. That means there would be a less number ... How does she know she's got one? Later we'll be grandparents ...'

Clearly it is a considerable intellectual achievement to realize that in enumerating Mary's ancestors in any generation we are not necessarily counting distinct individuals. But we are counting distinct relationships with Mary and it is interesting to analyze these relationships further. Consider the four grandparents in the following genealogical tree:

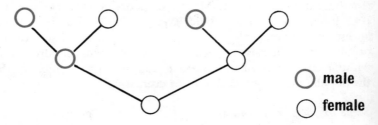

Fig.15

At one end is her father's father and at the other her mother's mother. We could say that she is related by a double male line to the one and by a double female line to the other. We could now group her father's mother and her mother's father together in the sense that she is related to them – in different orders – through one male and one female line. The four grandparents have been classified into groups of 1, 2 and 1. What is the corresponding classification of the great-grandparents? Here we consider relationships through three males, then two males and a female, then one male and two females, and finally through three females. A familiar pattern seems to emerge in another version of the genealogical tree.

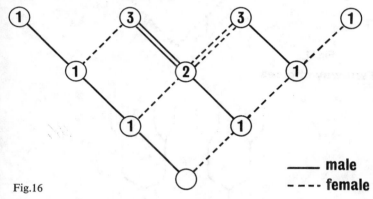

Fig.16

—— male
---- female

The pattern is clearly symmetrical since any male line is always balanced by a female line. Moreover, as the ancestry is traced back, the number of relationships in each generation doubles. These are familiar features of the Pascal Triangle pattern but can we be certain that the great-great-grandparents, say, also reveal the pattern and fall into groups of 1, 4, 6, 4 and 1? We need to show that the genealogical tree exhibits the additive property of the Pascal array. The schema in Fig.17 shows that there are indeed $3+3=6$ great-great-grandparents related to Mary through lines of 2 males and 2 females. Each generation adds an extra male or an extra female to each line so that the argument is in fact quite general.

It should not be surprising that the Pascal Triangle pattern can be imposed on the genealogical situation for, as we have seen, this pattern is fundamentally relevant to any two-way branching process and it is an essential feature of human ancestry that we inherit from two people.

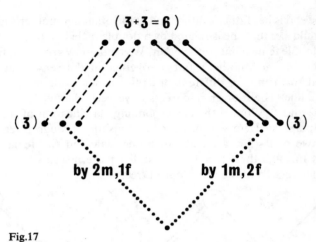

Fig.17

Two-way choices

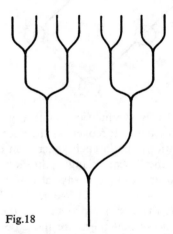

Fig.18

What does Fig.18 suggest? A formal representation of a bush? A candelabra? Upside down, a part of a large church-window in the Decorated style? Sideways, the plan of a tennis tournament? It might be the underlying scheme of a railway marshalling yard. We shall read it from the bottom up as a stylized representation of a general flow in a two-way branching process. As in the case of a truck threading its way through a succession of points in the marshalling yard, there are a series of choices to be made during the flow. At any stage there are two mutually exclusive choices that can be made; the flow is either this way or that way, male or female, off or on, left or right. By tossing a coin we could have the choice made for us – heads this way, tails that way. Thus any particular branch of the network could be described by the succession of heads or tails that would have had to be thrown for the flow to reach that branch. Fig. 19 shows a scrambled form of the network. The reader is invited to continue the coding of the branches in the network.

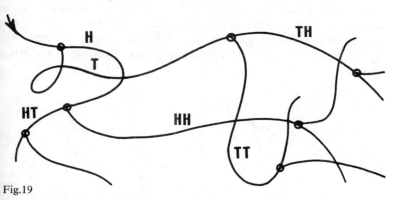

Fig.19

If we unscramble the network the Pascal pattern is quite clear. Thus, there are $2^3 = 8$ branches that can be reached in 3 tosses of the coin. These branches fall into groups of 1, 3, 3 and 1 in a way that can easily be indicated by their codes.

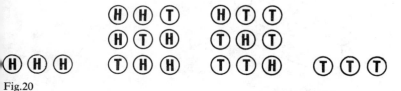

Fig.20

We see that the rows of the Pascal pattern enumerate the number of ways in which three pennies may be placed in order on the table. How many ways can four pennies be placed on a table? How many ways if the order doesn't matter? How many ways in which there are more heads than tails?

As a digression we note that combinatorial problems of this type are important. As they often arise quite naturally, the Pascal pattern emerges in unexpected guises. A class of children were making up different networks with Construct-o-straws, a plastic construction kit consisting of pliable straws which are joined in various ways by plastic wheels with varying numbers of protruding spokes on to which the straws fit. At one stage it was decided to investigate the topologically different networks that arise from specific restrictions on the number of wheels that could be used (see p.267). It was suggested that each person should use three wheels and could choose these from a pile of wheels with 1, 3 or 4 spokes. (The reader should consider why the class had decided it wasn't very interested in wheels with two spokes.) For some choices it was not possible to complete a connected network (Fig.21(i)); for others there were different networks possible within the particular choice of wheels (Fig.21(ii) and (iii)).

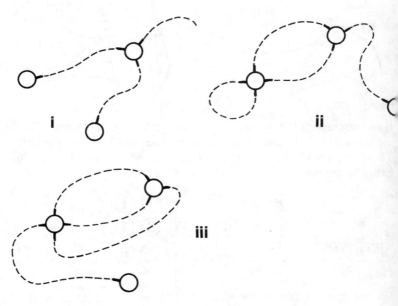

Fig.21

But the question of the number of choices of wheels was raised as a problem in its own right. When ten of these were enumerated successfully, further questions were raised. How many choices of four wheels can be made from a pile of four types? Of two wheels from five types? The answers were tabulated as in Fig.22.

		Number of types available			
		1	2	3	4
Number of	1			3	
objects	2		3	6	10
selected	3	1		10	
	4				

Fig.22

The reader will see the relation with the example discussed on p.207. With children the same problem may arise in many forms. It might be a question of choosing 3 bars of chocolate from a selection of 5 brands. Or consider a pile of blue, tan and yellow Cuisenaire rods lying on a table. A class of children is asked to come up and each child to take three from the table. In considering their selection some will spot that they have the same as others. How many distinct choices did the class make? Are there any others they could have made? How many choices were possible?

In the enumerative solution of such problems there will come a stage when recognition of the parts of a known pattern is not enough. The way the parts relate together is ultimately more important. At some stage of mathematical development it will not be enough to guess from the numbers of the table in Fig.22 that there are 4 ways of selecting three objects from two available types. The applicability of the Pascal pattern will need to be shown in full generality. It is impossible to legislate when and how the need for a particular type of deductive rigour arises. It certainly can never be imposed and primary school teachers rarely make the mistake of doing this. But at the same time it might be important to remember that induction can go wrong, as the example on p.53 shows. It is often a particular feature of the situations in which the Pascal pattern arises that the inner structure which makes it applicable can be grasped quite clearly. As indicated in Fig.16 the structure can be realized in a particular case and seen to hold quite generally. Relationships are in the mind and not in the m's and n's, the x's and y's of the text-books. A fully rigorous deduction of the Pascal pattern is made when such aspects as the symmetry, the doubling and the additive property of the array are perceived. Moreover, as we indicated before our digression into combinatorial problems, the structure is essentially established when a situation is understood to be a two-way branching process. The reader is invited to consider how the combinatorial problems contain such a process.

Returning to the classification of branches available after three choices, it is worth noting a way of re-coding the situation that has provided a powerful application of mathematics in our time. The two choices that were coded by the toss of a coin may be represented by the presence or absence of electric current in a wire. The branching points may be thought of as switches and the electrical state of the system can be coded as *off* or *on*, or, more conveniently, as 0 or 1. Any two-way system can be represented by an electrical network, and at the same time by a mathematical situation with symbols 0 and 1 and relevant rules of behaviour for these symbols.

The information in Fig.20 may now be presented in another way.

```
        001    011
        010    101
000    100    110    111
```

It may be noted that the eight forms that arise in this case occur when we write the numbers up to seven in binary numeration. This is not surprising since the binary system of notation involves a two-way choice for the entry in each place.

We return momentarily to sets. Many teachers will be familiar with such devices as the Venn diagram to aid classification. Consider then a particular set. How do we know what it consists of? It must have been defined by some rule even if this is only a dictionary list of all the things in it. A strange element lurks on the horizon and begs to be included in the set. We consult our rule, or list, and make a decision – *in* or *out*. The familiar closed curves of the Venn diagram can raise confusing issues, but their only function is to separate the sheep from the goats. (See p.299). Classification is therefore a two-way branching process. So we might employ other symbols to represent our thinking. Instead of

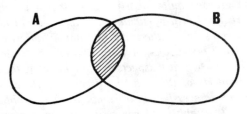

Fig.23

to denote the class of objects belonging to category A and category B, we might write

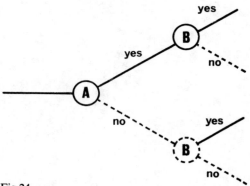

Fig.24

Indeed, if we use a 1,0 labelling system for *yes, no* respectively, we might write 11 to denote the class of objects we are considering.

10

Playing games

Certain activities can be labelled as obviously mathematical and others seem to be equally obviously something else. But there are borderline cases and history shows that it would be rash to assume that something at present considered to be outside the province of mathematics will always be so. In this chapter we set out deliberately to extend our notions of what constitutes mathematical activity in the classroom. One reason for doing this is that we can observe children acting out situations in their play which seem to be mathematically significant. These situations are rarely invoked in the classroom. Nor is it clear how they could be, for the mathematics is only implicit; it is being acted out, not thought about. Moreover when the adult observer does think about it, he finds that the mathematics involved can be difficult and very sophisticated. But as a teacher he will be less interested in a particular, mathematical end-product, and more interested in the fact that there seem to be situations which are potentially mathematical and which engage the whole child with an absorbed, passionate concentration not always found in the classroom.

Why are those children on the playground so completely engrossed in that skipping game? Among various reasons might be that there is no adult around. Geometry in the classroom is all about what the teacher has chosen to call geometry and is sometimes only looked at in the way he has chosen. Out on the playground the children can choose and what they choose is very complicated geometry indeed. A current example to be observed in many playgrounds is sometimes referred to as 'French skipping'. At least ten years old, this game is played with a large elastic band stretched round the legs of two children, while a third crosses in and out, altering the position of the band as in 'cat's cradle', but using his feet. Additions to the basic moves make the game more and more complicated. One is to make the band rise up the legs of the standing children to positions called *one-sie*, *two-sie* and *three-sie*, whilst the third child makes patterns of increasing complexity.

It might be claimed that what is in the feet cannot be called mathematics until it is put into the head. But we cannot be too certain that it is not there already. A teacher recently found some of his class hopelessly tangled up with the ribbons of a maypole. A girl who did not normally betray much mathematical ability in class was directing the group out of its tangle by a succession of clear instructions to individuals on how to move. Similarly, though we might be aware of the interesting cyclic patterns of counting chants we do not expect the child to be aware of them. But who has not met the cunning with which the seven-year-old can select one of many alternative endings to 'eenie, meenie, mina, mo' so as to count out a random group to her advantage? '*Out goes you!*'

Leave a group of children on their own for a time and they are soon playing some sort of game. Even Johnny, walking home from school alone, is playing a game – with himself. Now he is an agent delivering a message through enemy country; now he is a tiger stalking his prey. The stick in his hand bounces off the railings and the rhythm enlivens a tedious stretch of road. Shall he walk on the pavement slabs or on the cracks? Or some complicated, alternating combinations of these? Shall he shut his eyes for ten paces or hold his breath until the next car passes by? The world is his and he is making it. If the self-imposed rules prove too difficult he can cheat a little. How delightful to be able to do that, because, of course, when he is playing with a friend there is more than just his own conscience to keep him to the rules. A familiar feature of any group game is the intense litigation that the proper interpretation of the rules requires. This is often most hectic when the rules have been made by the group itself. Although many children's games are standard throughout the world, the really remarkable thing is the elaborate and spontaneous variations that occur. Children left on their own not only exhaust a particular game with repetitive concentration but they elaborate more and more versions with creative delight. The essence of this creative activity is the free choice of rules, which then in fact circumscribe consequent action.

Now mathematics can be viewed as a game in which we make rules and explore to the limit the consequences of these rules. Teachers have always harnessed the child's desire to play to the task of making the learning of mathematics more palatable. Many ingenious and attractive games have been devised to inculcate specific ideas that are felt to be important. These are no doubt useful, but the prime importance attached to inculcating the idea means that the full freedom of the game-playing activity is not invoked. Doing mathematics is one thing; making it is another. When Piaget asked an eleven-year-old boy whether everyone would want to play marbles according to a rule the boy had described, he replied that those who invented it would (Piaget [83], p.61). John will perhaps bring the full creative energy of the playground to the mathematics lesson only when he is given legislative rights.

Such universal suffrage brings other problems for the teacher. Given a free choice John might make up some rules which the teacher himself finds rather difficult to play to; John's group might even start playing games that the teacher would find difficulty in labelling as work. Such dilemmas would seem to be inevitable consequences of current movements for greater freedom and flexibility in mathematics teaching. We have only an inkling of what mathematics children might make if they were allowed to do so and, as we imply in our introduction, the mathematics that is accessible to them may be already quite different from the mathematics that was accessible to us. It is the teacher who has the greatest problem in the classroom: if he listens, how can he cope with what he hears? Perhaps he has to have some faith, and perhaps he has to have some confidence, that at least the initial game-situation he encourages the children to enter has some potential mathematical significance. Meanwhile we cannot see the variations of hopscotch or the complicated skipping games that are played without a momentary feeling of doubt about some of our naïvely contrived classroom situations. What is important about the skipping game is the continued creation of further challenges, the ever-changing nature of the rules being obeyed, and it is this aspect that should be kept in mind when reading the following brief descriptions of some games that are mathematically rewarding.

Noughts and crosses

At first sight there may not appear to be very much to say about the game of noughts and crosses. It is not long before a player finds that the game can always be played so as to lead to a draw, and that seems to be that. But a lot has already happened. At each stage of the game a player is faced with a number of choices. In making a correct decision he thinks ahead by asking the all-important question, 'What will happen if . . .?' Some of the choices turn out to be essentially the same as far as the outcome of the game is concerned. Thus the initial player starts with nine apparent choices:

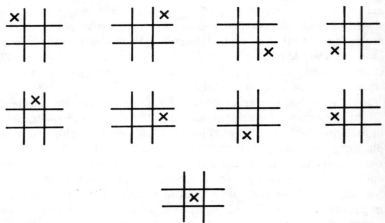

Fig.1

The first four figures look different, but after a few games the player knows that they are the 'same'. Each figure makes a different pattern on the page, but this depends on how the reader is holding the book. How should the book be moved to show that some of the figures are the same? Geometrical insights are developed as we reduce the initial choices to three.

1. Which of the three opening moves is the best?

Some interesting points arise when the first player considers his opening move against an inexperienced player. For each of his three moves, count the number of squares where his opponent's move leads to a draw. Is a centre start best when playing with an inexperienced player?

2. Consider the strategies involved in the 'reverse' game, i.e. when the object of the game is to lose.

3. Play a game with a rule that either player can play a nought or a cross at each move. In this game the first player can always win if he plays correctly. Describe his 'winning strategy'.

4. As in the game of battleships, the moves may be labelled with

'co-ordinates'. Number the rows and the columns and label each square with a number-pair – the number of the column and row in which the square lies. Write down the number-pairs of a winning set of three noughts and crosses. Find relationships to characterize these.

5. The object of the game may be said to be to get three-in-a-row (or column or diagonal). Extend the board and investigate the game of four-in-a-row.

6. The game is played on a 3×3 square board. Investigate a similar game on a $3 \times 3 \times 3$ cube.

7. Make up your own variation of the game.

8. A simple matchbox 'machine' that can be taught to play noughts and crosses is described in an article in *Science Survey 1961* [102], pp.129–45.

Nine men's morris

One variation of noughts and crosses is played with a limited number of symbols at the players' disposal. This is often played on a 3×3 square board, one player having three pennies and the other player three halfpennies. The coins are placed alternately on the board and can then be moved one at a time to any vacant adjacent position. Does adjacent mean along a diagonal? Well, shall it? We can play the game with either decision about the meaning of 'adjacent'. The distinction between the possible interpretations may be made clearer by transforming the actual board we play on. We started with nine squares and we now make nine dots, joining by lines those that we agree are to be called adjacent.

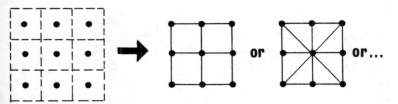

Fig.2

Such figures are scratched out in the dust, and the game played with pebbles, in many parts of the world. Clearly it can be played with any number of pebbles or counters with any configuration of points and lines. A convenient way of setting up a game today is to use pegs and a chalked figure on pegboard.

In an old English version called Nine Men's Morris, each player has nine counters and the following boards are used:

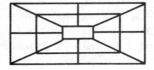

Fig.3

The first board was used by the Moors (hence 'morris') and the second is known in Anatolia. The reader may have observed that the third is the 'same' as the first. One version of the game has as its object to establish rows of three counters; on achieving this a player is then allowed to remove an opposing piece that is not already in a row of three. But there is scope for endless variations.

1. Draw a figure of points and lines joining them and play some form of the three-in-a-row game on it.

2. Play the game of five-in-a-row on a square lattice of points (pegboard). Some winning combinations are shown below. Determine others.

```
•  •  •  •  •  •        •  •  •  •  •        •  •  •  •  •
•  ⊙  ⊙  ⊙  ⊙  •        •  ⊙  •  •  •        •  •  ⊙  •  •
•  •  •  •  •  •        •  ⊙  •  •  •        •  ⊙  ⊙  ⊙  •
•  •  •  •  •  •        •  ⊙  ⊙  ⊙  •        •  •  ⊙  •  •
                       •  •  •  •  •        •  •  •  •  •
```

Fig.4

This Japanese game is used extensively by the Madison Project in the U.S.A., particularly for the development of work with co-ordinates [29]. A class of children can be formed into two teams and asked to call the co-ordinates of each move so that it may be marked on the blackboard. Consider the following situations in which the game was being played (by mistake!) on a 4×4 lattice. To complete the game the lattice must be extended. Suppose that extension is only permitted in certain directions. What are the choices open to the team playing the crosses at the stage shown below?

3 A Victorian version of five-in-a-row was played on a chessboard with twelve counters for each player, moves being allowed when the counters were exhausted. Investigate this game.

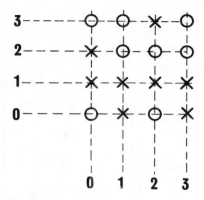

Fig.5

Squares

The object of a pegboard game need not only be to form rows. Thus consider a game for any number of players. They insert a peg of a particular colour in turn and try to get four of their pegs at the vertices of any square. When a player already has three pegs at the vertices of a square the next player must block by completing the square himself, or must set up a 'warning' device which acts as a force – the blocking move must then be made by another player before the move returns to the 'threatener'.

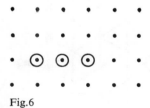

Fig.6

In a game with three players one of them has three pegs in a row in an otherwise unoccupied part of the board. Where should he place his next peg?

Note that a winning square can be of any size and have any orientation.

The reader is urged to play this game with children and see for himself how subtle are the strategies they soon develop.

Hex

Another family of games could be developed by taking the object of the game to be the establishing of a chain of counters or pegs from one side of the board to another. The figure below illustrates a win for black on a simple square board:

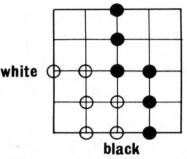

white

black

Fig.7

Which player began this game?
Is there a winning strategy for the first player?

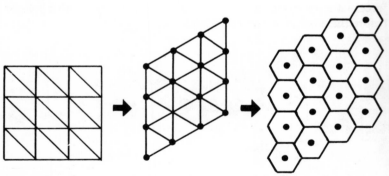

Fig.8

The above figure suggests a more complicated version of the chain game. Here certain diagonal connections are permitted. If we distort the network as shown, it is seen that the game may be played on a tessellation of hexagons. This form of the game, played on an 11×11 hexagon board, is known as Hex, and has been extensively studied by mathematicians in recent times. It has for instance been proved that the first player can in fact always win, though the proof does not tell him how to do this. A useful way of appreciating the interest of the game is to play on small boards at first.

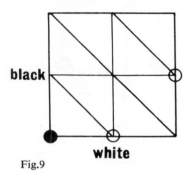

Fig.9

What is black's winning move in the game shown in Fig.9?
Devise some other problems for this board.
Further details about Hex can be found in Gardner [42], ch.8.

Go

A famous game that can also be played on pegboard is the Chinese game Wei-ki or the Japanese Go, said by connoisseurs to be more subtle than chess. Here the object of the game is to capture enemy pegs by surrounding them. As the partial enclosures that each player forms interlock, the situation becomes very complicated. Thus there is an obvious defensive move for white to play in Fig.10. But he could also play one space to the right.

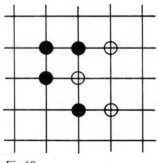

Fig.10

Nim

Another game that can be played on pegboard requires a spiral to be drawn, starting from a hole designated as base.

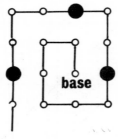

Fig.11

Three pegs are placed anywhere on the line other than the base. At each move any peg may be moved in along the spiral towards the base or indeed at it. On reaching base a peg is removed. The player who removes the last peg wins or loses according to the rule that has been agreed. The game can obviously be extended to include further pegs and the choice of moving more than one of them at a time.

This game is called Nim when it is in the form where a player removes one or more objects from one of three piles of objects, the winner usually being the one who forces his opponent to remove the last object. Full accounts of Nim and its mathematical theory can be found in various books (Gardner [42], ch.15, Rouse Ball [10], ch.1).

1. A particularly fiendish variation of Nim allows a pile to be broken up into two piles at any move. Investigate this game. What is the corresponding variation in the pegboard form of the game?

2. The Chinese play a removal game with two piles of objects. A game can be played with one pile. Here the players remove one or more up to an agreed limiting number of objects. Given the number of objects in the original pile, what is a suitable limit to choose?

3. In another version of the game with one pile, the players call out numbers from 1 to 10 and the winner is the player who takes the cumulative sum past 100. A form of this can be played with dice. After an initial throw, the players move by turning one or all of the dice being used to bring one of the sides to the top. Even with one dice and a goal of 30 this is an interesting game. Investigate some possible strategies.

4. Make up a 'removal' game.

Lucas' games

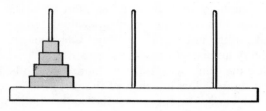

Fig.12

A set of rings of decreasing size are placed on a stick. One ring may be moved at a time but never on to a smaller one. The object of the game, which is for one player, is to transfer the pile of rings to another stick in the least number of moves. After a few games a general pattern is found that applies whatever the initial number of rings. The reader is asked to explore the game before attempting the following questions. Playing-cards with increasing value or rods of increasing size could be used as piles to be transferred.

1. What is the least number of moves required to move a pile of four rings?

2. Draw up a table showing the least number for different numbers of rings in the pile.

3. The relationship between the number of rings in the pile and the least number of moves is an example of a function. Can you guess what this relationship is? How would you express the function?

4. How many moves does the largest ring make? The next largest? The next? The smallest? This series of terms is an example of a geometric series. The sum of the series is the function found in the last question. Check this in some cases.

5. Suppose the rings are coloured alternately white and black. Play the game with different piles and observe the movements of each colour. What have the rings of the same colour in common?

6. How many choices of play are there at any stage? Can you still transfer the pile even though you make the wrong choice? Describe the right choice.

7. Play the game with four rings labelled, from the top, A, B, C and D. Write down a string of letters that indicate the movements in a transfer with the least number of moves.

8. Bisect a line-segment at the point D. Bisect each of the resulting

halves and label each new mid-point with a C. Bisect again, labelling resulting mid-points with B. Repeat once more with A. Read off the resulting string of letters along the line. It should be the same as the one derived for the last question. Why? Can you give a rule for labelling binary numbers to give the same string?

9. Generalize the game by considering more sticks to be available.

10. The first figure below is a map of the permissible moves in the game with two rings. The sticks are labelled 0, 1 and 2 and the nine states of the game are labelled with two-digit numbers to base 3. Investigate the second figure.

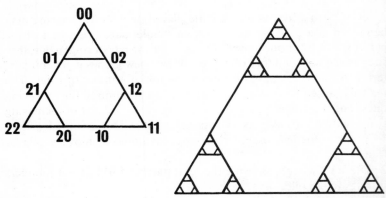

Fig.13

This game was invented by a French mathematician, Lucas. He also invented a story about it to the effect that somewhere in the East priests transferred rings from an original pile of 64. When the pile was transferred it would be the end of the world. Calculation shows that this is unlikely for some time yet. The game is referred to as the Tower of Hanoi (with a grim irony for the nineteen sixties!).

Another single-person game due to Lucas can be played with matchsticks in a row or with pegs of two colours on pegboard:

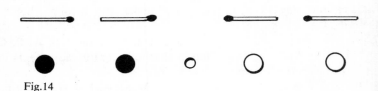

Fig.14

A black (white) peg can move into an adjacent space to the right (left) or jump one peg into a space to the right (left). In how many moves can the black and white pegs be interchanged? Again we can investigate a functional relationship between the number of pegs used and the minimum number of moves required. An interesting feature of the game is that there are positions in which one can be stuck if a wrong choice is made at some stage. We leave the investigation to the reader.

Both the Lucas games are used in the classroom by the Madison Project and are mentioned in the usual books on mathematical recreations (Gardner [42], ch.6; Rouse Ball [10], ch.11).

Crossroads

Crossroads is an intriguing game marketed commercially (p.338). It is played on a 5×5 square lattice with 25 counters and two markers, one for each player. The counters contain three 10's, three 5's and three units; these are positive or credit values. Negative or debit counters are coloured differently and comprise two 10's, two 5's and two 1's. In addition there are five master counters which are not numbered. The counters are placed at random on the lattice – numbers showing – for the start of the game.

The first player identifies a row by placing his marker along it. The second player now identifies a column and takes the counter in the identified row and column. The first player now identifies a new row to capture the corresponding counter, and the game proceeds with columns and rows being identified in turn. A master counter counts as positive 10, but it can be put back on an empty position of the lattice if a player wishes; for example, to avoid having to take a negative-numbered counter. In this case the marker is moved to the row or column required to identify the position now occupied by the master counter. The opponent cannot now take this master counter at his next move since he must move his marker before taking from the board.

If a player removes the last counter from a row or column the other must play by putting a master counter back into play. If he has none, the game is over and the winner is the player with the highest score, negative numbers counting against him. The player with the highest score at any stage may end the game in this way, so it is important to know both scores. Captured pieces are therefore displayed openly.

The essence of the game lies in each player having to select one of several possible moves in terms of their subsequent implications – the game forces the player to think ahead. A typical situation is shown in Fig.15. Player A has just played, having put his marker against the bottom row and captured a piece. It is player B's turn; where should he put his marker?

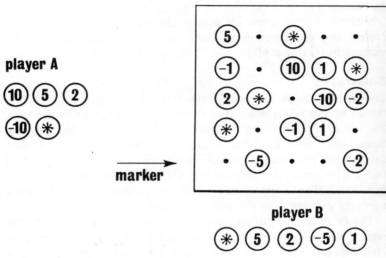

Fig.15

It is perhaps appropriate here to remind the reader that the preceding list of games, the discussion of them and the questions we have asked, are written for him. We are not saying that these are the games that primary school children should *play, that these are the questions they* should *be able to answer. We know primary school children who* do *enjoy these games and who* do *investigate them to the depth we have tried to indicate, but there is nothing remotely prescriptive about our account. We want to do more than give tips for interesting classroom activities – even though they may be tips worth having. Game-playing of the kind we have tried, perhaps not very successfully, to talk about is the purest form of mathematical activity. In it can be seen, at various times, the detailed exploration of a particular structure; the modification and elaboration of the structure by changing the rules ('What happens if . . .?'); the working out of the consequences by action or by argument ('This is what happens if . . .'). The game-player works out his own techniques, algorithms and strategies and he is involved in a social situation where others must agree with the procedure and be convinced when an endpoint has been reached.*

We do not want to say that this is the only kind of mathematical activity worth engaging in. But we believe that it has a value greater than the playing of a few well-known games to someone else's rules. We hope that the opening pages of this chapter have given something of this atmosphere.

**Pictures made by children after watching the film
'Dance Squared'**

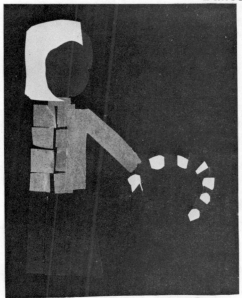

11

Open situations

*In choosing certain strategies a player in a game is formulating proced-
ures, and this activity is mathematical. The need to formulate procedure
is particularly evident when a group is presented with a so-called 'open'
situation – that is, some situation whose outcome is not necessarily
predetermined. In the classroom this means that the children are given
legislative rights. This may result in something that might be called a
game-playing activity. But the teacher is also in the game. She may
still wish to – or have to – exercise some legislative rights herself. The
open situation presents a difficult challenge to the sensitive teacher, but
invariably a rewarding experience for the children. The following is an
account of an attempt to meet the challenge.*

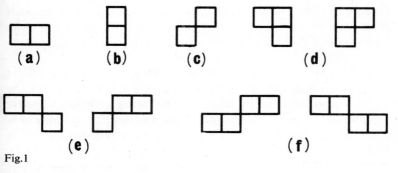

Fig.1

I gave geoboards to a group of girls, and having checked that all
of them could make a one-unit square on the geoboard I asked them
to make a second square touching the first one. When they held them
up I noticed that most of them had produced (a) or (b) (Fig.1) but
one girl had (c). I asked them to walk round and look at each other's
boards, and then to comment on what they had seen. I had to prompt

them with 'Are they all the same?' Then they chorused, 'Teresa's is different from ours.' I asked if they thought Teresa had in fact done what I asked, and after a long hesitation they decided that her squares did touch each other and so were acceptable. They had no hesitation in accepting the vertical and horizontal arrangements as the same, and so concluded that there were two shapes that could be made with two squares.

We proceeded to make shapes with three squares, and I first asked how many different shapes they could expect to find. The estimate ranged from two to nine. The girls then produced a variety of shapes and again I asked them to look at each other's and comment on what they saw. This time there was an animated discussion about which shapes were the 'same' and which were different. It was finally decided that two shapes were the 'same' if they looked the same when the boards were turned round, e.g. (d). The girls who suggested this were very anxious to convert the others to their point of view. Those who thought the shapes different seemed less sure of themselves and so were soon converted. Shapes such as (e) were agreed to be different as they could not be made the same however much the geoboards were turned round. We finally decided that there were six 'different' shapes by our definition.

The girls were anxious to go to four squares and estimated that there would be from four to nine different shapes. The majority thought that there would again be six shapes. There was keen competition to produce shapes that no-one else had thought of and again heated discussion took place about 'same' and 'different'. Eventually fifteen 'different' shapes were produced.

At this stage some girls were finding it difficult to understand what was going on and wanted to opt out of the situation. Others were keen to try a larger number of squares. Some brought shapes with five squares which they had drawn at home and wanted to know how many shapes there were so that they could try to find them all. I said I did not know but would see how many I could find. When I told them I had found thirty-four different shapes they wanted to see them all so I made a large diagram to put on the wall. A group of girls were discussing this diagram when Pauline said, 'You've put some of them in pairs. They go opposite!' She was referring to pairs such as (f). This led to further discussion and reconsideration of the shapes made with three and four squares to find opposites among them. From this followed further work on symmetry.

We notice that the form of presentation of the original situation led to the girls accepting certain shapes as proper answers. If the same question had been presented differently the response, too, might have been different. Would we expect a different set of answers if the girls had been given squared paper and scissors with which to cut out their shapes? It is likely that some shapes that were made on the geoboard would not arise in these circumstances (see the reference to polyominoes on p.145). Is there a best form of presentation of this question? This is unanswerable. The teacher was clearly not trying to teach a particular set of results that she already knew, but was encouraging the children to make an exploration. The nature of the material the girls had to hand was a part of the situation that was explored, so we should not be surprised if a different material were to produce different results. Perhaps some of the girls found this fact worth exploring, too.

Square grids

Geoboards, pegboard and squared paper have in common the idea that a flat surface can be covered (tessellated) with squares of the same size. Putting this another way, if a square is drawn on a plane and shifted a distance equal to the length of its side to the left, or to the right, or up and down; and if it is then shifted in the same way from its new position, and so on, it will generate a pattern of squares which can be extended to cover as much of the plane as we want.

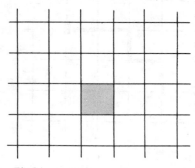

Fig.2

A square is not the only geometrical shape that will do this. Some other examples are given in the section about tessellations (p.131).

If we think of the network of straight lines which form the sides of the squares, we have a square grid; if we think only of the vertices of the squares, we have a square lattice. *Geoboards and pegboards are physical representations of square lattices; squared paper represents a square grid. There is no need, however, to stick rigidly to this distinction, as it is easy to think of the lines on a geoboard or to concentrate on the intersections on squared paper.*

Some obvious applications of these pieces of equipment are to a study of area and to simple co-ordinate geometry; these have been dealt with elsewhere. Both of these topics use a grid or lattice as a helpful accessory. It is as if one were mainly concerned with the geometry of shapes, lines and points, but constructed a grid in order to make it easier to find areas, or in order to give numerical labels to points. But the square grid suggests a geometry of its own, and it is instructive to explore this as a thing in its own right.

If we look at a piece of squared paper ($\frac{1}{2}$-in. squares are appropriate), we can play the game of supposing that the lines on the paper are the only ones we have. A story can be made up if we want to: the paper is a street-plan of some (American) city. This might launch us into a 'cops and robbers' problem. Whatever the setting, though, we will suppose that journeys or movements can take place only along the lines of the grid. The only points in the geometry lie on the lines of a grid, and all other places on the paper are inaccessible.

How can we get from A to B?

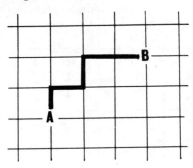

Fig.3

We can choose a variety of positions for A and B and discuss them. Some of the many ways we can travel from A to B suggest that we might compare the lengths of the different journeys. What is the best way to go from A to B? If A and B lie on the same line of the grid there is not likely to be any argument. But if they do not, there will be some choice (and disagreement) about the best way. Let us say that the 'best' way is the 'shortest' way. We find that there are several possible ways, all equally short, and we find we have a property which does not occur in ordinary geometry. (It quite often occurs in approximate form, though, in our experience of going by the shortest route from one place to another.)

In this discussion some decision will have been made about the measure or length of a particular journey. It will probably seem appropriate to give the lengths of journeys using a side of a square as a unit since we are interested only in comparing these journeys with each other.

One line of investigation is to find out how many shortest ways there are between two points on the grid. There are 10 between the A and B of Fig.3. Choose other positions for A and B and find the number of shortest routes. A number of things may be discovered: the length of a journey does not determine how many other journeys with the same length exist; a shortest route has (in general) two choices of direction in which to start, and two choices of arriving at the finishing-point. It is possible that this last fact may lead to some systematization of the answers and to a method of building up the numbers of journeys (see ch.9).

This is a simple example of a combinatorial problem – 'How many ways can . . . ?' It crops up in a variety of problem situations. The closest analogy to the one we have been investigating is the problem about the number of ways in which a rook on a chessboard can travel from a corner square to any other square of the board. The squares of the board act like the intersections of the grid. A part solution of the problem, for a fixed starting-point, is given in Fig.4. There is no need to suppose that all children will want to arrive at a complete solution.

Further games can be played with the shortest routes (or with any routes). A notation may be developed which can describe a route to someone who cannot see the path on the paper. It is interesting to throw this problem at the children and see what notations they can invent themselves. There seem to be two basic variants: one is an 'observer's' notation, the other a 'participant's' notation. The first kind will adopt some symbols to mean 'up', 'down', 'left' and 'right' (for example, the route shown in Fig.3 might be described as U R U R R). The second kind will invent a way of saying whether someone walking the route had to go straight on, turn left or turn right. Someone using the second kind has to find a way of saying

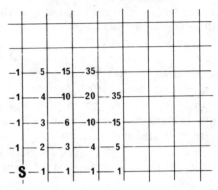

Fig.4

which direction he took first. So the same route might be described by saying 'I first went north, then R L R S'. There is plenty of freedom here for invention, and for the children to test the validity of their choice by seeing whether they are understood.

The children will think of additions to make to this basic game. Given the symbols describing one route, they may write other routes of the same length; or they may change from one symbolism to the other; or given a journey in one notation they may describe the reverse journey.

Another field for investigation leads to simple locus properties in this geometry, and a comparison with the corresponding results in ordinary geometry. Start with a point A at an intersection of the grid. Mark all the other points which are exactly 4 units from A.

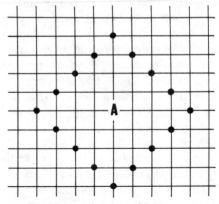

Fig.5

Given two points A and B, mark all the points which are exactly the same distance from A and from B. Given two points X and Y, mark all the points such that all the journeys from X to Y via the point have the same distance.

In ordinary geometry, these three questions give a circle, a straight line (the perpendicular bisector) and an ellipse, respectively. An interesting discussion can follow on the meaning of the word 'circle'. If we define the word to mean 'the set of points a fixed distance from a fixed point', Fig.5 certainly represents a circle!

These locus exercises can conveniently be worked out on a piece of pegboard, where the lines of the grid are understood from the children's experience with squared paper. When the children return to the paper, they can investigate what happens if the grid is refined by drawing additional lines parallel to the printed lines. Or they can be given paper marked in 1/10 in. squares so that they see the effect of making the squares smaller. Some children will certainly be able to imagine further refinements of the grid to a stage where it becomes impossible to mark all the lines, and make the mental jump from seeing each locus as a set of discrete points to the stage when each locus has an infinite number of points. In this way, with the former experience well understood, some children will be able to work in this geometry but draw their figures on plain paper.

In this work the children are experiencing a metric space *which is different from the usual Euclidean metric space. In their search for important structures, modern mathematicians have abstracted the idea of 'distance' from its familiar context and eliminated some of its properties until it becomes applicable in a large variety of situations, not all of them obviously geometrical. The properties that remain are (a) that a distance between two 'points' is measured by a non-negative real number, (b) that this number is zero only if the two points coincide, (c) that the distance from A to B is the same as the distance from B to A, and (d) that the sum of the distances from A to C and from C to B is always greater than or equal to the distance from A to B. The geometry we have played with has these properties. (Verify this.) See the article 'Distances' by Barbut [11].*

Exercises

1. In square grid geometry, explore the meaning of 'between'. (A point C is said to be between points A and B if the sum of the distances of C from A and B is equal to the distance from A to B.)

2. Will a similar kind of geometry exist on a grid of equilateral triangles? Or any other grid you know?

3. A grid (or a lattice) of squares can be used to generate Farey series. See Mansfield and Thompson [68], Book 1.

4. An interesting situation arises when we superimpose systems of circles on the square grid. A convenient and dynamic way of doing this is to draw the circles on acetate sheets which are then moved over the grid.

How many points lie inside a circle?

How does the answer depend on the radius?

How many lattice points lie on a circumference?

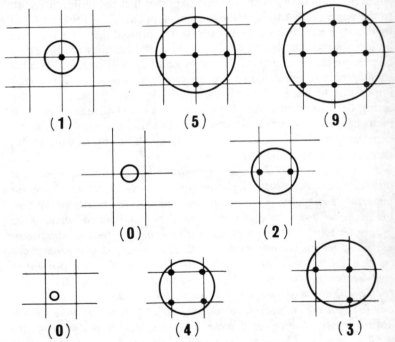

Fig.6

We may draw other figures on the acetate sheets.

How many lattice points lie inside a square?

How many squares have corners at lattice points?

And so on.

5. Make a cardboard square and construct the grid which it gener-

ates. Label the edges of the square **a,b,c,d** (mark both sides of the square, being careful to give the same edge the same letter). Put the cardboard square on an arbitrary square of the grid and mark this square I. If the cardboard square is turned over (or 'flopped') about the edge **a**, the square of the grid it lands on is labelled A. If it is first flopped about **a** and then flopped about **c**, the square it arrives at is labelled AC. By continuing in this way we can give names to all the squares of the grid. Find some rules for determining when two names are equivalent (i.e. describe the same square). Note that the cardboard square must always start from I and be put down on it in the same way each time.

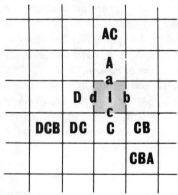

Fig.7

(This exercise shows another way in which a grid can be generated from a single square.)

6. On a limited grid explore some *longest* journeys. For example, what is the longest route from S to F on a 4×4 grid? What are the lengths of the longest routes from S to each of the 16 points of the lattice?

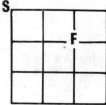

Fig.8

Spaces

In exploring what might be called the 'natural' geometry of the square grid it appears that we have to change our notions about some simple geometrical words like distance or space. But it is interesting to note the extent to which we already do this when we use geometrical metaphors to express our feelings and attitudes towards other people. We say that our friends are close to us; some people we keep at a distance, at arm's length. We place someone on a pedestal because they may fulfil our highest ideals. We look up to, as well as down on, certain people. A broad-minded person is not expected to have narrow views, an honest person is said to be straight. A flat voice may be recounting a low joke. In one idiom, the speaker may be a square. It is as if we make a geometry out of our emotional relationships. It is not surprising that the 'spaces' which we thereby create are not universal and absolute; they vary from individual to individual and from generation to generation. The 'space' created by the builders of Salisbury Cathedral is a world of movement. The atmosphere is quite different inside a Wren church; here the geometry is one of repose.

What space do we create and inhabit inside a room? From a conventional Euclidean point of view we are inside a rectangular box, but this does not help very much, especially when it is customary to make drawings and models of boxes from the outside. In fact very few of our conventional geometrical ideas are retained in the space we create. Someone in the far corner may be closer to us than the person sitting beside us. A room with one window may 'feel' more like a triangle or prism. In restaurants we may always seek a corner table, and in this case our room will be quite different from that of bolder spirits who sit in the centre. An adequate technical description of our particular space might involve some considerably 'advanced' mathematics. But the fact that we may not be able to make such an explicit analysis doesn't alter the fact that we know it implicitly.

We close this chapter with a few examples of some 'spaces' where children might roam.

Paper-clips

A group of ten-year-olds were given some ordinary paper-clips, asked to clip them on the edge of a piece of paper and then to draw what they saw. What was drawn?

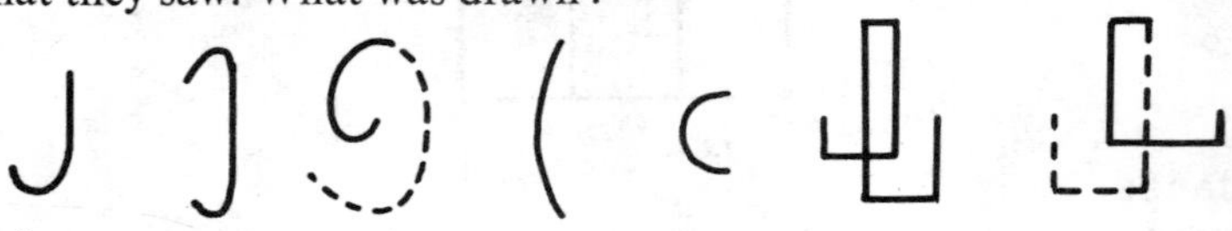

Fig.9

What was said?

'That's not right . . . yes, it is . . . it's the same as yours . . . it isn't because you've got the smaller bit on top . . . Oh, can you have the larger one? . . . you get it if you turn the paper over . . . you get the same shape . . . I don't . . . yours wasn't the same to begin with . . . but I can get it if I turn the paper upside down as well . . . I can put the clips on in all sorts of ways . . . they are all the same . . . look.'

The teacher gave up the attempt to follow the discourse when the group began attaching the clips together to make chains.

Cut-outs

Patterns can be made from a piece of paper by cutting out bits from an edge and placing them opposite the holes they occupied.

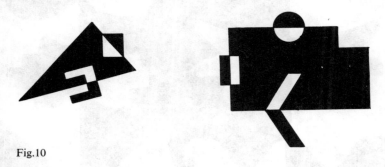

Fig.10

Interesting problems arise. What do you do if the cut goes through to another edge? What if the paper has different coloured sides? Where does the missing piece in the second figure go? A seven-year-old girl, having cut this, paused for a long time and placed it at the corner (see below). Faced with another problem she produced two solutions.

Fig.11

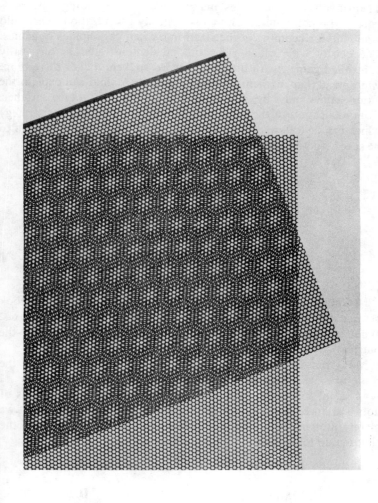

Strokes

Children can communicate their ideas to each other with a minimum
of words, aided by expression, intonation, sympathy between them
and the common ground of the intersection of their worlds of fantasy.
Their involvement in games, making rules and extending systems, is
part of this communication and is basically socialization. The child
who is unforthcoming in the classroom often participates in games.
The clarity with which rules can be demonstrated in physically
controlled games, with little or no word spoken, makes these more
widespread than mathematical paper games. A child can explain the
latter games only by demonstration to himself, not to another.
Communication to the other has to be in words, defining a strategy
which can be followed. Each has to seek out a strategy for himself to
be successful, invalidate the game, or to reach a stalemate.

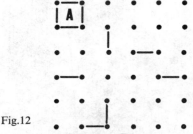

Fig.12

Making boxes from dots in a square lattice is a game we may look
at. Each person joins two dots by a line and tries to make boxes.
What strategy does the child follow? Is it better to start near the
outside? What makes the child decide?

Many puzzles are also concerned with dots and lines. Trace the
route to ... Find the path out of the maze ... Join up the dots ...
It is useful to look at simple situations involving arrangements of
dots and lines, as this is part of children's activity. It is fruitful if we
merely present the situation – with a few questions – and let the
children do the talking. Some examples follow.

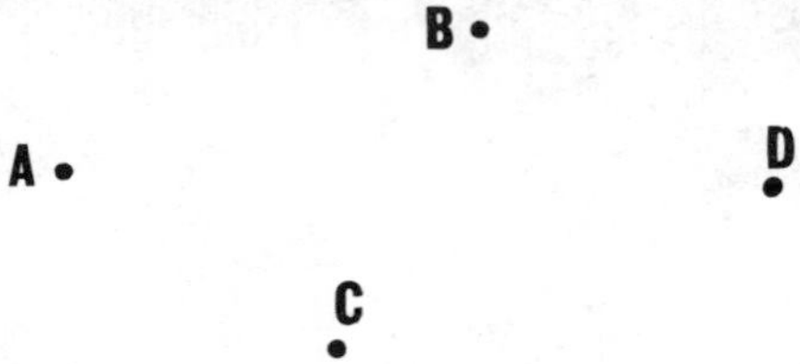

B •

A •   D
                                                       •

                          C
                          •

Fig.13

Join A to B and C to D. What can you say about these lines?
Join A to D and B to C. What can you say about these lines?
Join A to C, A to D and B to D.
Join A to C, A to D and A to B.
Join A to C, A to B and C to B.
Join the points in some other ways. Are all the ways you have drawn different? Join the dots in another way. In how many different ways do you think you could join them?

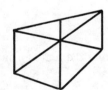

Fig.14

Talk about these. Could you draw round the shapes completely without taking your pencil from the paper? What about these . . . (Fig.15)?

Fig.15

Draw some more.

What can you see?
Make the pattern with matchsticks.
Talk about it.

Fig.16

Add one more matchstick. Draw the new pattern you have made. *Talk about it*. Make some more patterns, adding one matchstick at a time. Make drawings of the patterns and talk about them.

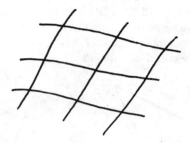

Fig.17

How many lines? Parts of lines? Spaces?

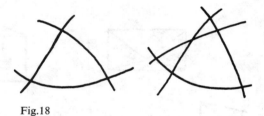

Fig.18

(See p.54 for an account of some more formalized activity on this theme.)

Fig.19

Bands

A familiar activity with a long narrow strip of paper is to make a so-called Moebius band. When we wrap the strip round so that the two narrow ends overlap we make a band which has manifestly two sides. But if we twist the paper once before we overlap the ends we find that we have a surface that has only one side – we can paint all the paper in one colour without our brush having to cross over an edge.

What happens if we give the strip two twists before overlapping the ends? Three twists?

It turns out that there are only the two possibilities that we have already met, the one-sided and the two-sided band. Moreover the number of twists put into the strip is the 'same' as the number of sides of the resulting surface in the sense that these numbers are both even or both odd. This type of sameness is often described by saying that the numbers have the same parity.

What happens when we press out some of our bands so that they lie flat on a table? In some cases this may not be as easy as it seems. A few possible results are shown below.

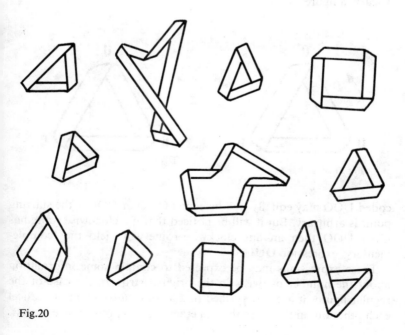

Fig.20

Are there any of these that are the same, and if so in what sense are they the same?

How many twists has each piece got?

Which of them are one-sided? Two-sided?

And inevitably the figures prompt further questions in themselves. Could any of them have been creased out in a different way? What is the significance of the fact that there appear to be groups of figures with 3, 4, 5 . . . corners? Some of the figures have cross-overs, some are re-entrant. Could this have been avoided? Can we always obtain a regular shape? If this were so each figure could be seen as a system of overlapping congruent trapezia. What are the angles of these trapezia? There seems to be no end to the questions we can ask (see Barr [13]).

A further point of interest that might be mentioned here is the nature of the fold at any corner. Consider the regular figures. In each case, as we approach a corner along the strip, the fold at the corner is either over or under (she loves me – she loves me not). We could label each corner with letters, say O or U, and code each figure by collecting their initials as we move round the corners in turn. Clearly a figure

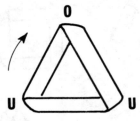
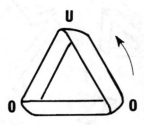

Fig.21

coded UOO may equally well be coded OUO or OOU – the starting point is arbitrary. But it will be noticed that if a clockwise route has given UOO then an anti-clockwise route will yield the 'complementary' expression OUU.

These expressions may be expected to contain some information about the number of twists in the original strip. In the case of the regular figures it is easily verified that a consecutive O and U cancel each other out in the sense that together they do not produce a twist.

The surplus number of O's or U's will then give the number of twists. This idea that elements of opposite parity neutralize each other has important applications.

The reader is recommended to investigate the irregular figures in the same way. Finally, we recall that the original strip of paper can be knotted in a simple over and under way and then flattened out to reveal a pentagon. Why?

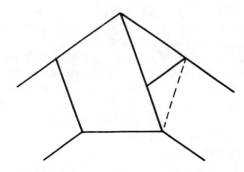

Fig.22

Connections

The basic set for a young child's railway consists of fourteen curved rails (each one-eighth the circumference of a circle) and a cross-over. The rails can be turned over and the 'track' is reproduced on the other side. The rails are joined by placing a stud on one rail in a hole on the next.

 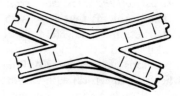

Fig.23

The purpose of the set is to make a track for a plastic train to be pushed round. If the train is to remain on the track without reversing the circuit must be closed. There are a large number of possible tracks that can be made using all the rails or only some of them. Variations can be made by introducing bridges and points. The making of these circuits can provide a wealth of experience for the child, but raises many questions. The first making of a circuit is probably fairly random, and decided by the way in which the rails are picked up from the pile; but sooner or later the question arises, can this particular circuit be closed, and if so how?

After several trials the child finds a satisfactory pattern for making a closed circuit. Does he now always keep to the circuit, or does he try to alter it, and, if so, in what way?

An eight-year-old child made a number of different closed circuits with the rails, but a three-year-old made only open-end circuits, and if a closed circuit was made for him to play with, often took it apart. Why did the eight-year-old make this closed circuit? Did he feel a sense of completeness? Or was it because only closed circuits were shown on the box in which the rails were sold?

Another three-year-old was given a similar railway in wood. It was not expected that his two-year-old sister would play with it. She did, although at first she was content just to fetch and carry. The three-year-old very quickly revealed a need for circuits, though frequently the girl was happy just to push her truck to and fro under the bridge, while the boy pushed the engine round and round, and over the bridge. During this play single pieces were frequently removed and replaced by the boy. Often a curved piece was turned over, necessitating much turning round and over before it was re-fitted. As interest waned this re-fitting was 'carelessly' done, and finally – the girl having by now toddled off elsewhere – the boy opened the circuit and ran the engine fast and furiously off the track and across the lino.

The problems that arise with a railway set can appear with other constructional toys. Here we discuss some further possibilities with the kit called Construct-o-straws that has already been mentioned in a previous chapter (p.220). Pliable, plastic straws can be fitted on to wheels (connectors) with varying numbers of projecting spokes. With the full set available, children will play freely and rapidly make a wider range of constructions than is possible with, for example, milk straws and pipe-cleaners. A tendency to want to use up all the spokes on a wheel is complemented by the desire to put all ends of the straws on to a spoke. This forces the production of circuits of various kinds.

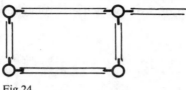

Fig.24

In the above situation, however, one straw is left dangling and immediate 'closure' would require the insertion of its free end on to a single-spoked wheel. The situation can be expressed in terms of the railway set if buffers are available.

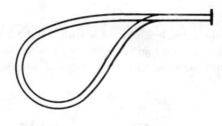

Fig.25

In problems that arise from the railway set we see that the 2-spoked wheels do not play an important role. Suppose the child is restricted to 3-spoked and 1-spoked wheels. What constructions are now possible?

Let us be more precise. Suppose he has two 3-spoked wheels and one 1-spoked wheel. What construction is possible using all these?

Given one 1-spoked wheel (or one buffer) what are the numbers of 3-spoked wheels (or points) that can be used to make a connected construction (or track)?

Fig.26

A connected construction is possible with two 1-spoked wheels and a certain number n of 3-spoked wheels. What restrictions can you place on n?

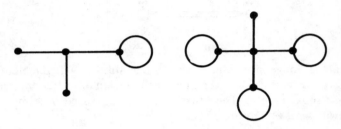

Fig.27

A connected railway track can be made with m buffers and n points. What relationships can you find between the numbers m and n?

Is a construction possible with two 4-spoked wheels and one 3-spoked wheel?

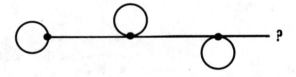

Fig.28

With three 4-spoked wheels and two 1-spoked wheels?

If it is possible with l 1-spoked, m 3-spoked and n 4-spoked wheels what can you say about the numbers l, m, n?

A construction is possible with one 1-spoked wheel, one 3-spoked wheel and one 4-spoked wheel. Some possibilities are shown in Fig.29. Two of them are the same. In what sense are they the same? How many different constructions are possible?

We can characterize a construction by making out a table that indicates when two wheels are directly joined by a straw. Thus, suppose we take two 1-spoked wheels, labelled A and B, and a 3-spoked wheel, labelled C (Fig.30).

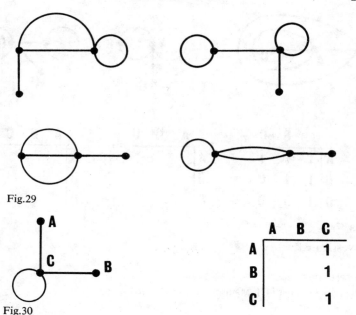

Fig.29

Fig.30

	A	B	C
A			1
B			1
C			1

Each square of the array, such as the one in column *C* and row *A*, is labelled with the number of connections between the corresponding wheels. Check the figures given and complete the table.

A construction has a table given in Fig.31. Can you complete the table? How many spokes have the three wheels *A*, *B* and *C*? Draw the construction.

	A	B	C
A	0	3	0
B		0	1
C	0	1	0

Fig.31

Complete the tables given in Fig.32. How many different figures are there in this case? Will two constructions with the same table be the same?

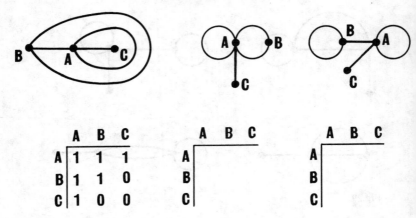

Fig.32

Investigate further.

References
Barr [13], Gardner [42], Madison Project [29], Rouse Ball [10].

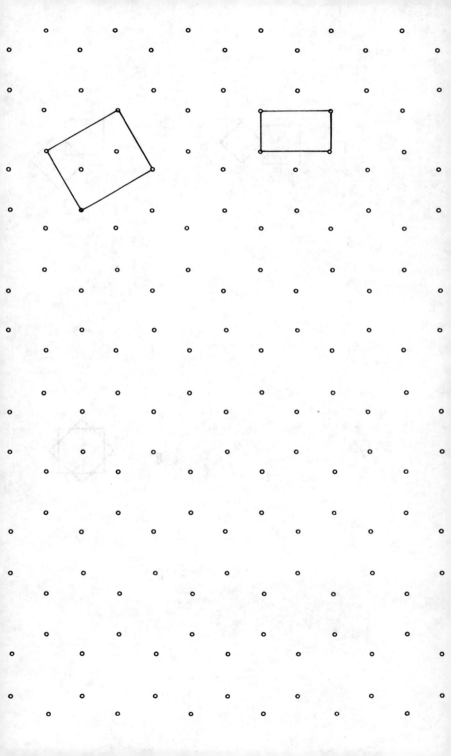

1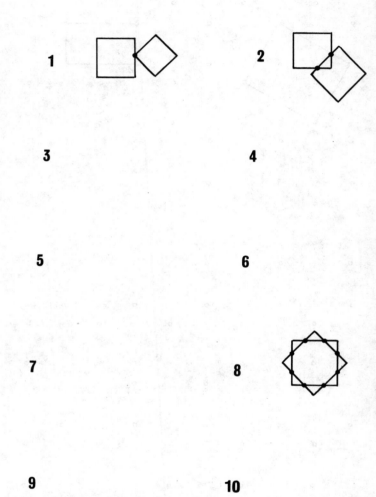

2

3

4

5

6

7

8

9

10

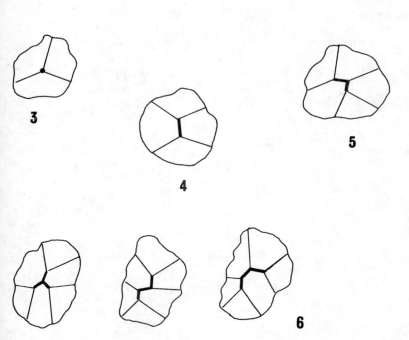

3

4

5

6

7

8

Lego is a toy. Kid's stuff. But Lego has structure and children will handle it. What do they make? A collection of shaped pieces means that they can use them to put things together. The activity is connected. A piece must go next and the one that is touched first is used. Is it discarded? If it is, why? What is the choice that was made? He picks another up. Does he look at it or does he try it? When does he start looking at the pile and not just taking? A space to be filled, let's fill it. How do the little ones fit with the big ones? He will not tell you any of these things because he is only two. Even when he is five, will he tell you? – or at seven – or ten? What is happening? Is the material teaching him about number or is he acting in the context of this material and developing the structures which fit his thought? Can we separate thought and action?

A chaffinch hops along a piece of ground patchy with bare earth and small lumps of grass. It avoids the clumps and pecks at the earth. Action and satisfaction are simultaneous. How is this with the free-playing child? When does he start working at the pile and controlling his play by abstracting? This would be an abstraction: to choose a piece by looking . . . He may still leave himself unsatisfied.

He makes a wall

and when he pushes his car against it it falls down. But he has made a wall – an extended surface which involves him in a precise structuring. The surface he required is filled. Shall we show him how to make a 'proper' wall? Why? When have we the right to show him? When he asks? This depends on his dependence. Has he seen that he can make

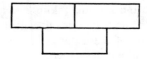

But this won't be flat . . . And why should he see a surface extended with this thing? And if he is shown, can he use it for anything else but this wall? When does he structure it for himself? He may make another wall like it, but has he 'understood'?

This is life – real life!

12

Like and unlike

We have become used to the idea that the word mathematics represents a classification of our activities of a particular, well-defined type. This is a fallacy. It is rather the reverse: it is when we have activities of a particular, well-defined type that we begin to exercise the language we speak and to use the word mathematics.

The first way of looking at it limits our understanding of mathematics to that which we know, while the second way shows us that many of our ordinary activities may well lead to a situation which we shall call mathematical. This does not necessarily mean that the activities lead to something which we recognize from our former experiences to be mathematics, but that the very act of dealing with a situation can itself be mathematics. It can be argued that in order to talk to anyone about such an act we would have to use some of the conventional language of mathematics. It is a characteristic of the development of mathematics that it often happens that conventional language has to be used to mean different and new things.

At this point it is rather important to gather some of the threads together and to look at the way the activity we call mathematics develops. It should be clear from much of the work of the book up to this point that our understanding of the word is not limited to its conventional use.

We are not at all clear about the modes of children's thinking; the variety that we can detect by listening and watching is often alarming in its range. The points of interest to the child often appear to carry a potential which escapes us. At times the child expresses his discoveries in a manner which we fail to match. We cannot continue the discussion with him except by ignoring him, bringing it back to words which we, the teachers, understand.

'*This . . . is . . . John.*' The child's finger hesitantly follows the words as he makes the sounds. We say that the child is learning to read, though we are not necessarily any clearer as to what he is doing when we have said this. '*This is John.*' It seems to be so simple and the next line in the reading book repeats the sentence. '*This . . . is . . .*' The child stumbles; can't he see that the next word is the same as the one he has just read? Patiently we move his finger to the end of the first line. '*John.*' Back in the second line there is still no response. But it is the same word; it looks the same so you say it's the same. We prompt the child; he reads on and sometime, somehow, we shall say that he has learnt to read. Whenever he sees the word 'John' in an English-speaking context he will mouth the same noise. He will have learnt to ignore the many, manifest differences between two particular appearances of the written symbol.

It is a salutary experience to try to see the two appearances of the word 'John' in the reading book with an innocent eye. The first ends a line. It is under a picture of a small boy with blue trousers and red pullover who is throwing a ball to his sister. The second is sandwiched between two lines of print and it is followed by some more words on the same line. Of course the two words are not the same, but the child has to learn that the many differences he can perceive and feel are in fact irrelevant to the matter in hand. *He has to choose to ignore the differences.* The important point here is that it is a matter of choice and that in many activities the word 'same' is used in a conventional sense. Thus we say that two things are the same when we have agreed to ignore certain differences. Learning to recognize sameness is not a matter of learning some intrinsic property of the real world; it is a matter of agreeing to, or making, an appropriate verbal convention. It is not surprising that in the learning of mathematics, which is very much an activity based on certain agreed conventions, we are concerned with deciding when two things are to be considered the same and the further implications of such decisions.

With this in mind, let us consider what is involved when a child is tackling a typical Piaget situation. Some sweets are laid out on a table in an extended line, or they are bunched together in a close group. In each case there is the *same* number of sweets. A cup of lemonade is poured into a wide, low container or into a narrow, tall one. The volume of the liquid remains the *same*. We say that the number of sweets, or the volume of lemonade, is conserved despite the various changes that are taking place and, as Piaget so successfully pointed out, that ideas about conservation are not somehow inherited at birth, they are acquired.

So we have come to think of children developing an understanding of conservation concepts. After a particular experiment of the above type we are tempted to say that the child has, or has not, got a certain concept. We may even be tempted further to suppose that the acquisition of certain concepts has to await a certain stage of development. We may even adopt a passive role towards 'number readiness'. On the other hand it may be more useful if we were to consider whether the child had, or had not, made the appropriate choices that govern the use of the word 'same' in the context involved. He still has to learn to make these choices, but to say that he has not yet made the choice has a different flavour from saying that he has not yet 'got' a concept.

In one of Piaget's experiments, Leo (4; 9) is shown a square and a circle. '*They are both round*', he observes. 'Are they both the same?' '*No, not the same thing*.' 'What are they like then?' '*They are round. This one is like this* [pointing to another circle], *and this one is not the same*.' Here we can say, as Piaget does, that the topological relationships seem to be completely mastered and that a start is being made on the discriminations between rectilinear and curved shapes.

The square and the circle are indeed the same in the sense that they are both 'round'. The next question subtly reminds the child that they are not the same in the sense of identical and he begins to explore the differences. It is interesting to contrast another account which has not the same happy ending. 'The experimenter presents two large squares and the subject (4; 6) recognizes their congruence. The experimenter then cuts one of the squares to form two rectangles and arranges them perpendicularly to one another: "Is there still the same amount of room on these (two rectangles) as there is on here (square)?" "*No, it's not the same any more because you've cut it*." "Is there more room on one side?" "*Yes, there's more room here* (two rectangles)." "But didn't these bits have the same room to start with?" "*Yes*." "Well haven't they the same now?" "*No, you've cut it*." ' In this case we may make the comment that the child's answers reveal a complete lack of understanding of the conservation concept involved; but this can, and unfortunately sometimes does, encourage a passive attitude in the teacher to the child's future experience. Piaget's work rightly emphasizes the importance of activity, but there is a tendency for us to act the doctor and after our diagnosis we may prescribe a heavy dose of 'experience'. Somehow, sometime, the patient will 'get' the concept. As in medicine this draconian measure has a certain degree of success which may prevent us from looking further.

It may be more important to analyze carefully the opposition between experimenter (teacher) and subject (pupil) in their use of the word 'same', for this would bring out into the open the underlying choices that have been made. It is in these choices that the essence of mathematics resides.

If certain choices about the use of the word 'same' lie at the heart of mathematical activity then mathematics starts in the cradle, for a sense of one's own identity from one moment to the next is one of the first lessons to be learnt. Mummy is quickly felt to be the same person when she comes and goes; it takes much longer for Daddy to acquire the same invariance. The rattle is seen from different positions and felt in different ways. Each perception is different but as it is explored helps to build up the idea of something permanent, something that is always the same. Later on it becomes more and more difficult to recapture the differences between our perceptions. We very rarely see a circle when we look at a penny, but that is the shape we say that we see when we are asked. In an agreed sense a circle remains the same from wherever we perceive it: in another agreed sense it does not. In one case a circle and an ellipse are the same, but in the other they are different.

The use of most nouns is, in fact, governed by agreed decisions of this sort. It is very important to note that we may make mistakes with such labels. This by no means implies that we are mistaken about the things being labelled. A child can be shown a square card held in a conventional position with sides horizontal and vertical and may correctly label the shape as a square. Turned through 45° the shape becomes a diamond. Is it still the same? Already the question is ambiguous and there appears a need to take a more sophisticated view. The awareness that certain properties remain unchanged, remain the *same*, after particularly chosen motions such as translations or rotations, allows us to call the piece of card a square in what ever position it is held. This particular situation reminds us how deeply rooted much geometrical experience is in our perceptions of horizontal and vertical. Once the child can stand upright he knows what a right angle is, but choosing to call the angle between an arbitrary pair of perpendicular lines the same is quite a different matter. *Will the angle still be the same if the lines are in Australia?*

Does it stay the same while I am asleep? We can make it so if we wish. In creating some permanency within a changing frame we consider possible changes and choose which are the ones whose effects we are going to ignore. As Dan says about one of his knots in a Piaget experiment, 'It's the same because if I pull it, it will make the same knot as before.' If we are moved in this way to use the word *same* to describe separate objects or events, it is likely that a more abstract step has been taken. Oliver (5; 10) having been making shapes on a geoboard which were the same, fell to discussing his brother and sister and the question of sameness. In particular he objected to being the *same* as his brother. 'No! We aren't the same. We are both boys but he isn't the same stuff as me' (pinching his leg as he spoke). Yet he had been making separate triangles on the board which were the 'same'.

When we eventually habitually use the word 'same' in this sense it seems that we abstract some property out of a set of properties and then consider other objects from which these properties can also be abstracted. Then we talk of people of the 'same sex', with the 'same name', of the 'same height', and it is a short step to using the word with respect to two persons.

The development and use of ordinary language we may call a 'folk-use' in order to distinguish it from specific technical uses. This does not mean that the two uses are not at times inextricably mingled. In fact they are most of the time. It is only when people explicitly, and sympathetically, agree to a usage that separation occurs.

It is significant that the use of the word 'same' reveals an incredibly complicated sequence of changes of viewpoints. To recognize that a child uses this word in this manner is to recognize some of the capabilities for abstraction which he is often denied. For instance, to talk of a group of people having the same heights is a case where the property we are momentarily concentrating on is explicit, and to call them the 'same' a temporary and well-defined event. On the other hand to ask the question, 'Which of these are the same?' is to invite choices of the property which will be tested for sameness. We stupidly do not realize what we are doing with this *instruction* to choose, with its implication that only one rational choice is possible. It can be very damaging to the independent development of thinking. We should recognize that this question opens the gates not merely to the property the asker had in mind, but to the extensive range of properties that the compulsion of the question may produce. The question

'*Are* these the same?' has a very different flavour. So has, '*I think these are the same, what do you think? Why?*' 'Some of these are the same and others are not. Can you see which?'

This situation is not made easier when we find children convinced that two things are the same but not able to make explicit the properties that make them so. This may be a problem of language where the folk-use tends to imply that 'sameness' is a property of the real world. A child may in this case believe that what he calls the same *is* the same!

It is possible to explore a little more closely the ways of deciding on sameness through an awareness, either explicitly or implicitly, of some property that interests one. The first action, and the most common, is to state simply, for example, '*John is the same as me!*' '*Why?*' '*Because we have the same birthday.*' '*Are there any others who have the same birthday?*' '*I don't know.*' This is usually the end of the matter – in public. But thinking goes on. What possibilities arise when the eight-year-old who started this conversation goes on thinking, 'I wonder if there is anybody else with the same birthday as me?' His picture may develop in this way:

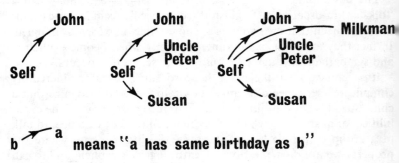

$b \nearrow^a$ means "a has same birthday as b"

Fig.1

He may ask his Uncle Peter if he knows anyone who has the same birthday. Later, it may be quite a long time afterwards, another conversation may start up.

'*There is a man works in the docks who has the same birthday as me.*' '*What are you talking about?*' '*He has the same birthday.*' '*Who?*' '*This man.*' '*But who is it?*' '*Uncle Peter knows him.*' '*Oh!*'

There the talk may languish, but the consequences develop.

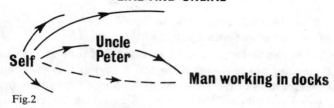

Fig.2

Or it may be another conversation:

'I have the same birthday as Uncle Peter.' *'Yes, I know.'* *'Oh, but you asked me if anyone else had the same birthday as me.'* *'Well?'* *'Uncle Peter has.'* *'Yes, he was in America when you were born.'*

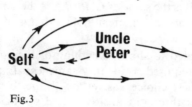

Fig.3

These two characteristic situations are the basis of the exploration of sameness relations and will occur in a variety of ways. The structure of the spoken sentences reflects the awareness of the relations and shows something of the mechanisms that may be set off in any learning situation where sameness is in question. This is not the whole story by a long way, but it gives some indication of the strength of folk-language in building up notions that will eventually be crystallized in mathematical argument.

Equivalence

We return to a constructed classroom situation where the number of different shapes that can be made with four cubes stuck face to face is being discussed. Questions like 'Are they the same?' will occur frequently.

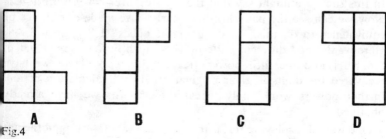

A   **B**   **C**   **D**

Fig.4

'*A and B are the same because you can turn B over.*'
'*B and C are the same because you can turn C round.*'

It may happen that a child will then say A and C are the same as a 'direct' consequence of these statements, though it may also happen that if the question of the sameness of A and C is raised a separate investigation will follow. '*Yes! Because you can turn C over.*'

To every act of identifying sameness there will be a set of associated operations, sometimes made explicit and sometimes not. What eventually becomes clear is that if we have objects which we can refer to as the same, then the *transitive* argument can hold; that is, if A is the same as B *and* B is the same as C, *then* A is the same as C. We also learn that the *symmetrical* argument holds; that is, if A is the same as B *then* B is the same as A.

We have attempted to show something of the complexity of the choices of action required to identify sameness. Exploration of the consequences of these choices, as we saw in the 'birthdays' illustration, is carried out through transitivity and symmetry; and we are left with Oliver's strong sense of identity, that no-one else is the 'same stuff' as he is. '*I am what I am, who cares or knows . . .*' – which reminds us that this identification with self, called *reflexive*, is ever-present in our use of the verb to be.

Mathematics is concerned with all types of relations, but the relation that links the things that are considered to be the 'same' in a specific situation seems to play a very important role. A relation that satisfies the properties of sameness listed above is called an *equivalence relation*.

When we square the digits 1 to 9 we get $1, 4, 9, 16, 25, 36, 49, 64, 81$, and we may observe that the units digits in this sequence form a symmetrical pattern (p.36). From the point of view of our interest in this pattern the tens digits are irrelevant and 25 is the 'same' as 5. In this sense we might say that the squares 'are' $1, 4, 9, 6, 5, 6, 9, 4, 1$. Now we can see the pattern more clearly – we made our choice of equivalence to do this. What about the cubes? $1, 8, 7, 4, 5, 6, 3, 2, 9$. Here we detect a different pattern. The fourth powers 'are' $1, 6, 1, 6, 5, 6, 1, 6, 1$ and the fifth powers $1, 2, 3, 4, 5, 6, 7, 8, 9$. Here we have recovered the digits in their original order and calculation of any further powers would only repeat the patterns we have already obtained.

One way of displaying this is to draw up a table starting in the left hand column with the digits 1 to 9, and indicating at the top the power to which the numbers have been raised:

1	2	3	4	5	6	7	.	.	.	.	.	.
1	1	1	1	1	1	1	.	.	.	.	.	
2	4	8	6	2	4	8	.	.	.	.	.	
3	9	7	1	3	9	7	.	.	.	.	.	
4	6	4	6	4	6	4	.	.	.	.	.	
5	5	5	5	5	5	5	.	.	.	.	.	
6	6	6	6	6	6	6	.	.	.	.	.	.
7	9	3	1	7	9	3	.	.	.	.	.	
8	4	2	6	8	4	2	.	.	.	.	.	
9	1	9	1	9	1	9	.	.	.	.	.	
a	b	c	d	a	b	c	.	.	.	.	.	

We label the different columns of figures. This gives us an opportunity to investigate the operations we have performed, as we see that the columns a, b, c, d are repeated. The calculations we originally made may be represented as

$$a \times a = b$$
$$a \times a \times a = c$$
$$a \times a \times a \times a = d$$
$$a \times a \times a \times a \times a = a.$$

But there are other statements which are consequences of these, for example
$$a \times b = c$$
$$c \times d = c.$$

A multiplication table for the elements a, b, c and d can be drawn up. Note that $a \times c$ means that corresponding numbers in columns *a* and *c* are multiplied together and their last digits put down. Can you use the table to say what $a \times c$ is equal to without working it out? Moreover, the question which asks, 'What letter will label the column of the 27th power?' reveals that the multiplication table for a, b, c, d is linked with an addition table for 1, 2, 3, 4, where again we may choose 'equals' to have a special meaning (p.83).

Just as we may create different arithmetics we can create different algebras or different geometries. The Euclidean geometry to which we are so accustomed, arises from specific agreements as to what shall be called the same; one of the equivalence relations here is usually described as congruence. When we classify different perceptions of a coin as being the same we are extinguishing the differences between, say, an ellipse and a circle and choosing to call different appearances the same. This particular activity tends to the development of a particular geometry where such 'samenesses' are part of the agreed definitions. In further refinements we may drastically enlarge the class of transformations which will be said to preserve some property. In topology, a triangle, a circle, an ellipse and a closed clover-knot are all the 'same'. (The elaboration of different geometries has taken place historically in the order just presented.) One of the most dramatic implications of Piaget's work has been the suggestion that in children's developing understanding of spatial concepts this order is reversed. The infant's closed squiggle 'is' a square. The transitions from topological, through projective, to Euclidean notions of equivalence require increasingly complex co-ordination of different actions. These actions give us our 'intuition' of space, but as Piaget has emphasized, this intuition is not a 'reading' or apprehension of the properties of objects, it is very much something that is under our control. We do not 'discover' our geometries from without; we impose them from within.

This has some important implications for the teaching of mathematics. If in our enthusiasm for providing active experience for young children we do no more than provide the springs and balances, the sand and water, with requests for a recording of what happens in certain selected situations, then we run the danger of abdicating from mathematics altogether. We certainly encourage the same abdications if we think in terms of children 'discovering' relations in certain external situations. Some of the most important mathematical relations stem from the earliest mental and emotional activity of the infant. We make sense of our environment by imposing these relations upon it. In developing our understanding and control of these relations we further provide the possibility of a control of the environment. In order to develop the fullest resources of the human mind it may be more important to think of creating mathematics rather than discovering it. In the creation of likes and unlikes we detect 'the mind at work creating works of the mind'. And this is mathematics.

It's all in the mind

Make a pattern using two orange, three dark-green and one red Cuisenaire rods.

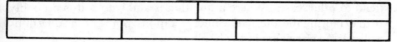

Fig.5. $o+o=d+d+d+r$.

The following statements could be made about this pattern.

(i) $10+10=6+6+6+2$

(ii) $3\times6=20-2$

(iii) $(2\times10)-(3\times6)=2$

(iv) $20\div6=3$, remainder 2

(v) $(10-6)+[10-(6+2)]=6$

(vi)   the number which is written 20 in base ten is written 32 in base six

(vii) $2\times5=(3\times3)+1$

(viii) $\frac{1}{3}$ of $10=3\frac{1}{3}$

(ix) $(3\times\frac{3}{5})+\frac{1}{5}=2$

These are a very small sample indeed of the total possible number of meaningful mathematical statements that could be made. Each can be 'read' from the pattern. Write some more statements derived from the same pattern.

The pattern is the same in each case, but the mind has read a number of different things into the pattern. The pattern acts as a prompt, but it does not dictate exactly what may be said. The differences that manifestly exist in the nine statements are not differences in the situation which is being interpreted. In this sense, the mathematics of the above statements is in the mind and not in the material.

We have seen that the mind generates equivalences (makes classifications) by choosing to think of different things as essentially the same. Here we see it generating equivalences by operating on the same thing to produce differences.

How many?

'How many?' occurs several times in this book. Such questions often depend for their interest on a degree of ambiguity which relates to the interpretation given to the word 'different'. Look at the report on the 'How many shapes with n squares?' question (p.247). Other types of ambiguity exist, however, as can be seen from the report on line crossings (p.58).

In the following questions, particular numbers and other details are given, but these are mostly arbitrary and the investigations should extend to other cases. Where a question is ambiguous it is probably worth exploring the alternative interpretations. Some of the questions are discussed elsewhere in the book.

1. (a) How many different weighings can be made with a pair of scales and one each of 1 oz., 2 oz., 4 oz., 8 oz. weights?

(b) A classroom has four electric light switches. How many different ways may lights be put on?

(c) How many different lengths can be made with white, red, pink and brown Cuisenaire rods if no length may contain more than one rod of any one colour?

2. A set of five cards is made, each with one digit written on it. The digits used are 1, 2, 2, 5, 7. How many different numbers can be shown with the set of cards?

3. How many different subsets can be chosen from a set of six different objects?

4. How many ways can a cube be painted with two colours?

5. Take a piece of pegboard and 36 pegs. How many different rectangular shapes can be made with the pegs?

6. By putting rods end-to-end make rows equal in length to the pink rod. How many different rows can be made?

7. Using only whole numbers and addition, write as many different expressions for the number 5 as possible.

8. Draw five straight lines so that each one crosses each of the others in distinct points. How many regions are enclosed by the lines?

9. On a geoboard or pegboard make as many different shapes with an area of 2 sq. units as possible.

10. Make a connected network (it need not be closed) with five matches. How many different networks are possible?

11. Make a row of four different objects. How many different orders of the objects are possible?

12. Make an expression using four 4's (but no other figures) and any other mathematical signs you like. What is the numerical value? How many different numerical values can you make?

13. How many different things do you think of connected with the number eight?

14. How many odd numbers are there smaller than 100, say, without the figure 3 occurring in them?

15. How many words can you find implying 'two' (e.g. duet, brace)?

16. How many different-sized groups can you make from 24 blocks (counters, shells, etc.)?

17. How many lines can you write of a tale like this:
'At home we have one (car?)
                    two (dogs?)
                    three (children?)
                    four (?)
                    five (?), etc.'
or 'I have one –
     I have two – , etc.'

The specific activities implied by the question 'How many?' carry in a fairly direct way the essence of mathematical investigation. The first psychological advantage of the question is the variety of answers that can be given. In particular the variety arises on two counts; the one where different or inadequate methods were used to deal with the problem, and the second where different assumptions were made as to the meaning of the problem.

For example, given a set of differently coloured rods, how many ways can rods be used to produce the same lengths? Recalling the discussions on p.52 and p.201 we can make decisions about the same length and then decisions about the same way.

Thus (a) it might be simply interpreted as aligning *single equivalent rods* until there were no more left in the box; or

(b) it might be interpreted that any rods of equivalent length or less can be used *in combination* to make the given length. Here decisions may be made as to the number of rods in such combinations.

(c) A further interpretation might be that the length can be produced as the *difference* between two rods in alignment.

(d) And so on. (Usually 'and so on' or 'etc.' means 'I can't think of any more', or 'I can't be bothered to think of any more'. Here, though, we have an open situation where an interpretation might well take a form which the teacher or child, whoever proposed the problem, had not thought of.)

In case (b) a question arises as to whether the same selection of rods placed in different orders is recognized as the same or different.

All this provides material for active group work and discussion, especially as freedom with imposed restrictions (self-imposed?) is felt by the child exploring. '*What if we allow this?*' rather than '*Are we allowed to do this?*' The importance of the different answers that are obtained is that the onus is thrown on the children to discuss the differences among themselves. The teacher is not looked on as the provider of the answer.

The second advantage of these situations is the lack of any need for any special techniques. This could be seen as a disadvantage, for it means that full rigorous solutions are hard to establish. But the simple direct approach which sets out (a) to exhaust all the possibilities, once the conditions are set, and (b) to ensure that there are no repetitions, is beginning to see the nub of the problem and the criteria that any later abstract treatment has to satisfy.

Let us look at another example. 'How many addition calculations will make 6?'

First, we have to decide what extra conditions we shall put. What kind of numbers may we use? How many may we add together? Note that as the question stands we are free to decide.

Suppose we decide to find all possible whole number additions with up to six numbers. Is this all right?

John produces:

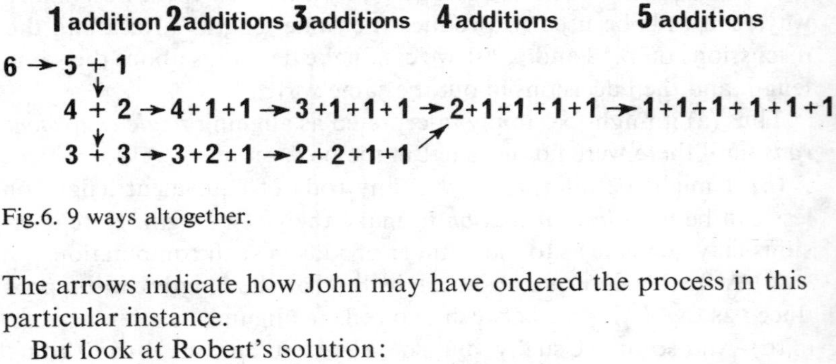

1 addition
2 additions
3 additions
4 additions
5 additions
6
5 + 1
4 + 2
4+1+1
3+1+1+1
2+1+1+1+1
1+1+1+1+1+1
3 + 3
3+2+1
2+2+1+1

Fig.6. 9 ways altogether.

The arrows indicate how John may have ordered the process in this particular instance.

But look at Robert's solution:

6
5+1
4+2
4+1+1
3+3
3+2+1
3+1+1+1
2+2+2
2+2+1+1
2+1+1+1+1
1+1+1+1+1+1

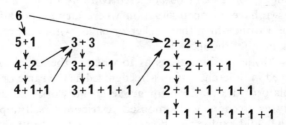

Fig.7

John has 9 answers and Robert has 10. The kind of steps taken by each to deal with the situation will be subject to criticism and argument – not necessarily conclusive. For instance, John may quickly see that Robert has $2+2+2$ and be satisfied that this makes the tenth solution. On the other hand he may not be satisfied and may argue for other methods. He will run into difficulties of avoiding repetition, especially as the particular routines given above are most unlikely to be picked on by juniors. Confusion and discussion about things like $2+3+1$ and $3+1+2$ happen, but the main point is that there are the conditions to satisfy and problems to resolve.

The third advantage is the finite nature of the situation. There is an attainable limit to most 'How many?' questions.

Fourthly, they are questions that just happen. The children themselves may pose such a question; it may force itself on to a group; the teacher may introduce it deliberately. It is a type of question that is always around. This leads to the fifth advantage that if it is always around, in many different situations, and children are free to explore them, then similarities between problems will be stumbled on, genuinely discovered; that is, discoveries will be made of relationships that the teacher was unaware of.

It has not been the custom to introduce this sort of problem early in mathematical work for, as was said above, complete solutions of the problems are sometimes difficult. This poses a dilemma. Should we only tackle mathematical situations to which we can see the end? Many will say that children like to finish a task; but isn't this a conclusion drawn from observing them in an atmosphere where they must finish the task in order to please the teacher?

'How many?' questions set a genuine research situation. The mathematician opening up new fields does not really know the full consequences of his work; nor is he absolutely certain that there are no fallacies in his arguments. The social interchange with other mathematicians which follows his published discoveries takes the process a stage further. Children can have this experience too. They can suggest and argue with each other; they can be satisfied as a group, until someone else joins in and upsets their conclusions. This someone else is not necessarily the teacher, who may or may not know whether they are 'right'.

But if they are 'wrong', they are not wrong because someone has misinformed them authoritatively; they are wrong because their activity has for the moment ceased. New stimuli will tend to re-create the situation and extend the activity they have felt to be important.

Half-an-inch square

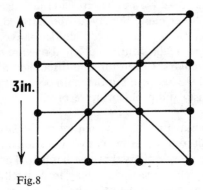

Fig.8

A figure was being investigated on the geoboard.
How many inch squares inside the three-inch square?
Nine.
How many inch squares inside half the three-inch square?
Three.
No. Four-and-a-half.
There aren't. There are only three inch squares; the others are bits. Yes, but they're half and there are three of them, so that makes one-and-a-half.
They *aren't* inch squares.

The whole class is now involved in various states of anger.
It takes a long time . . .

Decisions

We have spent some time talking about, and referring to, children's games; the ones they invent and discard, the formal ones they enter into, the ones where rules are implicit in their actions and the ones where the rules have to be explained. What is the mathematical significance, one may ask? We usually ask this question because we are thinking of mathematics as a body of knowledge, a set of interesting procedures enabling us to solve problems. We ask the question because we are not used to seeing as mathematical the acts of becoming aware of procedures, and further, the possibility that children will invent procedures which we have not thought of.

If we think of these things as mathematical, then we may see the significance of the game situation as we have described it. Work elsewhere (that of Dienes, for example) has, by emphasizing the first aspect of mathematical knowledge, deliberately invented games that the children might play which implicitly carry certain mathematical structures. We put another point of view. As in the first part of this chapter, we have tried to indicate how the basic linguistic problem of identification or classification ('sameness') has the structures that we wish to study in mathematics, so now we maintain that games, and the decisions that have to be taken, carry in them the seeds of developing mathematical awareness.

One of the great sadnesses that spreads over systematic education is the effect of the thought that children only learn what we teach them. We deny this and deny it vehemently. We deny it because we know that the activities freely indulged in by children are paramount in developing independence. Thoughts developed under duress, no matter how pleasant, tend to be ephemeral. The game situation carries within itself the core of the mathematical choice – to conform or to break away. The child of six playing draughts who suddenly decides to move backwards is not conforming. The child of ten who has mastered the combinations of moves and a certain ability to control abstractly the future situation in the game, is content to conform to the rules. This is right, for the freedom his insight gives him counterbalances the price of conformity.

Here we have a characteristic of mathematics and of education as a whole, and one which cannot be overemphasized. The balance between conforming and breaking away is something that cannot be allowed to correspond, as it usually does, to the activity in the classroom and the rush away from it afterwards. The child has to be given, in the classroom, the opportunity to break away and explore as well as the opportunity to conform. Given a confident classroom atmosphere he will do both. When faced with an open situation, a child is his own master; what course of action he takes is his own decision. He can make up his mind whether

  to follow the aspect of the situation that takes his fancy
  to do what he thinks the teacher wants him to do
  to do what his next door neighbour is doing
  to do what his next door neighbour wants him to do
  to dismiss the whole lot and do something else.

Whichever of these he chooses, the ensuing action takes control of the situation; the open situation has passed and a new state has been reached.

What a child does in these situations is dependent on the atmosphere which has developed between the teacher and a class, a group, or a particular child. Whether the child wastes time, works, or works hard, is also mainly dependent on this. The amount of work produced varies, but generally, when the child is personally involved in something of his own, the amount is large. Often the most productive command is, 'and you can present your work in any way you like'. This produces books, folders, leaflets, wall-charts, complete exercise books, models; the self-expression of the child is not restricted to the mathematics involved. The freedom to choose has consequences beyond our expectations.

The Figure 12.

The figure twelve is a funny little thing he often hops from place to place sometimes he is inches and other times he will be feet, sometimes you just don't know what he will do next. One day he said to me that he did not want to be feet and inches any more and he wanted to have a go at being little men.

Fig.1

After he had been little men he thought of his name which was 12. He said to himself well my name is even and if you double it it becomes 24 and if you half it it becomes 6.

Think of a number	=12
Double it	=24
Half it	=12
Half it again	=6 half of 12

Think of a number	=12
Double it	=24
Take away the number	=12
Half it	=6

The verses above are all about my name 12. On the table in my room there was twelve pennies so I thought if 12 inches were 1 ft and 12 ft are 4 yds why can't twelve pennies be 1/–. Then suddenly thought of something if my name was twelve there must be an eleven, ten, nine, eight, seven, six, five, four, three, two and one. So if I took:—

$$10+2=12$$
$$12-10=2$$
$$11+1=12$$
$$9+3=12$$

they would all include me and my friends. I wonder how many 12s of me would be in 366. 'Now let me think   30 r 6'
12)366

So me into 366 will go 30 times with six over. If you turn me round I will make 21 then I could say that 21 shillings make one guinea but I think I will stay as I am. Somebody wrote my name like this:—XII but I think that was Roman Numerals. Then one day I saw somebody write XXI but they were thinking of my friend 21. You know if there was twelve of me there would be 144.

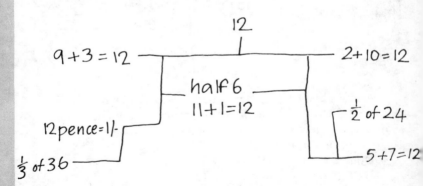

Just some things about me.

One day my friends and I played this game which was very easy it went like this my friend No 2 stood on the line first then came 4 and 6 in between each of them we placed a Mr.+. After six came the = and then came me 12.

$$2+4+6=12$$

Now you know enough about me 12 and I am a very intelligent 12 as you know.

even	$5+7=12$
double 24	$11+1=12$
turn round 21	$9+3=12$
Half it 6	$\frac{1}{2}$ of 24
Treble it 36	$\frac{1}{3}$ of 36
$2+10=12$	12 pence $=1/-$
12 inches $=1$ ft.	$3\times12=36$

Sets

It may have come as a surprise that little mention has been made of sets in the book. In one sense this is because it is being treated in other books. In another sense it is because the approach to sets by putting rings round pictures and talking about sets of objects is to come in at the wrong end. Of course there are sets of things. Of course it is a fundamental idea. But the notions that have led to this new topic were adult notions born of a hindsight into those mathematical activities that the creative mathematician wished to investigate.

It is not, you may say, the reasons for the inventions of the notion of sets that concern us, but that once having been invented the more simple aspects can be taught to children.

And so they can.

But we have endeavoured to paint a picture of children learning – we have emphasized that anything really understood must be understood by the child and that the ways of coming to this understanding are many and devious.

Yes, you can teach sets. You can set up a programme for it.

But let us look again. The really exciting thing about the more recent mathematical creations is not so much that they can be simplified for use in school, but that their own properties throw light on what children do. The adult's approach involves definitions; but if you are a child and you know what's in your set, you can talk about acting with, and operating on, all sorts of things long before someone introduces the magic word 'set'.

Ah! But the concept of 'set' allows you to talk more clearly about useful and defined things. You know what to act with. Yes, indeed, at a level when you are prepared to do so. No amount of interesting introductions to the concept of set will prevent the multitude of reactions described earlier to the questions about 'same'. '*Are these* the same?' 'No!' 'Have they the same angles?' 'Yes.' 'Are they the same?' 'Yes.' Exchanges of this kind are common and they reflect the uncertainties surrounding classification.

What seems to have been forgotten in the excitement of introducing a new idea is that the useful aspect of the notion at the elementary level rests on the concept of a *well-defined* set. That is, that its description is possible by listing or by a characterization in which there is no ambiguity. Our experience is that children, unaware of the value that such agreement to define will bring, delight at this stage of putting on the pressure to find differences or exceptions within same-nesses. This cannot, must not, be ignored. It is once more a question of conformity and non-conformity. The child acts like the mathe-matician who on hearing of a new theorem goes nosing round look-ing for loop-holes – looking for exceptional cases in an attempt, one may sometimes say, to show that he is rather clever. More charitably, though not more truthfully, we may decide that this is a characteristic of the search for truth. But the child who asks about his half-brother when teacher has decided to talk about brothers, is followed by others bringing in foster brothers and brothers-in-law. When the class has stopped discussing the implications of the set of people called 'broth-er', the original neat little set is a bit disturbed.

But sets are modern and useful. No they are not. There are two notions mixed up here. The sets that are part of our experience, and hence folk-language, are as old as, and indeed older than, our language. The sets that mathematicians have used to free themselves from the shackles of the classical style of argument – which have allowed the vigorous flowering of modern mathematics and applied mathematics – must be seen as the result of a growth from previous ideas. To take a simplified version and give it to children is to do damage both to the real freedom arising from a genuinely voluntary acceptance of the limitations involved in a strictly defined *set inclusion*, and also to the opportunity to use the growth of children's language as the starting-point for mathematics.

A game with a group of children:

'Put up your hands if you have a brother.'	10 hands
'Put up your hands if you have a sister.'	5 hands
'How many children are there?'	14
'Put up your hands if you have a brother . . . now if you have a sister . . . how many?'	

Some concern here: some wanted to put two hands up, some were suddenly concerned about more than one; but eventually the number of children with hands up was found to be 12.

A record on the board showed:

C		14
B		10
S		5

and the teacher put up   B   S   12

and then added 'or':   B or S   12.

(The atmosphere around this activity was not one of firm direction; the 'or' was tentative.)

    Some of the children reacted to this action and one said 'No! Don't put "or".' 'What is it then?' 'Well, it's "B or S or B and S".'

    Nothing was put there – the space was eventually left blank – but during the following discussion any reference to that number 12 was as 'Brothers or Sisters or Brothers and Sisters'. And this was consistently upheld.

There is a considerable point to be made from this story.

The children had never heard of sets before – they didn't hear during this session. The language they used for precision was their own: well-organized, efficient and relevant. The children who objected gave their attention to the suggestion by the teacher that he could use the word 'or' to link B and S, when the situation *they* saw was a number (12) made up from those with brothers only, those with sisters only and those with both brothers and sisters. If this is looked at in terms of those diagrams that everyone seems to think are essential (the children didn't suggest any diagrams), we can see the distinction being made:

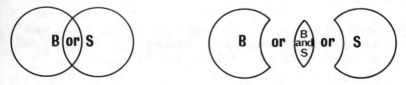

Fig.1

Once we recognize intellectually that the 'or' the teacher suggested is an inclusive 'or' and that normal language usually uses 'or' as a disjunction (exclusive 'or') then once more we have shown the danger of artificially introducing sets too early. Those children may eventually see their way to the value of the inclusive 'or' as a useful device, but for the present they reject it.

In case you are not sure about inclusive or exclusive 'or's:

'Did you go to the theatre or the cinema?' 'Yes!'

This is a perfectly correct answer if the 'or' is inclusive, though it gives one a little shock until one can think of a context in which the inclusive 'or' would be used naturally. Such a question and answer may well be part of a police questioning, where questions about several alternative activities are being presented on an inclusive basis. Usually the context and tone of voice tell the person being questioned whether the 'or' is inclusive or exclusive. But in set theory the 'or' is always inclusive – the more uncommon use in ordinary language.

There is a large and growing number of books which set out to explain the use of sets in the conventional sense, and the introductions are more or less interesting. But the interest lies only in stimulating the reader or child to understand a conventional, and highly efficient, specialist use of language. The chief danger in the deliberate teaching of sets as if it were an elementary aspect of a more complex mathematical structure, which the children will eventually grasp, is its narrowing effect. The traditional curriculum of the primary school with its undue emphasis on computation did not stop children from thinking and learning about things and their relationships, even if this was not deliberately called mathematics. The introduction of collections of objects, contents of mother's handbag, furniture in the room, etc., in order that the child shall be 'led' to think more clearly, is a threat to the child's imagination. He is *already* experiencing these things as collections. He is *already* operating with them. What is important is that he knows about a collection not by defining it and being able to describe it, but through some action or thought towards it. His recognition of the word 'chairs' is likely to be linked at first with the act of sitting, not by using a language to describe what is available for the act of sitting. The complex relation that must exist between all his range of experience of sitting and all the acts of talking about chairs is a necessary part of his development as a person. If this is narrowed down because he is compelled to talk about well-defined sets then great mischief could be wrought.

There are some publications which warn the teacher against using the word 'set' unless he is sure a situation warrants it. But suppose the child himself uses it. Does one stop him talking about his father's set of false teeth? Or his mother's tea-set? It is a folk-word and one must not demean the language by procuring it exclusively for a strictly defined mathematical usage too soon.

The challenge is wider; for a set is just a collection of elements and in one sense there is no restriction on how we can know about it. Good. But the theory of well-defined sets which leads to the development of a particular algebra, which is useful in coping with certain mathematical situations, is out of place as a direct teaching activity in the primary school. For the child to develop an awareness of 'knowing what we are talking about' is important. So the teacher should know about some of the language that the mathematician uses to distinguish his actions. But it shouldn't be forced on children – we don't know enough yet.

Variety

We have suggested that over-enthusiasm for *sets* should be curbed, pointing as we have done to the inevitable circumscription that can have a blinkering effect. We shall try to build a picture into which this useful but narrow concept of *set* can be put. What seems important to us is that, whatever we do, we should always guard against unnecessarily restricting thought by an over-rigorous use of language. Language should be free. The invention of printing has gone some way to limiting this freedom, even though there have been other benefits, and we should take care when dealing with children who are learning, that the offer of a wider scope of activity should not be accompanied by stereotyping. This danger is very real when we see books describing lists of things for children to discover. The jokes made about schools by the score busily timing toy trains are bitter, for then the stereotyping has already happened and what was once exciting and free has been trapped.

There are two things which we must be clear about. One is that children (and people as a whole!) get along by doing things – *operating*. Secondly, teaching and learning anything (not only mathematics) usually involves at some stage the necessity of talking about the operations. Unfortunately these distinct activities are often confused and we find that the *repeating of the words* is substituted for the *doing of the operations*. The example on p.304 of the child concerned with 'sitting' and 'chair' is a particular case of this.

Now, as we live we operate all the time, so that at every point in our lives we have things which we may want to communicate about.

We hence use any means we can to communicate. But there are many, many acts which we carry out without any wish to talk to anyone about them or to show them to anybody. It is a necessary understanding by the teacher that this rich, continuous and ever-present operational state of the child is the only source for the child's learning. We use the word 'only' here to indicate at once the totality of the operational state and also to avoid the confusion that arises when differently described ways of tapping this experience are promoted to being different sources of learning (for example, learning by rote, learning by discovery, learning by association).

There is a big difference between the commonly imagined random experiencing of children, which we as teachers then organize into productive channels, and the kind of picture we wish to portray here of an active, self-stabilizing, operating human being (a thinking human being, in other words!) who uses these properties to respond to the acts of the teacher and so develops through his own actions (see, for instance, the story of the child with the 'Lego' material on p.277).

Some of the examples that are given in different parts of the book reflect our concern for this point of view. It is a point of view which says, essentially, that nothing a child does is useless, and if the teacher expects progress in a particular direction it will always be, in the end, by the child's own wishes that the progress is made. These truisms are often resisted because they sound as if it is being suggested that children *left to themselves* will learn all that is necessary. This is not true and has never been suggested. We are talking about the actual mechanism. The most heavily-directed child takes action on his own – in some cases he has no option but to respond in the only way he has been allowed to experience – but even in this tight, formalized way it is still *his* way. There is always a spark of originality though all conspire to crush it.

We want to draw attention to ways in which *variety* is experienced; variety in language, in use of language, in the possibility of choices, in the ways of limiting thought, in the ways of extending thought. We want to encourage thinking about the child learning and not only about the teacher teaching. This means we must look at what actually happens.

A teacher reported something that took place in the classroom:

The children met with a need to add two two-figure numbers as a result of some work they were doing, so I wrote them on the board one

under the other: 25, and asked the children what the answer was. The
    32
majority wrote 57 and I asked how they got it. They said, 'We added
2 and 3 to get 5 and 5 and 2 to get 7'. Next I put on the board 25 and
                                                    38
asked the children to do this. After some thought several children
said 'It cannot be done!' When asked why they replied 'Because 5 and
8 make 13 and there is nowhere to put the 1'. I then showed them how
to add the units first and carry the one.

Was this in fact necessary? Does it matter whether we add the units
first? Or perhaps the children were oblivious of this tens and units
business – only being sure that there were adjacent columns of figures.
They may well have learnt something about the procedures and
learnt to operate in a limited way. Our difficulty as teachers is that
we find it hard to distinguish when they are operating in a fully
organized way or in one in which the associations between their
actions and what they know are limited. For instance, another
teacher reports:

I gave a small group of eight-year-old children 5 shillingsworth of
pennies and asked them to make a graph on the desk arranging
them in date order. The dates on the pennies ranged from 1851 to
1963. Although they were quite conversant with notation to thousands
they had the greatest difficulty in doing this. I tried various groups of
children; some groups never did manage it, others took a very long
time.

Some time later I used 5 shillingsworth of pennies and asked them to
arrange them in piles according to the King or Queen's head. This was
apparently easy, but a difficulty again arose when I asked them to
arrange the piles chronologically. Again they seemed to be unable to
use the dates as a guide.

Here was a situation to which they had not associated their knowledge of place value – whatever this was. This 'associated' learning
is often taken to be understanding, because the situations later to be
solved (problems presented, oral questions, practical exercises) are
usually themselves associated with the original situation. It is only
when a new question comes from an unexpected direction (a mere
change of units, a bicycle sold instead of a car, the speed of a train
instead of a man walking, is not necessarily radical enough) that the
learning will be fully examined. It may then be determined whether
or not the new situation is 'associated' with the old. The situation

with which learning may be 'associated' may be created in a number of ways. It may be a 'real' situation in the practical sense of the infant classroom; for example, the weighing of objects on scales. It may be created by structural apparatus or materials. It may be presented by language written, spoken or otherwise symbolic. It may be narrowed by the pattern of a particular method used. Any or all of these situations may be all that seems to happen at school.

Consider some of the limitations in the use of language. What often happens is that the language used confines potentially varied situations to the one that is familiar. For example, over-emphasis on the word 'share' so that it appears to cover division; the universal 'makes'; the repeated pattern of words when dealing with mechanical methods – 'goes into', 'turn upside down and multiply'. Neither is this readily solved by the strict employment of 'true' mathematical terms; for example, attempts to clear confusion in $\frac{1}{2} \div \frac{1}{4}$ ($\frac{1}{2}$ *divided by* $\frac{1}{4}$) by merely using earlier forms of words: 'count $\frac{1}{2}$ in $\frac{1}{4}$'s' or 'how many quarters in $\frac{1}{2}$?' Unfortunately this 'real' situation language is often neglected as soon as symbolic language is used. Perhaps this is where much of the trouble lies. Is the child really aware that the mathematical symbols stand for a variety of situations which can be expressed in a variety of ways; for example, '$+$' as 'put together', 'more', 'count on', 'add', 'plus', etc? Even the earliest experienced symbols – the numerals – are, not necessarily, seen at the outset as a shorthand (symbolic) way of writing what is *said*, but acquire a mystic quality instead.

These observations should give us serious cause to consider how far language should be made 'exact' or how far it should be deliberately developed as a flexible, changeable instrument. Similarly with the notational situations; the teacher in the first example attempting to guide the children to 'carry' sees only the technique. We must know that the children have become aware that the second column has a greater power than the first. The 25 is a matrix representation of $(2 \times 10) + 5$. Going back to the sum 25, what other things can we

do with it? If we write it as

$$
\begin{array}{r}
38 \\
20 \\
5 \\
30 \\
8 \\
\hline
\end{array}
$$

we can start adding at the bottom and

go upwards. The above pattern is $8 + 30 + 5 + 20$. There are several arrangements:

20	20	30	8	5
5	30	20	5	8
30	5	8	30	20
8	8	5	20	30

and others.

| (a) | (b) | (c) | (d) | (e) |

All of these give the same answer, yet, if we start at the bottom and add upwards (b) and (c) may imply adding the units first and (d) and (e) may imply adding the tens first. What way do you do it in your head? Is this the same way you would use if you did it with pencil and paper? A child faced with this problem without instruction in a definite method could use any of these ways of addition, all quite correct. A possible way of setting out if adding the tens first is:

```
25
38
—
50
13
—
63
```

but there are many other ways that children will use if they have the freedom to do so.

Does this freedom exist in all calculations, and if not, what does it depend on? We can use these different ways because addition is (a) *commutative*, that is, if we have $3+4$ the number produced is 7, and if we take a different order, $4+3$, we still get 7; and (b) *associative*, that is, $3+(4+5)=(3+4)+5$. (With two additions it is irrelevant to the final answer which is done first – they can't be done simultaneously. The brackets mean 'do this operation first'.) Both of these facts the children learn in the early days of work with numbers, but see p.321 for a discussion of this work. This means that given some numbers to add we can do so in any order. The same is true of multiplication, but it is not true of subtraction and division:

$$3-4\neq4-3$$
$$(10-6)-3\neq10-(6-3)$$
$$10\div5\neq5\div10$$
$$(48\div8)\div2\neq48\div(8\div2).$$

We feel that it is very important for children to realize that they have some freedom in the use of operations. The investigation through action of what this freedom is, for instance that certain operations may be done in any order, is an essential prerequisite if later confusions are to be avoided as number systems are developed. Another example: 25 is not the same as 52 and perhaps children should have 38 83

$$\frac{25}{38} \qquad \frac{52}{83}$$

the chance of experimenting to see why not!

The experimenting and exploration is like a jigsaw – a jigsaw that never ends. Just as we build up a 'real' puzzle by completing a small bit of the border here, a little of the house in the picture there, a little more border or a chimney and eventually, finding that all the portions we have seen as small separate entities fit into place, yielding a satisfying picture, so, it seems, does our awareness of mathematics develop.

We learn that 2, 3, 4 are numbers. We soon find that 23, 34 are numbers too and that now the 2, 3 and 4 are digits too. Soon we find that we need numbers like $\frac{2}{3}$, $\frac{3}{4}$ which happened first as fractions. We find that 23 and 34 are decimal numbers and that numbers can be operators as well. We meet rationals, irrationals, complex, and imaginary numbers. We find that we can 'do without' the numbers and make generalizations, allowing letters (or other symbols) to act for numbers.

Thus as we progress we use terms that we met first, perhaps, in a homely untechnical sense, in a limited specific sense, and then with wider and wider possibilities – from which we learn to choose the meaning appropriate to the task in hand. What is more, this vocabulary is always growing and developing as mathematics itself develops, so we must be ready to allow our thinking to grow with it: mathematics is dynamic, not static, and the language must be flexible. On similar lines must the whole of our mathematical thinking grow too. We start with a few small 'pieces' only, perhaps some feeling for sameness or difference, from which we learn to classify, appreciate number, shape, pattern and relationships and from which we abstract and generalize and make structures. We use our previous abstractions, generalizations and structurings as the elements of the next phase of growth. Now we get a new idea of the pieces of our puzzle: some will now be seen to fit together but others for the time being still appear not to 'fit in'. These may be just the points from which our next growth will spring, or they may have to await some further development before they seem to 'belong'.

So gradually our 'picture' appears, but unlike the concrete jigsaw puzzle from which the analogy started, our jigsaw of mathematics is never completed! As long as there are men and women of creative imagination, so long can the mathematical picture develop. We may be able to offer situations and material from which we think our pupils will extract certain ideas, and which we think will help their previous experience to 'fit in', but we cannot predict precisely what they will think or in what directions their creative imagination may lead. May they not perhaps devise sets of rules quite different from those by which we are at present playing? And is it not in this unimaginable picture of mathematics that the pieces of the jigsaw may one day have to take their place or be rejected? It is not *we* who must 'make sense' of our pupils' mathematics, but they.

Turning round

'I don't like the way the furniture is in this room', says Mummy, 'I'm going to move it round.' What she means is that she is going to change the positions of some of the pieces of furniture, which may in fact involve very little or no circular motion. 'Go round to the shop and get two pounds of sugar', says Mummy on another occasion. This usually means that the shop in question is not in a direct line from the home, and may involve one or more turns of 90°. One child was asked to go round to the shop by her mother, and this involved a journey like this:

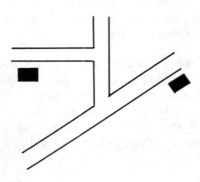

Fig.2

At meal times the children and their parents sit round the table, although the table is most commonly rectangular. In the evening they sit round the fire or the television set. 'Come and play round my house', says one child to another. 'Stop running round!' says Mummy, although the child may in fact have been running up and down.

A plate is round, so is an orange; a penny is round, so is a ball; a wheel is round, so is a balloon. Thus, long before the child reaches school, the experience of the word 'round' is full of a wide variety of meanings. Admittedly a lot of the confusion has arisen from the use of the word 'round', when what is meant is 'around', but at school the process is continued and even intensified. A teacher may laboriously explain to a child the difference between round and around, yet the first time she sees a child whose attention has wandered, she will say, 'Turn round and get on with your work.' A number of children may be detailed to take round the milk, someone else may be asked to take a message round to the other classes. A child painting a pattern may be advised to put a certain colour round the edge, although this may be any shape. Rectangular sheets of paper are given out to the children; some have them one way, some another, so some of the children are told to turn theirs round. The very last thing that teacher wants is that they should turn their paper right round, so under these circumstances the child soon learns by bitter experience that turning round means moving through 90° if it is a piece of paper, but when it is applied to himself, it may mean anything up to 360°. He may have been asked to draw round a triangle, a square, a hexagon, or even a horse. Many more things are round—a milk bottle, a globe, a clock face, a pencil. The head teacher comes round, so does the caretaker. If the child is absent from school, the attendance officer comes round, and a child who has fainted comes round.

Occasionally teacher might even say, 'You're making my head go round with all that noise!' The first time he hears this, Charlie is all attention to witness this new marvel, but when he sees that teacher's head is quite static and not gyrating like a top, he adds this statement to his already overflowing collection of adult idiosyncrasies and goes back to the far more satisfying business of hitting Jane round the head.

Conservation

Nigel (7) was playing with water in the water-tray. He had a pint milk bottle and a quart measure, and when asked which would hold the most water replied, 'This one, it's bigger,' pointing to the pint bottle. When he poured water from one to the other and found that the less tall measure held more water, Nigel was immediately intrigued and quietly continued pouring water carefully from one receptacle to the other.

The world in which the child operates is not the same one that the adult sees. Even the implied complexity that a child using the word 'round' must be involved in, does not necessarily align him with adult conceptualization. One of the most useful concepts that we use to control our world is that of *conservation*. It becomes so much part of our thinking that it is hard to believe when children's actions demonstrate the lack of this concept. Piaget has produced situations which show the young child unaware of the conservation notion.

Much that has been written in this country about his work gives undue stress to this particular concept. It is often assumed that conservation is a kind of natural necessary concept that must be acquired. This is a dangerous assumption. Conservation is an intellectual concept of an extremely useful kind but there are many situations in which we have to operate where the concept does not help.

It seems laughable that a young child should think the number of counters in a row changes as we re-arrange the row, but what is his normal experience? When he goes away for a minute big brother takes one of his toy cars to play with – 'Brian can't count yet. He won't know!' – or Daddy walks past his pieces of chocolate on the table and eats one absentmindedly. *Is* there conservation of substances with time for Brian?

Many adults mis-answer the question 'Are there more brown beads or more wooden beads' when presented with a handful of brown and white wooden beads. When the question is concerned with pictures of birds and other animals, how many adults appreciate that birds are members of the animal kingdom with sufficient certainty to see birds as a sub-class on the spur of the moment? 'Where did David leave his tadpoles?' If Mother let him take them up to the warm playroom, they will not be forgotten, but if he had to leave them in the garden it is not surprising if there is no water left in the jar when David goes to it again. Is there, for him, conservation of substance with time?

Today Josie can reach the shelf that she just couldn't reach not so long ago. Why should the width of the cupboard be the same as it was a week ago if the height has 'changed'? A six-year-old was measuring the playground with the help of a visitor to the school.

When the visitor returned a week later he ran up with great excitement – 'Miss, Miss! we measured it again, and it was the same!'

Stephen, aged 10, measured the shelf from left to right, 'Does it
measure 2 ft. 4 in. the other way too?' he was asked. 'I don't know',
said Stephen, and thought hard. 'Oh, I'll measure it', he said. 'Yes,
it does', he said, after measuring carefully from right to left. He then
went on to measure a few more things 'both ways to be sure'.

The Infant Lower Junior class of a village school had made a scale
of their heights by standing against the wall thus

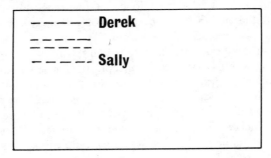

Fig.3

They then laid the sheet on the floor. One after the other Sally and
Derek lay down. They drew round Sally and coloured her picture in,
and drew round Derek's head as it appeared above her (they were
very careful to have his feet at the bottom of the sheet!) and coloured
his face and hair. They stood back to admire their work. 'Sally's not
that tall' they said. Picking the sheet up to measure was no good;
Sally had to lie down again to check and then stand up beside it too.
The concept of conservation of length with change of position is *not*
obvious. After all, when you hold the window pole up it won't go
through the doorway, but when you tilt it, it will.

One of Piaget's questions is about two 'fields' of equal size and
shape with a cow in each, and he 'builds' houses in them, the houses
being detached in one and terraced in the other. After a number of
houses have been 'built' the children are misled by the appearance
and think there is more grass left for the cow in the field with the
terraced houses, even though the same number have been 'built',
detached, in the other field. But Joyce said, 'Of course there's less
grass for the cow, because these (the detached) would have bigger
gardens!'

This kind of observation should pull us up sharply when we too easily refer to 'a daily period of twenty minutes of planned experience'. This suggestion is made when a child has not acquired an appropriate concept. The great danger in using the findings of Piaget is that deliberate steps will be taken so that the child's experience becomes distorted. We have the threat – and indeed they exist already – of formal 'discovery methods'.

An intriguing example of the relationship between intuition and intellect is the problem of finding the area of an irregular flat shape. One will find many reports of young children finding the areas of leaves, making guesses and hypotheses about which is bigger. They may well use discrete bricks or tiles to cover the leaves and find the area. There are other activities too, like taking a closed loop of string, say 3 ft. long, and pulling it into different shaped rectangles, calculating the area, drawing graphs of the results, etc. Again areas can be made with a given number of square tiles and the perimeter investigated, with many different shapes. There is a great variety of situations linked with the relation between area and perimeter.

But after all this, we must look keenly at the other situations that may be created. The conjecture that equal perimeters enclose equal areas is a strong one. If we are to generate a realistic mathematical attitude, we must allow the children to develop critical powers. These are not developed by avoiding questions. If we make a conjecture like the one above, then it cannot be sustained if there is one example where it is not true. But with a strongly satisfying conjecture people tend merely to adjust and say, well, it's true for all except that kind of case. For instance, what does pulling a fixed string loop into distinct rectangles tell us about distorting a fixed string loop?

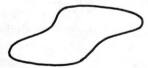 

In other words, there are many shapes which *appear* to have the same area and there is no reason to suppose that the conjecture is not true – indeed able thirteen-year-old children have been known to reject the 'counting squares' method for a 'string round the perimeter'.

Conservation as a 'concept' is to do with intellectual acts and convictions, not only with intuitions and special cases.

Calculations

What follows is the beginning of an attempt to look much more closely at what we actually do when we calculate and use words as instructions for what to do with numbers. It is an attempt to show the relation between the reality of language and action and the developing structure of mathematical properties.

Let us look at addition. This is something that unfortunately we find only too easy. It seems to be so susceptible to ease of handling, of giving rules, of giving simple operational instructions on how to check, that by the time we have finished and all the children in the class can in fact get their sums [sic] right, we are satisfied that they understand about addition.

But let us look closer.

When do we first know that we can add? And when we use the word 'add', are we necessarily meaning abstract numbers? The word 'add' is used in a large variety of situations which are not modelled by the natural number system; for example, in a recipe for making a cake, the force of an extra argument on the total debate, additional power for an engine, 'the people came from the city and added to the number of refugees'.

Adding is an activity involving things, sometimes countable, sometimes not. Even if the things are countable it does not necessarily follow that the adding is going to conserve numerical relationships. The operation may occur in a way which is not in accord with conserving the counting that preceded it: for example, adding piles of sand to a big pile. 'There are half-a-dozen piles there and another three round the corner; just stick it all in the yard with the rest, will you!' To look at this and say, 'Well! There are nine altogether', is to take an unimportant property and to misconstrue the situation deliberately.

Money is particularly interesting, for a given sum, say 6 shillings, can turn up in a variety of ways. The ways of splitting it up are not simply the partitions of 72 – they are governed in a quite different way by the coins available to make 6 shillings. Notice the difference between asking, 'What is the change for 2s. 6d. out of 6s.?' and *asking for change* for 2s. 6d. out of 6s. We can always work out an answer to the former but we cannot always give the change. So that, for example, the sum of three florins is different from a florin, two shilling-pieces and four sixpenny-pieces for the purpose of giving change.

Examples can proliferate, it being of particular interest to observe those uses of 'add' which are nearest to the numerically conserving use. A man travels 2 miles and then a further 3 miles; 'How far is he from his starting point?' Again we can see a different meaning for this as against, 'How far has he travelled?'

We use the word 'folk' to refer to words or phrases that are used in everyday life. In this sense 'add' is a folk word and implies an action. The character of the action varies considerably with the situation and, although we have specialized the use of the word in mathematical work, it is still used in its folk way in other circumstances. We should like to show some connection.

When a child is introduced to the specialized notion of adding associated with numbers, it is likely that he brings to this situation a variety of experiences of adding, including adding numbers of things. Most of these experiences he will not have described or attempted to verbalize at all. In the case of numbers he may well have experienced doubt when he noticed that he did not get one of the extra sweets that had been handed out, and we know from Piaget's work that his precise knowledge is tenuous.

He is told, 'You have 3 apples and I give you one more'; then asked, 'How many will you have?' He may already have realized that this is a special game in which he is not allowed to do anything except imagine that he holds three apples and receives one more. This is a different situation from the one where he had three beads on the table in front of him and he took another from the box and placed it with the others, then counted 'four'. In both situations he is faced with something given, in the former asked to imagine something else added, and in the latter actually carrying out an adding action.

Consider now a different situation in which he is playing with a pile of bricks. From the pile he takes a handful and builds a wall. His actions are of adding bricks to the wall. It is very unlikely that he starts with one brick and then adds three bricks (at once) to it. But in the case of the hypothetical apples or the beads he could quite easily have been in the position of increasing a single one by three to four. The boy may be asked how many he would have if, possessing one apple, he was given three. He may answer 'four' immediately or he may act quite differently and add (on) one at a time. He is unlikely to think, 'If I give my apple to the teacher, he will have four and then he can give them all to me.'

Is it trivial to consider the different instructions:
'*Add three to five*',
Add three and five',
'*Three add five*',
'*Add on five to three*'?

These almost certainly suggest different practical situations, and although we may use the cardinal number property '3+5=8' as a check in each case, we see that, for example, the *commutativity of addition* of numbers is not necessarily a true model of the world we diligently use to demonstrate number properties. It also appears that the concrete situations in which children find themselves, and which teachers prepare for them, have attributes which may be as important – sometimes more so – than the cardinal number properties that are so assiduously sought.

Within a formal mathematical system we study sets of elements of one kind or another. Sometimes we have strict definitions of these sets and at other times the definitions are not so severe. The sets are related to each other and it may be the case that one set of elements is a generalization from another. Contained in the definition of these sets, either explicitly at the formal level, or implicitly at a less formal level, are the things that they do, and also what can be done to them. For instance, when we refer to the set of natural numbers, this is a formal construction for which we have formal actions implying a description of the relations within the set. Thus Goodstein [49] on this basis can refer, in his informal description of the natural numbers, to addition of numbers as 'the uniting of two collections'. This can be identified by the symbolic representation '6+5=11'. We can be sure of the truth of the relation through the *act* of counting before and after the *act* of uniting.

But we made the suggestion previously that when children add they are 'adding *to*' in a very practical sense; and we can certainly detect a variety of practical situations where the 'something already there', with 'something else' that is to be 'added to' it, is more important that the cardinal number property which is formally described in the uniting of two collections.

We should be clear about the distinction that is being made. Every situation which we know as 'adding' in the numerical sense *can eventually be described and thought of* in the formal sense of uniting or combining two collections, independently of the order of combining. And from this we can move into the abstract set of natural numbers, with the action of addition as a *composition relation* between elements. That is, when one is aware that for *any* two elements a unique third can be chosen which is the *sum*, we can use the term 'composition relation'. (It is strange that the word 'operation' is often used to describe this relation, as it seems clear that an operation implies the existence of an operator and an operand. However, we shall discuss this later.)

Let us take an example from a slightly different point of view. If a young child is aware of a set of elements and they turn out to be some part of the 'intuitively-arrived-at' natural numbers (as opposed to the formally defined set of natural numbers of which he is as yet unaware), and he attempts to 'double' some of them, what can he say?

It is not certain that the double, if it can be made, is immediately going to be recognized by the thinker as a natural number in the sense in which this is understood by him at that moment. This will depend on:

(a) whether he can perform the doubling action with, say, counters (if he cannot, the double does not yet exist in his universe);

(b) whether, having performed the action, he has accidentally extended his set. (*This is a more subtle situation depending on the mechanism of doubling that is being used. For instance, if Cuisenaire rods are being used, then there is a sense in which doubling a dark-green rod produces a new length and a decision has to be made:*
(i) *I can't; because there is no single rod to which it is equivalent;*
(ii) *I can; because I have a new length and it must have a name*);

(c) whether the double is already clearly identifiable in the set he knows.

We have deliberately chosen the less well-defined area of the growing thinker rather than the apparently organized natural numbers of the adult. In the latter case the act of doubling is seen as a thing *to do to* the numbers. If the thinker has a mechanism for constructing all the natural numbers, or at least as many as he is likely to think of, then we can see the doubling act as an *operation* which it is possible to perform on the elements. (It may be linked with an already understood *relation* in the set itself, where 2 can be associated with every number to produce a unique third element known as the product; or it may be linked with the operation of adding *to* the number the same number again.)

Whatever the action taken to find the consequence of this operation (*that is, doubling*), *it remains an operation performed on a* single *element of a set. We shall call it a* unary *operation.*

A game has elements (counters) and moves. The move is something that can be thought about and carried out. In playing draughts, halma and all board games, there is an early development stage in the composition of moves. This develops by such thoughts as, 'If I do that, then he will do that or that, and I can then do this or this.' This is complex, but it is probably in such informal and often only half-thought actions that a consciousness of the consequence of the composed operation occurs. It is the consciousness we are concerned with, for all our lives are filled with unschematized operational activities and their compositions. 'I shall go home' is a single statement of an intention to carry out a single operation. The fact that we know, and we might have said, 'I shall go outside. I shall catch a No.21 bus. I shall walk up the hill to my home', is irrelevant. The accepted composition of such operations through acting them out, rather than schematizing them, is probably a feature we can use to divide activities in general into non-mathematical and mathematical kinds. (We are making this suggestion as a social observation, for it is clear by implication that at any given stage any such identifiable operations *may* be linked into a schema and earn the adjective 'mathematical'.)

We can look at an intuitive situation or act in it – calling it free play, messing about, doodling, investigating, exploring – and we can schematize by choosing the operation and the elements whose actions and consequences we will particularly study.

Unary operations

In most writings on early work the unavoidable clash between understanding and memorizing is rarely resolved. Mostly this is left to hope, with lots of good wishes and concern for general welfare. 'It is important to know and understand the 81 addition number facts . . .'

Apart from the worth of the aim stated in this way, the mere statement of such an exhortation goes nowhere in helping teachers, who may well agree with the sentiment expressed, but who do not see a clear path through the many suggestions that are made. It is not sufficient merely to say that experience of a particular numerical operation (in the conventional sense) must be as varied as possible and that it should be seen in many different circumstances. Merely to quote a so-called Principle of Variability does not help, especially when one must also quote a Principle of Manifest Difference. (This latter indicates that within a variety of different examples of an event there must inevitably be different attributes which allow children to make distinctions and develop an ability to classify, compare and contrast properties of sets of events. This can enhance their understanding of the non-uniformity of the use of operations. See our discussion earlier about 'same'.)

It appears that the unary operational notion can be of assistance in clearing up some difficulties which inevitably arise if it is believed that there is a separation between understanding and learning.
Let us look at some appropriate unary operations:

'*add four to*'
'*take away five*'
'*three of*' or simply '*three*'
'*one quarter of*'
'*share between five*'
'*multiply by six*'

From the appearance of these examples we see a considerable development from those folk-operations which are performed rather than thought about; thinking, though, can be seen as an extension of action, and in this sense the composition of such operations has taken place.

Thus to be aware that an order 'add four to' can be given, carries with it implicitly the composition of 'add one to' and 'add one to' and 'add one to' and 'add one to'. Conversely, it also means that the order 'add four to' carries the implication that, in doing the task, the person can 'add one to' and 'add one to' and 'add one to' and 'add one to'. It is in this way, and this way only, that an awareness develops that the 'four' in the operation has the same characteristic of cardinality as the elements of the set on which the operation can act.

Clearly the general unary operation of 'adding to' is going to change its characteristics according to the various classifications of the sets on which it acts. Thus we can see that the bringing of 3 pebbles to add to a collection of 4 pebbles, on the order 'add 3 to', may allow the development of an appreciation of the cardinal properties of collections of pebbles under the composition relation of addition. But the 'add 3 to' in the sense of bringing £3 to £4 of hard-earned savings at a few shillings per week, may carry attributes to which the cardinal property is irrelevant. Further, 3 stones weight added to a man's load of 4 stones weight has properties to which general cardinal properties have little relevance.

So, although it will be seen in the examples that we have already developed unary operations so that they contain variables, it is important to recognize, and it cannot be over-emphasized, that the elements arising within these unary operational structures do not in the first place belong to the same set as the elements on which they are operating.

If we now look at such operations with more complex materials, we can begin to see a pattern emerge that will be seen throughout mathematical activities. Let us look at a pile of Cuisenaire rods. There are many primitive, non-schematic (in the technical sense in which this has been used) operations which we shall carry out, such as 'taking a handful' and 'pushing them around'. In particular, we can see 'putting rods end-to-end' and 'putting rods side-by-side'. Compositions of these operations are unary in the sense that they are *external* to the set of rods and operate variously on subsets of the heap of rods. (Note, that when we operate to put two rods together this will eventually be seen as a composition relation between two rods within the set producing a length which may or may not be in the set.) Amongst the operations in free play will be 'filling a gap with', 'standing upright', 'placing cornerwise to' and so on. These operations always exist for anyone playing with the rods. Our concern is with the development of a schematization for *some* of these operations into a system which we feel, socially, to be valuable. There is no reason why a child should not develop schematizations of his own based on operations of his choice, but here is not the place to discuss the relationships between these two activities. It is only necessary to say that freedom to do both must exist.

In the discussions that develop through similar acts to those described with the pebbles, it can be seen that cardinal numbers will be used in operations of the kind, 'three of the', applied to reds of different lengths or colours. The cardinality will have been established by counting operations (that is, a recitation of sounds accompanying one of the many possible unary operations, or the bodily action of pointing to each in turn). The issue here is that we shall have interesting situations arising, say when 'three of the reds' and 'three of the greens' occur. '*Can anything be said about this all at once?*' If such a phrase as 'three of the reds and greens', or 'three of the yellows' arrives, it is a matter for exploration. The operational ingredients, however, will be there:

Fig.4

Different operations may show:

Fig.5

Or we can simply make a collection of pairs of red and green; or take a red and green, replace by a yellow, and then take two more yellows.

The consequence of exploring, for example, 'three of the reds' and 'four of the greens', or 'two of the reds' and 'four of the reds' after this, will show a variety of responses, and it is important to recognize that the investigation has three elements:

(a) the relationships of the rods themselves;

(b) the external operations,

  (i) using unary operations involving actions,

  (ii) involving the special case of the set of cardinals;

(c) the development of the *internal* properties of the intuitive natural number system.

At this stage we may list some unary operations and alongside them the corresponding composition relations in the set of natural numbers.

Unary operation	*Composition relations*
'add to'	'sum'
'take from'	'difference'
'of'	{ 'product' 'quotient'

It is important to note that, although the 'sum' and 'product' are *closed* in the set of natural numbers – that is, for any two elements there exists a unique element which is the sum and a unique element which is the product, in the case of 'difference' and 'quotient' this is not so.

The connection between 'add to' and 'sum' has been discussed but, because the notion of the sum of two numbers as an internal *relation in the set of natural numbers has developed, we should not assume that the anticipatory unary operation is now no longer used. In order to find the sum of two numbers it is often necessary to use the unary operation in one of its many executive forms. Often the command will be, for example, 'add 5 and 6 together'. This may be answered by already knowing the result; or by using a constructed algorithm (for example, numbers placed in vertical array and careful attention paid to order of operation); or by putting one number on a machine and using the unary operations of turning handles and knobs to 'add to it'; or by reducing to simpler operations.*

'Of means multiply' is a false rule, for it is the very reverse that is the case. The notion of multiplication arises analogously to the development of the cardinal numbers as operation elements in some of the unary operations on the rods. That is, if 'add three to' is repeatedly applied then the 'of' operation is developed and we note that we, for example, 'add four of the threes to'. Usually the repeating of addition is not met until the operational language has taken on the form 'add 5 and 6 together' (see above) which satisfies the internal composition relation. So, instead of developing the repeated 'addition to', as one is able to do with Cuisenaire rods or in other structural situations, it is dealt with as repeated 'addition together'. This can give a false impression as the following two calculations show:

Repeated addition together	*Repeated subtraction from 35*
7	35
7	7
7	—
7	28
7	7
—	—
35	21
—	7
	—
	14
	7
	—
	7
	7
	—
	0
	—

It would appear rather different if the first preposition were 'to' and we had:

Repeated addition to 0	Repeated subtraction from 35
0	35
7	7
—	—
7	28
7	7
—	—
14	21
7	7
—	—
21	14
7	7
—	—
28	7
7	7
—	—
35	0
—	—

But whatever the means of developing this new operation, in its first form it is '5 of 7' and any practical example that may be chosen to illustrate it has this characteristic. Note that the phrase '5 times 7' is quite adequate, though archaic, and more appropriate than some other phrases since the '5' precedes '7' in the way that it does in '5 of 7'. '5 of' or '5 times' is certainly in this sense a unary operation, and once more we have a set of *external* operational elements acting on a set of natural numbers. The system is growing in richness as this new multiplier operates on numbers which have some fully organized internal relations (that is, sums and differences).

At this stage further investigation of what is already a complex system will lead to further structuring. We may start from

(a), (b), (c), (d), (e), (f), ... (elements of our original set)

and a, β, γ, δ, ...   (operational elements).

Then we develop various relationships:

$(a) + (b) = (c)$ $(a) - (b) = (d)$

a of $(a) = (e)$

a of $[(b) + (c)] = [(a$ of $(b)) + (a$ of $(c))]$.

a of $[(b) - (c)] = [(a$ of $(b)) - (a$ of $(c))]$.

And (*discovery!*) $[(a$ of $(b)) + (\beta$ of $(b))] = [\{a + \beta\}$ of $(b)]$.

A new *relation* appears in $\{\alpha+\beta\}$ and from this development comes the identification of the properties of the set of the operational elements with some of the properties of the original set.

Explore [α *of* (β *of* (a))].

As the properties of $\{\alpha, \beta, \gamma, \delta, \ldots\}$ become those of $\{a, b, c, d, \ldots\}$, so the possibility of a composition relation of multiplication develops. But when it does it still has to be *computed* by using the external operation.

It was said that 'of means multiply' was wrong and we have shown that the 'of' operation is fundamental. It is important to see that the practical applications often have limited properties: for instance, 4 of 2 oz. In this case '2' belongs to a set where we have sums, differences, and a zero. '4' on the other hand belongs to a set which has sums, differences, zero, unity and composition by 'of' amongst other properties. It is certainly clear that the straightforward view that 4 of 2 oz. and 2 of 4 oz. are the 'same' is not necessarily valid.

This double structure is basic to mathematics. It allows for the development of the study of mathematics by attention to the sets and the relations in sets that are created. At the same time, the operations which originally gave rise to the sets being formally constructed, permit the development of the techniques through which mathematics acts as a structural tool.

Extending the set of numbers

It may have been hard to follow some of the discussion in the last section. This is largely because adequate language for the ideas expressed has not been fully worked out. There *is* a simplified picture of how our knowledge of number is extended but this is really hindsight – being wise after the event. Often in telling stories in mathematical history we fall prey to the innocent distortion caused by using the operations available to us which were not available at the time about which we are attempting to speak. So it is with children. At the risk of falling into this trap – although once we have said that there is one, the reader may well look around more warily himself – a brief outline is offered of how ideas of number are extended. This is independent of the more practical, though more complicated, operational concepts of the last section as it assumes that there is a fully internal operation.

For example, in the set of counting numbers, addition is always possible and an addition table can be built up. *Any* two numbers will give rise to a third. But if we think of differencing and try to make a table there will be gaps, as we clearly cannot select *any* two numbers in the ordinary counting sense. Once we say, 'But surely we can have negative numbers', then we are using hindsight. Children, when faced with tables like:

Sum: $a+b$

+	1	2	3	4	5
1	2	3	4	5	6
2	3	4	5	6	7
3	4	5	6	.	.
4	5	6	.	.	.
5	6	7	.	.	.

Difference: $a-b$

−	1	2	3	4	5	6
1						
2	1					
3	2	1				
4	3	2	1			
5	4	3	2	1		
6	5	4	3	2	1	

will fill in the left hand one and will have strange discussions about noughts and nothing when the empty spaces are considered in the right-hand table. ('Nothing' goes at $2-5$! 'Nought' at $3-3$!) These tables are interesting areas of exploration and the matter gets even more difficult as we look at other operations. As more operations are defined, so the number properties of things and the things we call numbers go on getting more complicated.

The general outline of the story is something like this:

(1) We start with a particular set of numbers.

(2) In this set of numbers we define an operation.

(3) The set of numbers is *closed* for this operation (that is, we can perform our operation on any pair of our numbers and get an answer within the set of numbers. (It is an internal operation.)

(4) We become interested in the possibility of 'undoing' our operation – that is, we define the inverse operation (we have the answer and one of the pair that made it – what is the other?).

(5) This new operation tends not to work throughout the whole set; in other words, our original set is not closed for this new operation.

(6) Certain sums involving the inverse operation are therefore 'impossible'; we can make them possible by inventing some more numbers, so . . .

(7) We invent new numbers, we *extend* the set in order to close it for this operation.

(8) So that we do not lose what we already have, we make our new set of numbers contain the old set (or *embed* the old set in the new set).

(9) In our new set we have, perhaps, another operation and closure.

(10) We become interested in the possibility of 'undoing' this operation, but, alas . . .

Examples

1. In the set of counting numbers, addition is always possible. But subtraction is not: 'seven from three we cannot'. Negative whole numbers (and zero) are needed to 'close the set for subtraction'. So we obtain the set of *integers*. We identify our old counting numbers with the positive integers.

2. In the set of counting numbers, multiplication is always possible. But division is not: 'seven into three won't go'. Fractions (or unsigned rational numbers) are needed to close the set (except that we exclude division by zero anyway). So we obtain the unsigned rational numbers. We identify our old counting numbers with the rationals which have unit denominators. (*Note:* there is a distinction between fractions and unsigned rationals which is not gone into here.)

Schematically, the development of the number system proceeds as follows:

$$N \underset{F}{\overset{I}{\rightleftarrows}} Q \rightarrow R \rightarrow C$$

(*N:* set of natural numbers; *I:* integers; *F:* fractions; *Q:* rationals (signed); *R:* real numbers; *C:* complex numbers).

E. Begle [15] *points out that the advantages of extending the set of numbers involves certain losses as well:*

'*For example, in proceeding from* I *to* Q *one gains the advantage of being able to solve equations of the form* ax=b. *At the same time one loses the advantages of being able to decompose a number into prime factors. In proceeding from* Q *to* R *one gains the advantage of being able to extract square roots of non-negative numbers but one loses countability. In proceeding from* R *to* C *one gains the advantage of being able to solve quadratic equations but one loses the advantage of linear order.*'

At primary school level, problems of the relations between counting numbers, measuring numbers, directed numbers, fractions and rational numbers abound, and the discussion in the previous section opens up some issues that may well help, but which will have to be discussed in detail elsewhere.

Arrows for operators

Finally in this section on operations, which we see as a growing point for a great deal of work and thought in the classroom, we look briefly at a practical issue which has been introduced into school over the last ten to fifteen years in a variety of forms. We refer to the use of an arrow to express a relation and, in the sense of the previous work, an operation.

Professor Papy has used this notation extensively (see [78]); it has been used here as a game situation (p.94) and several times has been used to denote what we have called here a unary operation.

A 'Papy-graph' uses arrows to indicate that a relation between two things exists. For example, given a set of people represented by a set of points, we can draw an arrow to represent the relation 'is the brother of', etc. (see [40]). All these examples are of *binary* relations because the arrow links *two* things each time.

The arrow game referred to is one in which a collection of numbers is put on the board and the person in control at the moment chooses a relation. He then draws some arrows (or all possible arrows) and the rest try to find out the relation he is using (and put in more arrows).

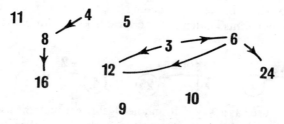

But in action the arrows seem to take on an extra significance. Instead of merely recording a relationship ('12 is twice 6' for instance), in a particular game the arrow can take on a dynamic meaning. If the game is first played in the original way, so that the relationship is discovered, it can be continued by putting more *arrows* in and asking the children to put in the necessary numbers. The arrow then acts like an instruction – to double, say. The arrow now means *an operation* on a number to produce another number: that is, a unary operation.

This emerges more clearly in more complex 'graphs' where more than one relationship is involved, and where *the relations are themselves related* (see Figs. on pp.111-12).

What we find here is a very real way in which children can make the kind of discovery referred to on p.325. That is, that the relations between the operations have properties similar to the things that they are operating on. The deliberate use of a signified arrow, that is, one with the unary operation marked, is a much better symbolism for dealing with operational activities. It is important and easy to see then that

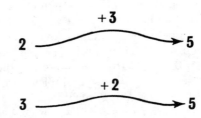

is different from

and this difference can be explored. The sum $2+3=5$ is seen to be of a different order. (Some writers have used the analogy of the calculating machine and the way instructions are written for the machine.)

Developing this idea of labelling the arrow with the operation which it represents, statements of various kinds can be written; for example:

It *could* be used as a way in to simple algebra through the usual 'think of a number' problems; for example 'Think of a number, add 2 to it, then multiply by 3. If the result is 24 what was the original number?' can be shown by

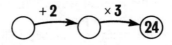

Reversing the arrow inverts the operation. Also the sequence of inverse operations will be in the reverse order.

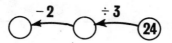

The 'unknown' can be represented by a symbol, or a letter, if desired.

The above can lead to simple equations if formalized. If the unknown is an operation, one gets a variant of an arrow game. It is obvious that in most (all?) cases, the provision of all the numbers does not lead to unique answers for the operations.

Unfortunately, like all other ideas this could be a liability if it were overdone, and if all the processes were formalized too far. It is merely a suggestion for a way in which the arrow notation *may* be extended if the appropriate circumstances arise.

Bibliography

We acknowledge gratefully the help of the staff of the Institute of Education Library, Southampton University, in checking the details of this list.

[1] Adams, L. D. *A background to primary school mathematics.* London: Oxford Univ. Press, 1953

[2] Adler, I. *The magic house of numbers.* London: Dobson, 1958

[3] Adler, I. *The giant colour book of mathematics.* London: Hamlyn, 1961

[4] Adler, I. *Mathematics: the story of numbers, symbols and space.* New York: Golden Press, 1958

[5] Adler, I. *The new mathematics.* 2nd edn. London: Dobson, 1964

[6] Adler, I. and Adler, R. *Numbers old and new* (The reason why series). London: Dobson, 1961

[7] Asimov, I. *Realm of numbers.* London: Gollancz, 1963

[8] Association of Teachers in Colleges and Departments of Education. *Primary mathematics for schools and colleges.* A.T.C.D.E., 151 Gower Street, London WC1, 1964

[9] Association of Teachers of Mathematics. *Mathematical films and film-strips* (Mathematics Teaching pamphlet No.1). Rev. edn. Nelson: A.T.M., 1966

Association of Teachers of Mathematics, *see* British National Committee for Mathematics, Fletcher, T. J., *and* Harrison, P. G.

[10] Ball, W. W. Rouse. *Mathematical recreations and essays.* Revised by H. S. M. Coxeter. 11th edn. London: Macmillan; New York: St. Martin's Press, 1959

[11] Barbut, M. Distances. *Mathematics Teaching,* No.23 (Summer, 1963), pp.15–20

[12] Barnett, N. M., *and others. Juniors learning mathematics.* 2nd edn., Educational Supply Association, 1962 (now supplied by Ward Lock through any bookseller)

[13] Barr, S. *Experiments in topology.* New York: Crowell, 1964

[14] Beberman, M. Searching for patterns. *In:* O.E.C.D. *Mathematics today: a guide for teachers* . . . Paris: O.E.C.D., 1964, pp.148–64

[15] Begle, E. G. Pre-university algebra. *In:* O.E.C.D. *Mathematics today: a guide for teachers* . . . Paris: O.E.C.D., 1964, pp.36–41

[16] Biggs, J. B. *Anxiety, motivation and primary school mathematics* (Occasional publication, No.7). National Foundation for Educational Research, 1962

[17] Bowman, M. E. *Romance in arithmetic: a history of our currency, weights and measures and calendar.* London: Univ. of London Press, 1950

[18] Bowran, A. P. *Sets for schools.* London: Macmillan; New York: St. Martin's Press, 1964

[19] Bracewell, H. The new look in primary mathematics. *Mathematics Teaching* No.24 (Autumn, 1963), pp.20–6

[20] British National Committee for Mathematics. *The development of mathematical activity in children; the place of the problem in this development* (a report prepared by the Research and Development Panel of the Association of Teachers of Mathematics). Nelson: A.T.M., 1966

[21] Chivers, K. G. and Rosewell, G. H. W. *Mathematical experiments for juniors.* 3 vols London: Cassell, 1965

[22] Chivers, P. K. *A basis for primary school mathematics.* 6 pupils' books and 3 teacher's books. London, Melbourne: Ward Lock, 1966 (in progress)

[23] Churchill, E. M. *Counting and measuring: an approach to number education in the infant school.* London: Routledge & Kegan Paul, 1961

[24] Churchill, E. M. *Piaget's findings and the teacher.* National Froebel Foundation, 1962

[25] Coxeter, H. S. M. *Introduction to geometry.* New York, London: Wiley, 1961

[26] Cundy, H. M. and Rollett, A. P. *Mathematical models.* 2nd edn. Oxford: Clarendon Press, 1961

[27] Dantzig, T. *Number, the language of science.* 4th edn. London: Allen and Unwin, 1963

[28] Davis, D. *Some thoughts on mathematical apparatus in the infant school.* Welwyn: Nisbet, 1962

[29] Davis, R. B. *Discovery in mathematics: a text for teachers.* (About the Madison Project). Reading (Mass.): Addison-Wesley, 1964

[30] Dienes, Z. P. *Building up mathematics.* London: Hutchinson Educational, 1960

[31] Dienes, Z. P. *A short introduction to the use of the algebraic experience materials: 'A.E.M.'* (Revised version). National Foundation for Educational Research, 1961

[32] Dienes, Z. P. *An experimental study of mathematics learning.* London: Hutchinson, 1963

[33] Dienes, Z. P. *Mathematics in the primary school.* Melbourne: Macmillan, 1964

[34] Dienes, Z. P. *The power of mathematics.* London: Hutchinson Educational, 1964

[35] Dienes, Z. P. *Modern mathematics for young children.* Harlow: Educational Supply Association, 1965

[36] Downes, L. W. and Paling, D. *The teaching of arithmetic in the primary schools.* London: Oxford Univ. Press, 1958

[37] Dumont, M. *Algébre I. Classes de 5ᵉ et 4ᵉ.* Paris: Dunod, 1965

[38] Escher, M. C. *The graphic work of M. C. Escher.* London: Oldbourne Press, 1961

[39] Flavell, J. S. and Wakelam, B. B. *Primary mathematics: an introduction to the language of number.* 4 course books, 3 teacher's books and 4 supplementary books. London: Methuen, 1959–65

[40] Fletcher, T. J., *editor. Some lessons in mathematics.* By members of the Association of Teachers of Mathematics. London: Cambridge Univ. Press, 1964

[41] French, P. and Rickard, R. J. *Exploring mathematics.* Glasgow: House of Grant, 1963
French, P. *Introducing polyhedra*
Introducing sets
Number patterns
Number systems old and new

[42] Gardner, M. *Mathematical puzzles and diversions.* London: Bell, 1961
(Paperback edn., Harmondsworth: Penguin, 1965)

[43] Gardner, M. *More mathematical puzzles and diversions.* Bell, 1963
(Paperback edn., Harmondsworth: Penguin, 1966)

[44] Gardner, M. *New mathematical diversions from Scientific American.* New York: Simon and Schuster, 1967

[45] Gattegno, C. *Modern mathematics with numbers in colour.* Reading: Cuisenaire Co., 1959

[46] Gattegno, C. *Mathematics with numbers in colour.* 7 vols. (Books 1–6 issued 1963–4). Reading: Educational Explorers, 1963 (in progress)

[47] Gattegno, C. *'Now Johnny can do arithmetic': a guide for the use of the Cuisenaire materials.* Revised edn. Reading: Educational Explorers, 1963

[48] Gattegno, C. *For the teaching of mathematics.* 4 vols. Reading: Educational Explorers, 1963 (in progress)
Vol.1: *Mathematics and the child; Pedagogical discussions*
Vol.2: *Psychological studies; On films*
Vol.3: *Elementary mathematics*
Vol.4: *Miscellaneous topics; Mathematics teaching and society; Book reviews*

[49] Goodstein, R. L. *Fundamental concepts of elementary mathematics.* Oxford: Pergamon Press, 1962

[50] Goutard, M. *Mathematics and children: a reappraisal of our attitude.* Reading: Educational Explorers, 1964

[51] Goutard, M. *Talks for primary school teachers on the Cuisenaire-Gattegno approach to the teaching of mathematics.* Reading: Educational Explorers, 1963

[52] Hames, J. and Wyvill, R. *Number patterns.* 87 Borough High St, London SE1, Copyprints Ltd, n.d.

[53] Harrison, P. G. *On teaching sets to children* (Mathematics Teaching pamphlet No.10). Nelson: A.T.M., 1963

[54] Hogben, L. *Man must measure: the wonderful world of mathematics.* Rathbone, 1955

[55] Holt, J. *How children fail.* New York: Pitman Pub. Co., 1964

[56] Hunter, J. A. H. *Figures for fun.* London: Phoenix House, 1957

[57] Hunter, J. A. H. and Madachy, J. S. *Mathematical diversions*. Princeton (N.J.): Van Nostrand, 1963

[58] Irwin, K. G. *Man learns to measure*. London: Dobson, 1962

[59] Isaacs, N. *The growth of understanding in the young child: a brief introduction to Piaget's work*. 2nd edn., Educational Supply Association, 1963 (now supplied by Ward Lock through any bookseller)

[60] Isaacs, N. *New light on children's ideas of number: the work of Professor Piaget*. Educational Supply Association, 1960 (now supplied by Ward Lock through any bookseller)

[61] James, E. J. *Mathematical topics for modern schools. Second year . . . Book 2: Curve stitching*. London: Oxford Univ. Press, 1960

[62] Johnson, D. A., *and others. Exploring mathematics on your own*. by Donovan A. Johnson, William H. Glenn, M. Scott Norton, St. Louis: Webster Publishing Co., 1961–3 (English edition published by John Murray, 1964–5)

    Glenn, William H. and Johnson, D. A.:
        Computing devices
        Adventures in graphing
        Fun with mathematics
        Number patterns
        The Pythagorean theorem
        Short cuts in computing
    Johnson, D. A.:
        Curves in space
        Logic and reasoning in mathematics
        Probability and chance
    Johnson, D. A. and Glenn, W. H.:
        Invitation to mathematics
        Sets, sentences and operations
        Topology: the rubber sheet geometry
        Understanding numeration systems
        The world of measurement
        The world of statistics
    Norton, M. Scott:
        Basic concepts of vectors
        Finite mathematical systems
        Geometric constructions

[63] Kline, M. and Crown, A. W. *The language of shapes*. 4 vols. Leeds: E. J. Arnold, 1956

[64] Land, F. W. *The language of mathematics*. London: John Murray, 1961

[65] Land F. W., *editor. New approaches to mathematics teaching*. London: Macmillan; New York: St. Martin's Press, 1963

[66] Lietzmann, W. *Visual topology*. Translated from the German by M. Bruckheimer. London: Chatto & Windus, 1965

[67] Lovell, K. *The growth of basic scientific and mathematical concepts in children*. London: Univ. of London Press, 1961

Madison Project, see Davis, R. B.

[68] Mansfield, D. E. and Thompson, D. *Mathematics: a new approach*. Book 1 and teacher's book 1. London: Chatto & Windus, 1962

[69] Marsh, L. G. *Let's explore mathematics.* 4 basic books, 3 group booklets and teacher's book. London: Black, 1964 (in progress)

[70] Mathematical Association. *The teaching of mathematics in primary schools.* London: Bell, 1955

[71] Moss, G. *Think of a number.* 2 vols. and teacher's book. Oxford: Blackwell, 1958

[72] Moss, G. *Geometry for juniors.* 4 vols. Oxford: Blackwell, 1960

[73] National Council of Teachers of Mathematics. *27th Yearbook. Enrichment mathematics for the grades.* Washington: N.C.T.M., 1963

[74] National Council of Teachers of Mathematics. *29th Yearbook. Topics in Mathematics.* Washington: N.C.T.M., 1964

[75] New Education Fellowship. *Approaches to science in the primary school.* Edited by Evelyn Lawrence, Nathan Isaacs, Wyatt Rawson. Educational Supply Association, 1960 (now supplied by Ward Lock through any bookseller)

[76] Niven, I. *Mathematics of choice:* New Mathematical Library No.15. New York: Random House, 1965

[77] Nuffield Foundation – Mathematics Teaching Project:
  Computation and structure
  I do and I understand
  Pictorial representation
  Shape and size
Nuffield Foundation, Mathematics Teaching Project. These booklets are trial editions, issued for limited circulation only. Revised versions for publication by John Murray and Chambers, 1967

O.E.C.D., *see* Beberman, M., Begle, E. G. *and* Papy, G.

[78] Papy, G. *Mathématique moderne.* Vol.1. Brussels and Paris: Didier, 1964

[79] Papy, G. Methods and techniques of explaining new mathematical concepts in the lower forms of secondary schools. *In:* O.E.C.D. *Mathematics today: a guide for teachers* . . . Paris: O.E.C.D., 1964, pp.99–147

[80] Pearcy, J. F. F. and Lewis, K. *Experiments in mathematics.* 2 vols. London: Longmans, 1966

[81] Peel, E. A. *The pupil's thinking.* London: Oldbourne, 1960

[82] Péter, R. *Playing with infinity.* Translated by Z. P. Dienes. London: Bell, 1961

[83] Piaget, J. *The moral judgment of the child.* Translated by Marjorie Gabain London: Routledge & Kegan Paul, 1932

[84] Piaget, J. *The child's conception of number.* Translated by C. Gattegno and F. M. Hodgson. London: Routledge & Kegan Paul, 1952

[85] Piaget, J. and Inhelder, B. *The child's conception of space.* Translated by F. J. Langdon and J. L. Lunzer. London: Routledge & Kegan Paul, 1956

[86] Piaget, J. and Inhelder, B. *The growth of logical thinking from childhood to adolescence* . . . Translated by Anne Parsons and Stanley Milgram. London: Routledge & Kegan Paul, 1958

[87] Piaget, J., Inhelder, B., and Szeminska, A. *The child's conception of geometry.* Translated by E. A. Lunzer. London: Routledge & Kegan Paul, 1960

[88] Polya, G. *Mathematical discovery: on understanding, learning, and teaching problem solving.* 2 vols. New York, London: Wiley, 1962–5

[89] Polya, G. *Mathematics and plausible reasoning.* Vol.1: Induction and analogy in mathematics. London: Oxford Univ. Press, 1954

[90] Quiggin, A. H. *The story of money.* London: Methuen, 1956

[91] Ravielli, A. *Adventures with shapes.* London: Phoenix House, 1960

[92] Razzell, A. G. and Watts, K. G. O. *Mathematical topics.* 6 vols. London: Hart-Davis, 1964
    1: *4 and the shape of four*
    2: *Circles and curves*
    3: *Symmetry*
    4: *Probability*
    5: *3 and the shape of three*
    6: *A question of accuracy*

[93] Reid, C. *From zero to infinity: what makes numbers interesting.* 2nd edn. London: Routledge & Kegan Paul, 1965

[94] Renwick, E. M. *The case against arithmetic.* London: Simpkin Marshall, 1935

[95] Renwick, E. M. *Children learning mathematics.* Ilfracombe: Arthur H. Stockwell, 1963

[96] Rowland, K. *Looking and seeing: a four-part book for a new subject.* London: Ginn, 1964–6
    Part 1: *Patterns and shapes*
    Part 2: *Development of shape*
    Part 3: *The shapes we need*
    Part 4: *The shape of towns*
    Notes for teachers, parts 1–4

[97] Saunders, J. G. *Mathematics alive.* 3 vols. and teacher's book. London: Hamish Hamilton, 1964–5

[98] Sawyer, W. W. Not classical, not modern, but mathematics as a whole. *Mathematics Teaching*, No.25 (Winter, 1963), pp.29–32

[99] Sawyer, W. W. *Vision in elementary mathematics* (Introducing mathematics Series No.1). Harmondsworth: Penguin, 1964

[100] Sawyer, W. W. *A path to modern mathematics* (Introducing mathematics series No.4). Harmondsworth: Penguin, 1966

[101] Schools Council for the Curriculum and Examinations. *Mathematics in primary schools* (Curriculum Bulletin No.1). 2nd edn. H.M.S.O., 1966

[102] *Science Survey* 1961. Part 2. Harmondsworth: Penguin Books, 1962

[103] Sealey, L. G. W. *The creative use of mathematics in the junior school.* Oxford: Blackwell, 1961

[104] Skemp, R. R. The teaching of mathematical concepts. *Mathematics Teaching*, No.20 (Autumn, 1962), pp.13–15

[105] Smith, D. E. *Number stories of long ago.* London: Ginn, 1948

[106] Smith, T. *The story of measurement.* Series 1. Oxford: Blackwell, 1955
    1: *How measuring began*
    2: *The yard, the foot and the inch*

   3: *Measuring land and large spaces*
   4: *Measuring roads and long distances*
[107] Smith, T. *The story of measurement.* Series 2. Oxford: Blackwell, 1956
   1: *The story of weight*
   2: *The story of money*
   3: *The story of capacity*
   4: *The story of time*

[108] Southampton University Institute of Education Library. *Mathematics for the primary school: guide-lines to recent literature.* Southampton: the University, 1966

[109] Steinhaus, H. *Mathematical snapshots.* Rev. edn. London: Oxford Univ. Press, 1960

[110] Stern, C. *Children discover arithmetic.* New York: Harper, 1949

[111] Valens, E. G. *The number of things: Pythagoras, geometry and humming strings.* London: Methuen, 1965

[112] Weyl, H. *Symmetry.* Princeton (N.J.): Princeton Univ. Press, 1952

[113] Whittaker, D. E. *Mathematics through discovery.* 3 vols. and teacher's book. London: Harrap, 1965

[114] Williams, E. M. and James, E. J. *Oxford junior mathematics.* 5 pupils' and 5 teacher's books. London: Oxford Univ. Press, 1962–6

Some materials mentioned in the text

Construct-o-straws: manufactured by R.J.M. Exports, Great Rollright Manor, Chipping Norton, Oxon., for Parker Bros. and distributed through educational suppliers

'Crossroads', a board game: manufactured by the Spicer Magic Corporation, Philadelphia 18, U.S.A., for Tell Products, Pa., U.S.A.

Cuisenaire rods, 'Numbers in Colour': manufactured and distributed by the Cuisenaire Company Ltd, 40 Silver Street, Reading, Berks

'Dance Squared', a film by René Jodoin from an idea by Trevor Fletcher: produced by the National Film Board of Canada

Gattegno Geo-Boards: manufactured and distributed by the Cuisenaire Company Ltd, 40 Silver Street, Reading, Berks

Multibase Arithmetic Blocks, devised by Z. P. Dienes: distributed by the Educational Supply Association, School Materials Division, Pinnacles, Harlow, Essex

Index